Keyboarding / **T**ypewriting

For Personal Applications

6E

Berle Haggblade

**Professor, Information Management
California State University, Fresno**

John Kushner

**Vice President for Academic Affairs
Detroit College of Business**

South-Western Publishing Co.

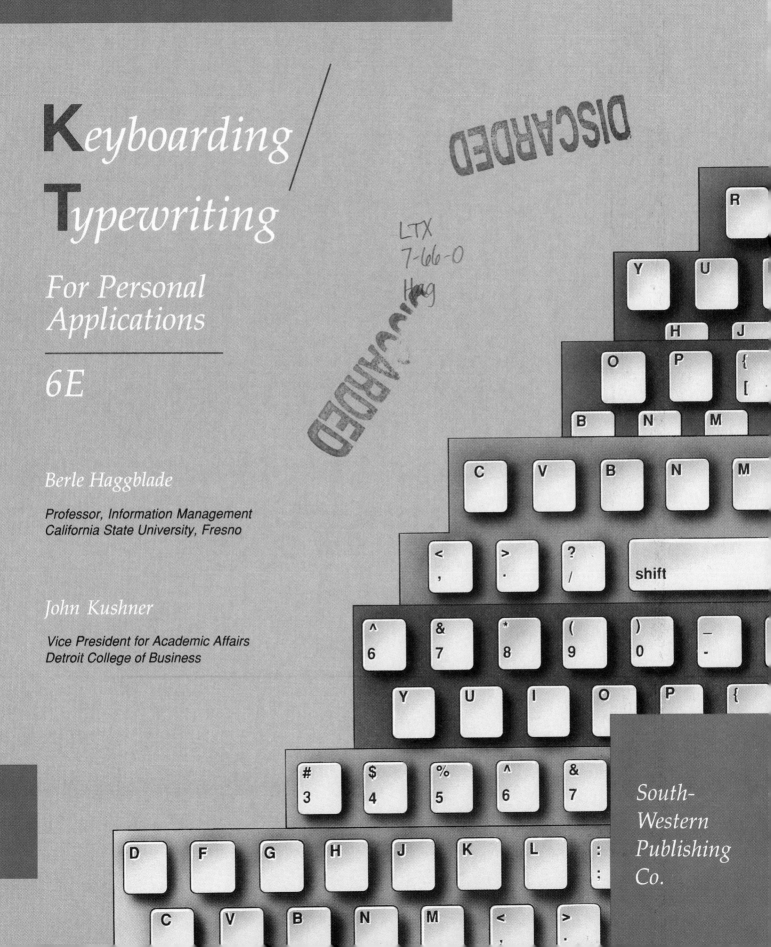

Copyright © 1993

by SOUTH-WESTERN PUBLISHING CO.
Cincinnati, Ohio

ISBN: 0-538-60411-5

Library of Congress Catalog Card Number: 91-60539

3 4 5 6 7 8 H 9 8 7 6 5 4 3

Printed in the United States of America

ACKNOWLEDGEMENTS

We greatly appreciate the feedback received from students and teachers who have used previous editions. Their comments and suggestions have been most helpful in the preparation of this edition. We also want to extend our appreciation to Dr. S. J. Wanous, who wrote the original edition of the text and contributed so much to its success over the years.

Berle Haggblade

John Kushner

Other Contributors:

Senior Acquisitions Editor:	Karen Schmohe
Senior Developmental Editor:	Richard E. Adams
Production Editor:	Deborah M. Luebbe
Associate Editor/Production:	A. Yvonne Stearns
Production Artist:	Steven McMahon
Photo Editor/Stylist:	Devore M. Nixon
Associate Photo Editor/Stylist:	Linda Ellis
Associate Director/Photography:	Diana W. Fleming
Marketing Manager:	Al S. Roane

Cover Photo:	Fredric Petters

PREFACE

The Sixth Edition of KEYBOARDING/TYPEWRITING FOR PERSONAL APPLICATIONS reflects the gradual transition from the teaching of keyboarding solely on typewriters to the teaching of this vital skill on computers. The text is appropriate for instruction on either type of equipment.

These broader applications of keyboarding skills have increased the importance of acquiring keyboarding proficiency in the middle and junior high schools, the grades for which this book is designed. Topics covered in both skillbuilding and problem copy are geared to the needs, interests, experiences, and reading levels of learners at this age. Activities provided call for the development of problem-solving skills for students of varying abilities.

OBJECTIVES

Students who complete the text should accomplish several major objectives:

- Achieve sufficient keyboarding skill to be able to operate the machines by touch.

- Master correct techniques of position, fingering, and stroking, and develop appropriate response patterns.

- Attain optimum speed and accuracy according to their individual capabilities.

- Review and improve basic English skills of punctuation, spelling, proofreading, and word division.

- Develop the ability to transfer thoughts (compose) from their heads directly to the keyboard.

- Acquire the habit of using their machine as a basic communication tool in the preparation of personal and school papers.

ORGANIZATION

KEYBOARDING/TYPEWRITING FOR PERSONAL APPLICATIONS, with a total of 140 lessons plus a numeric keypad unit and a simulation, contains ample instructional material for a full 2-semester course.

Organized into four cycles, the text may also be used for shorter courses designed primarily to cover basic key locations.

The first 70 lessons are devoted to skill development and personal writing tasks. Drill and timed writing copy is easy in the early lessons and advances in gradual stages to average difficulty. The second 70 lessons provide a thorough review and advanced work.

Keyboarding Skill. Special technique drills are included in nearly every lesson. Speed and control aids are generously placed throughout the entire book. Exercises progress from simple to complex; copy appears first in print, then in rough draft and script to help students develop keyboarding skill under realistic conditions.

Keyboarding Applications. Beginning with Cycle 2, the book covers personal notes and business letters, reports, outlines, book reviews, speech and class notes, minutes, agendas, tables, and other personal papers. Students work first from model copy containing detailed reminders and later from unarranged copy.

Language Arts Development. After students have acquired desirable techniques, they are introduced to numerous language arts and composing activities. **Special Index.** A Special Index lists the location of:

- Language arts skills
- Timed writings (including speed ladder paragraphs)
- Formatting problems
- Key location drills
- Manipulative and preapplication writings
- Technique builders
- Skill builders
- Skill comparison sentences and paragraphs
- Guided writings
- Continuity and fluency practice
- Control builders
- Speed builders
- Rough draft sentences/paragraphs

This index provides students with easy reference to each activity that can aid them in problem areas.

FEATURES

More than 75% of the copy in this edition is new, much of it related specifically to the Information Age, environmental concerns, and other current topics.

Spacing and arrangement of the drills, problems, and directions provide for attractive appearance and maximum readability.

Color is used effectively throughout to highlight information deserving particular attention.

Special icons make it easy to identify important activities and instructions.

Six pages of new drill material have been added to the keyboard introduction lessons.

Every fourth lesson of the introductory unit is devoted to key location reviews and technique reinforcement.

A convenient reference section contains a Glossary of Computer and Keyboarding Terms, as well as other needed explanations and illustrations.

An office simulation, popular in previous editions, gives students an opportunity to apply their keyboarding skills to the production of jobs required in a typical school office.

A new unit, ''Learning to Operate the Ten-Key Numeric Keypad,'' appears in the Appendix.

CONTENTS

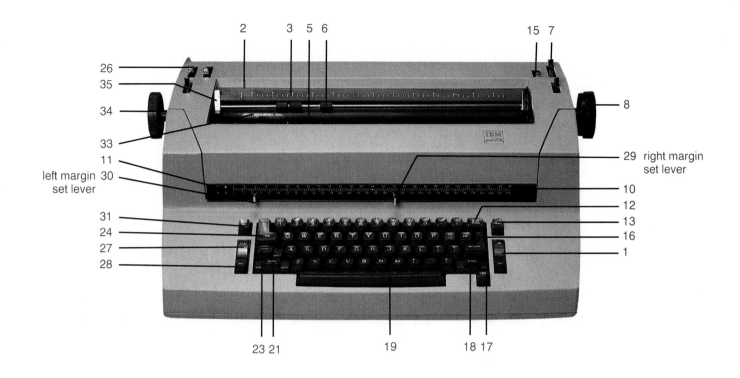

The diagram above shows the parts of an electric typewiter. Illustrated on pp. viii–x are other machines to which your keyboarding skills will transfer.

Since all typewriters have similar parts, you will probably be able to locate the parts on your machine using one of these diagrams. However, if you have the User's Manual that comes with your machine, use it to identify the exact location of each machine part, including special parts that may be on one machine but not on another.

1 ON/OFF control--used to turn machine on or off (not shown on Brother EM-811--under left platen knob)

2 paper guide--used to position paper for insertion

3 paper guide scale--used to set paper guide at desired position

4 paper support--used to support paper in machine (not on Selectric)

5 platen (cylinder)--used to feed paper into machine and to provide a hard surface for daisy wheel or element to strike

6 paper bail and **paper bail rolls**-- used to hold paper against platen

7 paper release lever--used to adjust position of paper after insertion

8 right platen knob--used to turn platen manually

9 paper insert key--used to feed paper into machine and advance paper to proper position for keying (not on Selectric); some machines also have an eject key

10 line-of-writing or **format scales**-- used to plan margin settings and tab stops

11 print point indicator--used to position print carrier at desired point (on Selectric--red piece behind left margin set lever)

12 backspace key--used to move print point to the left one space at a time

13 paper up key--used to advance paper one-half line at a time; can be used for paper insertion and ejection; also called **page up key** and **index key**

14 paper down key--used to retract paper one-half line at a time (not on Selectric); also called **page down key**

15 line space selector--used to select line spacing, such as single spacing or double spacing

16 return key--used to return print carrier to left margin and to advance paper up to next line of writing

17 correction key--used to erase (''lift off'') characters

18 right shift key--used to key capital letters and symbols controlled by left hand

19 space bar--used to move print carrier to the right one space at a time

20 code key--used with selected character or service keys to key special characters or to perform certain operations (not on Selectric)

21 left shift key--used to key capital letters and symbols controlled by the right hand

22 caps lock key--used to lock shift mechanism for *alphabet characters only* (not on Selectric)

23 shift lock key--used to lock shift mechanism for *all* keyboard characters

24 tab key--used to move print carrier to tab stops

25 repeat key--used to repeat the previous keystroke (Selectric has a feature that causes certain keys to repeat when held down)

26 pitch selector--used to select pitch (type size); some machines adjust pitch automatically depending upon the daisy wheel inserted

27 tab clear key--used to erase tab stops

28 tab set key--used to set tab stops

29 right margin key--used to set right margin

30 left margin key--used to set left margin

31 margin release key--used to move print carrier beyond margin settings

32 print carrier--used to carry ribbon cassette, daisy wheel or element, correction tape, and print mechanism to print point (not visible on Selectric)

33 aligning scale--used to align copy that has been reinserted

34 left platen knob--used to feed paper manually; also **variable line spacer** on machines with platen knobs

35 paper bail lever--used to move paper bail forward when inserting paper manually (Selectric has one at each end of the paper bail)

The diagram above shows the parts of an electronic typewriter. Illustrated on pp. vii, ix, and x are other machines to which your keyboarding skills will transfer.

Since all typewriters have similar parts, you will probably be able to locate the parts on your machine using one of these diagrams. However, if you have the User's Manual that comes with your machine, use it to identify the exact location of each machine part, including special parts that may be on one machine but not on another.

1 ON/OFF control--used to turn machine on or off (not shown on Brother EM-811)--under left platen knob)

2 paper guide--used to position paper for insertion

3 paper guide scale--used to set paper guide at desired position

4 paper support--used to support paper in machine (not on Selectric)

5 platen (cylinder)--used to feed paper into machine and to provide a hard surface for daisy wheel or element to strike

6 paper bail and **paper ball rolls**--used to hold paper against platen

7 paper release lever--used to adjust position of paper after insertion

8 right platen knob--used to turn platen manually

9 paper insert key--used to feed paper into machine and advance paper to proper position for keying (not on Selectric); some machines also have an eject key

10 line-of-writing or format scales--used to plan margin settings and tab stops

11 print point indicator--used to position print carrier at desired point (on Selectric--red piece behind left margin set lever)

12 backspace key--used to move print point to the left one space at a time

13 paper up key--used to advance paper one-half line at a time; can be used for paper insertion and is also called **page up key** and **index key**

14 paper down key--used to retract paper one-half line at a time (not on Selectric); also called **page down key**

15 line space selector--used to select line spacing, such as single spacing or double spacing

16 return key--used to return print carrier to left margin and to advance paper up to next line of writing

17 correction key--used to erase ('lift off') characters

18 right shift key--used to key capital letters and symbols controlled by left hand

19 space bar--used to move print carrier to the right one space at a time

20 code key--used with selected character or service keys to key special characters or to perform certain operations (not on Selectric)

21 left shift key--used to key capital letters and symbols controlled by the right hand

22 caps lock key--used to lock shift mechanism for alphabet characters *only* (not on Selectric)

23 shift lock key--used to lock shift mechanism for all keyboard characters

24 tab key--used to move print carrier to tab stops

25 repeat key--used to repeat the previous keystroke

26 pitch selector--used to select pitch (type size); some machines adjust pitch automatically depending upon the daisy wheel inserted

27 tab clear key--used to erase tab stops

28 tab set key--used to set tab stops

29 right margin key--used to set right margin

30 left margin key--used to set left margin

31 margin release key--used to move print carrier beyond margin settings

32 print carrier--used to carry ribbon cassette, daisy wheel or element, correction tape, and print mechanism to print point

33 aligning scale--used to align copy that has been reinserted

34 left platen knob--used to feed paper manually; also **variable line spacer** on machines with platen knobs

35 paper bail lever--used to move paper bail forward when inserting paper manually

■ ELECTRONIC (Brother EM-811fx)

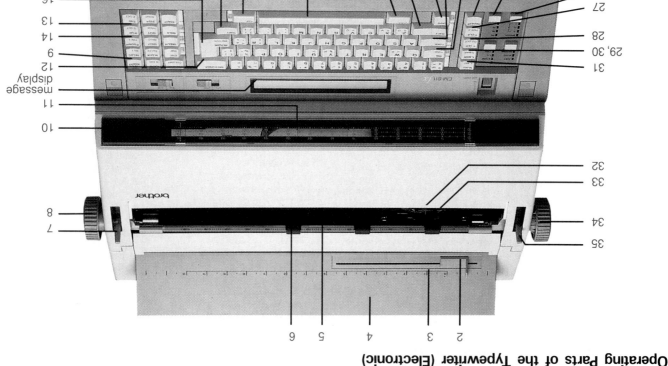

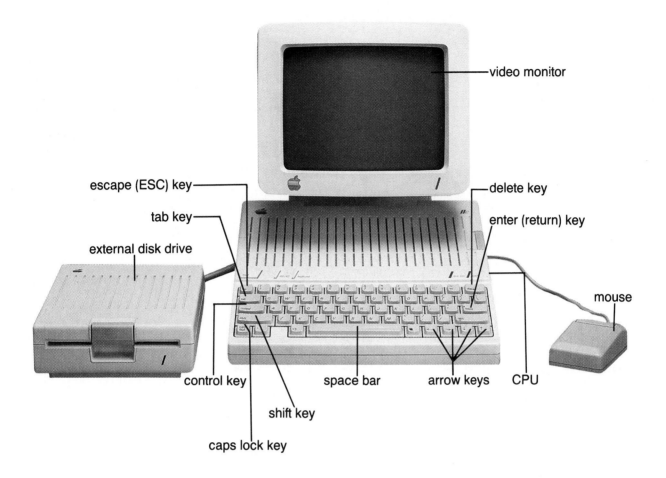

video monitor

escape (ESC) key

delete key

tab key

enter (return) key

external disk drive

mouse

control key

space bar

arrow keys

CPU

shift key

caps lock key

■ THE APPLE IIC

The diagram above shows the various parts of the **Apple IIc.** Microcomputers/word processors have similar parts, though the names of these parts and their arrangements may differ. With the help of the User's Manual for your equipment, you should be able to identify each item labeled in the illustration above.

The particular word processing software that you use will determine the specific uses of so-called "function keys." Therefore, you must familiarize yourself with the User's Manual for your software as well as the one for your equipment.

The number in parentheses with some items in the alphabetized list at right refers to a comparable machine part on an electric or electronic typewriter (pp. vii–viii).

"arrow" keys--used to move cursor in the direction of the arrow

caps lock key--used to lock shift mechanism for alphabet characters only (22)

control (CTRL) key--used with selected function keys to perform certain operations

CPU (Central Processing Unit)--the piece of equipment that holds the hardware or "brain" of the computer

delete key--used to remove characters from screen one by one

enter (return) key--used to return cursor to left margin and down to the next line; also, to enter system commands (16)

escape (ESC) key--used to cancel a function or exit a program section

external disk drive--reads information from and writes information to disks, just like the built-in disk drive

mouse--moves a marker across the screen

ON/OFF control--used to "power up" or "power down" the system

shift key--used to key uppercase letters and the upper character on 2-character keys (18, 21)

space bar--used to move cursor to right one space at a time or to add space between characters (19)

tab key--used to move cursor to tab stops (24)

video monitor--the piece of equipment used to display text, data, and graphic images on screen

■ The IBM Personal System/2 Model 30

The diagram above shows the various parts of the **IBM Personal System/2 Model 30.** Microcomputers/word processors have similar parts, though the names of these parts and their arrangements may differ. With the help of the User's Manual for your equipment, you should be able to identify each item labeled in the illustration above.

The particular word processing software that you will use will determine the specific uses of so-called "function keys." Therefore, you must familiarize yourself with the User's Manual for your software as well as the one for your equipment.

The number in parentheses with some items in the alphabetized list at right refers to a comparable machine part on an electric or electronic typewriter (pp. vii–viii).

"arrow" keys--used to move cursor in the direction of the arrow

caps lock key--used to lock shift mechanism for alphabet characters only (22)

control (CTRL) key--used with selected function keys to perform certain operations

CPU (Central Processing Unit)--the piece of equipment that holds the hardware or "brain" of the computer

delete key--used to remove characters from the screen one by one

enter (return) key--used to return cursor to left margin and down to the next line; also, to enter system commands (16)

escape (ESC) key--used to cancel a function or exit a program section

ON/OFF control--used to "power up" or "power down" the system

shift key--used to key uppercase letters and the upper character on 2-character keys (18, 21)

space bar--used to move cursor to right one space at a time or to add space between characters (19)

tab key--used to move cursor to tab stops (24)

video monitor--the piece of equipment used to display text, data, and graphic images on screen

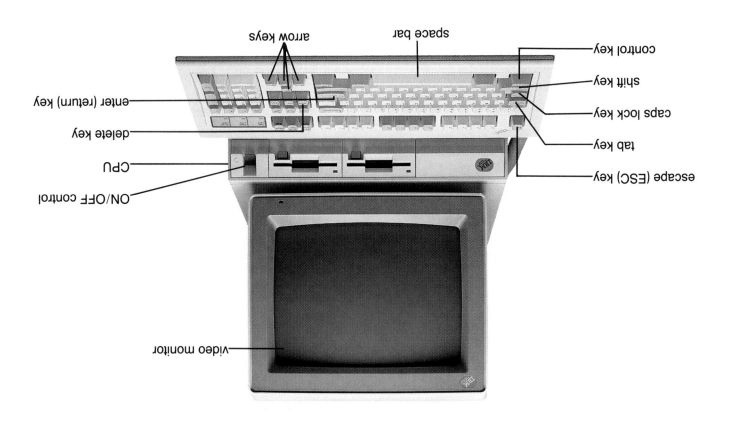

arrow keys

space bar

control key

enter (return) key

shift key

delete key

caps lock key

CPU

tab key

ON/OFF control

escape (ESC) key

video monitor

Operating a typewriter or computer involves more than learning to stroke the keys. This page and page xii contain information regarding machine adjustments which you must know for the particular model you are using.

Pica and Elite Type

Some machines are equipped with pica type; some with elite type. Pica is larger than elite. The line-of-writing scale (10) range is from 0 to about 90 on pica type; from 0 to about 110 on elite type.

Pica: f j f j f j f j f j (10 letters per inch)

1 inch

Elite: f j f j f j f j f j (12 letters per inch)

Setting the Margin Stops

Two major kinds of typewriter margin sets are described below. Determine which kind of margin set your machine has; then follow the appropriate directions.

Push-Lever Margins

1. Push in on the left margin lever set, and slide it to the desired position.
2. Release the left margin lever set.
3. Set the right margin in the same manner, using the right margin lever set.

Electronic Margins

1. Use the space bar to move the carrier to the desired left margin position and strike the left margin key.
2. Space to the desired right margin position and strike the right margin key.

 Note: On the microcomputer these stops may be preset for you.

Clearing and Setting the Tab Stops

Tab Clear Move the carrier to the extreme right of your machine. Depress the tab clear key (No. 27) and hold it down as you return your carrier to the left margin.

Tab Set Move your carrier to the desired tab stop position; then press the tab set (No. 28). Repeat this operation to set as many tab stops as are needed.

Paper Guide and Centering Point

There is at least one scale on every typewriter, usually the line-of-writing scale (10), that reads from 0 at the left to 90 or more at the right, depending on the width of the machine and style of type—either pica or elite. The spaces on this scale are matched to the spacing mechanism on the machine.

To simplify directions, your instructor may ask you to insert paper into your machine so that the left edge corresponds to 0 on the line-of-writing scale. The center point of 8½" × 11" paper will then be 42 on the carrier scale for pica type and 51 for elite.

If this procedure is adopted, adjust the paper guide (2) to the left edge of your paper after it is inserted with the left edge at 0 on the scale. Note the position of the paper guide. Move it to this point at the beginning of each period.

 Note: If you are using a microcomputer, follow set-up directions for your printer.

Daily Care of Your Machine

1. Brush the dirt and dust from the bars.
2. Keep desk free of dust, especially the area under the machine.
3. Cover the machine when it is not in use.
4. Shut off power on an electric machine after each use.

Weekly Care of Your Machine

1. Clean keys, using approved cleaner.
2. Move the carrier to extreme end positions. With cloth moistened with oil, clean the carrier rails on each side.
3. Clean cylinder (platen), feed rolls, and paper bail rolls with cloth moistened with cleaning fluid.

Changing the Ribbon

In replacing a typewriter cartridge ribbon, note how the old ribbon was threaded. Then remove the old cartridge and follow this general procedure in changing your typewriter ribbon.

If your machine is not equipped with a cartridge ribbon, install the new one according to the manufacturer's instructions.

1. Wind the used ribbon on one spool. Usually, it is best to wind it on the right side of your machine.
2. Study the route of the ribbon as you wind. Note especially how the ribbon winds and unwinds on the two spools.
3. Lift the right spool slightly off its hub to see if both sides are the same. Study both sides of the spool so you will replace it properly.
4. Remove the ribbon from the carrier, and remove both spools. Note how the ribbon is attached to the empty spool.
5. Fasten the new ribbon to the empty spool, and wind several inches of the new ribbon on it.
6. Place both spools on their hubs, and thread the ribbon through the carrier. Make sure the ribbon is straight.

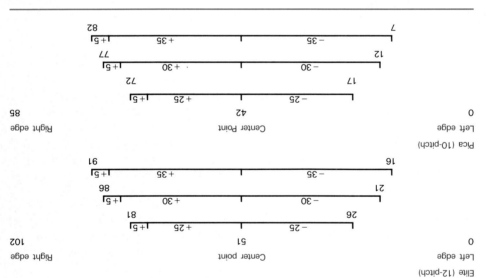

Pica (10-pitch)

Left edge 0	Center Point 42	Right edge 85
−25	+25	+5
17	72	
−30	+30	+5
12	77	
−35	+35	+5
7	82	

Elite (12-pitch)

Left edge 0	Center point 51	Right edge 102
−25	+25	+5
26	81	
−30	+30	+5
21	96	
−35	+35	+5
16	91	

Determining the Margin Stops

You may set the margin stops (29 and 30) for any length of line desired, such as 50-, 60-, or 70-space line. To have equal left and right margins, take these two steps.

Step 1 Subtract half the line length from the center point (42 for pica; 51 for elite). Set the left margin stop at this point.

Step 2 Add half the line length, plus 5 spaces for the end-of-line signal, to the center point. Set the right stop at this point.

Position of Hands

When keying, keep your fingers deeply curved. Fingernails should be neatly trimmed.

Hold your hands directly over the keys. Turn the hands inward slightly to get straight strokes. Do not permit your hands to turn over on the little fingers.

Keep your forearms in a parallel line with the slope of the keyboard. Hold your wrists down near, but not resting on, the front frame of the machine. Do not buckle your wrists upward.

Barely touch the home keys with your fingertips. Feel the keys; do not smother them.

When a finger makes a reach from its home position to strike another key, the other fingers remain on or near their home keys. Such reaches are made by the finger without twisting the wrist or moving the arm or elbow.

Forearms parallel to slant of machine

Reach with the finger

Fingers curved

Keep arms and wrists quiet

Keying Rhythm

Your goal is to strike the keys at a steady pace, without breaks or pauses. At first, you will think each letter as you key it. Later, you will think and key short, easy-to-key words and phrases as a whole. You will key longer, hard-to-key words by letters or syllables. Finally, you will combine whole word keying with letter or syllable keying into a smooth, fluent, steady rhythm.

Stroking

Center the stroking action in your fingers. Keep your elbows, arms, and wrists quiet as you key. Your fingers should be deeply curved. Use quick, sharp strokes. Release the keys quickly by snapping the fingers toward the palm of the hand. Strike the keys squarely with short, quick, straight strokes.

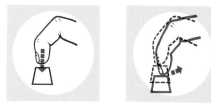

Posture

Good posture is vital in learning to key well. Given below are 10 guides of good form. Study the guides carefully. Observe them whenever you work at your machine.

1. Book at right of machine on bookholder or with something under top for easier reading.

2. Table free of unneeded books and papers.

3. Front frame of the machine even with the edge of the desk.

4. Body centered opposite the h key, 6 to 8 inches from front frame of machine.

5. Body seated back in chair, shoulders erect with body leaning forward slightly from waist.

6. Elbows held near the body.

7. Wrists held low with forearms parallel to the slant of the machine. Do not rest lower hand on frame of machine.

8. Feet flat on the floor, one just ahead of the other.

9. Head turned toward book with eyes on copy.

10. Fingers curved and held over second row of keys.

Spacing Between Words

Almost one in every five strokes is made with the space bar (19). Learn to operate the space bar correctly.

1. Hold the right thumb curved under the hand just over the space bar.
2. Strike the bar with a quick down-and-in motion of the thumb.

3. Keep the wrist low and quiet as you strike the bar.
4. Keep the left thumb tucked under the hand.

Control of the space bar

 Note: On microcomputers check the user's manual.

Shift and Shift Lock Keys

The left shift key (21) is used when capital letters are keyed with the right hand. Use a one-two count as you shift.
ONE Depress the shift key with the little finger and hold it down.
TWO Strike the capital letter with the opposite hand; then quickly release the shift key and return the little finger to its home row position.

The right shift key (18) is used when capital letters are keyed with the left hand.
To key ALL CAP items, depress the shift lock (23) with the left little finger and key. To release the shift lock, depress either the right or left shift key.

Control of left shift

Control of right shift

Return (Enter) on a Microcomputer

When using an electronic typewriter with automatic return or a microcomputer with word wrap, operate the return key at the end of each drill line.

Returning on an Electric or Electronic Typewriter

1. Reach the little finger of your right hand to the return key (16).
2. Tap the return key quickly.
3. Return the finger at once to its home-key position.

Electric return

Electronic return

Computer return

Carbon Copies

Before copying machines became commonly used, extra copies were often prepared with carbon paper as follows:

1. Place the carbon paper (with glossy side down) on a sheet of plain paper. The paper on which you will prepare the original is then laid on top of the carbon paper.
2. Place the sheets between the cylinder and the paper table (glossy side of carbon facing you). Roll into the typewriter. The dull surface of the carbon should be facing you.

Erasing and Correcting Carbon Copies

1. Move the carrier to the extreme right or left so that the eraser crumbs will not fall into the machine.
2. To avoid moving the paper out of alignment, turn the cylinder forward if the erasure is to be made on the upper two thirds of the paper; backward, if on the lower third of the paper.
3. To erase on the original sheet, lift the paper bail out of the way and place a small card in back of the original copy and in front of the first carbon sheet. Use an eraser shield to protect the letters that are not being erased. Use a hard typewriter eraser. When you complete the erasure, brush the eraser crumbs away from the machine.
4. Move the card in front of the second carbon sheet if more than one copy is being made. Erase the errors on the carbon copies with a soft (or pencil) eraser first, then use the hard typewriter eraser used in erasing on the original copy.
5. When the error has been neatly erased on the original and all the carbon copies, remove the card, position the carrier to the proper point, and key the correction.

Cycle 1

Learning to Operate Your Keyboard

GET READY TO KEY

Adjust Your Machine

The numbers in parentheses following names of machine parts are those assigned to machine parts on pages vii–x.

1. Paper guide (No. 2): Adjust the paper guide so that the left edge of your paper is on "0" on the line-of-writing scale (No. 10).

2. Line-space selector (No. 15): Set the line-space selector at "2" for double spacing.

3. Margin stops (Nos. 29 and 30): Set the margin stops for a 50-space line (center-25; center+25+5). When a standard sheet of paper (8½ × 11 inches) is inserted into a machine with the paper guide set at 0, the center point for pica type is 42 on the line-of-writing scale. The center point for elite type is 51.

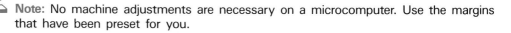

Note: No machine adjustments are necessary on a microcomputer. Use the margins that have been preset for you.

Insert Paper into Your Machine

1. Place paper to the left of the machine.

2. Pull the paper bail (No. 6) away from the cylinder (No. 5).

3. Grasp the paper in the left hand.

4. Place the paper behind the cylinder (No. 5) and against the paper guide (No. 2). At the same time, bring the right hand to the right cylinder knob (No. 8) and twirl it with a quick movement of the fingers and the thumb.

5. Adjust the paper bail (No. 6) so that it holds the paper against the cylinder. If necessary, adjust the paper-bail rolls (No. 6). The paper-bail rolls should be about 2 inches from the left and right edges of the paper.

6. If the paper needs straightening after it is inserted, release it long enough to straighten it. Use the paper-release lever (No. 7).

Note: If you are using a microcomputer, follow set-up directions for your printer.

Check Your Position at Your Machine

See page xiv for a larger posture illustration.

1. Place this book to the right of your machine on a bookholder, or put something under the top of the book to raise it for easier reading.

2. Have the front of the keyboard even with the edge of the desk. Your body should be centered opposite the **h** key.

3. Your body should be 6 to 8 inches from the frame of the machine.

4. Don't slump; sit erect. Hold your elbows near your body.

5. Place your feet on the floor, one just ahead of the other in order to give you good balance.

Unit 1 ■ Learning to Operate the Letter Keys (Lessons 1–15)

Learning Goals:

1. To key all letter keys by touch, using correct fingering.

2. To locate and use correctly the machine parts introduced in Unit 1.

3. To insert and remove paper from the machine, return the carrier, operate the shift keys, indent for paragraphs, adjust the paper guide, and set the margin stops.

4. To key with good techniques and form, paying particular attention to the posture guides and technique goals introduced in Unit 1.

LESSON 1

1a ● Find the Home Keys, Space Bar, and Return Key

hands upright over keys

fingers deeply curved

1. Place the fingers of your left hand on **a s d f**.

2. Place the fingers of your right hand on **j k l ;**.

3. Take your fingers off the home keys. Replace them. Say the keys of each hand as you touch them. Repeat several times to get the "feel" of these keys.

4. Hold your right thumb over the middle of the space bar. Strike the bar with a quick, inward motion of your right thumb. Keep the left thumb out of the way.

5. Curve your fingers. Hold them very lightly over the home keys. Key the line below. Say and think each letter as you strike it.

```
ff jj dd kk ss ll aa ;; fj dk sl a; fj dk sl a; fj
```

1b ● Use Proper Techniques

Hand Position

Hold your hands directly over the keys, keeping your fingers deeply curved.

Do not permit your hands to turn over on the little fingers. Turn your hands inward slightly to get straight strokes.

Hold your wrists down near, but not resting on, the front frame of the machine. Keep your forearms in a parallel line with the slope of the keyboard.

Barely touch home keys with the fingers.

quick finger stroke

Stroking

Center the stroking action in your fingers. Keep elbows, arms, and wrists quiet as you key. Your fingers should be deeply curved. Use quick, sharp strokes.

Release the keys quickly by snapping the fingers toward the palm of the hand. Hit the keys squarely with short, quick, straight strokes.

space with right thumb

Spacing Between Words

Hold the right thumb curved under the hand just over the space bar. Strike the bar with a quick down-and-in motion

of the thumb. Keep wrist low and quiet as you strike the bar.

Lesson 1

3

Lesson 6 ■ Review/Measurement

6a ● Number Review

Read down each column, keying the numbers as they appear. Strike Enter after the final number in each line.

Drill a	Drill b	Drill c	Drill d
395	3.15	26.54	15.61
164	8.03	47.02	23.96
786	4.20	71.29	78.13
519	7.42	84.38	69.09
207	2.58	32.06	53.47
140	9.61	89.65	77.80

6b ● Keying Numbers Containing Commas

Although commas are often used to separate groups of numbers, they cannot be entered on the ten-key pad.

Ignore the commas as you key the numbers in Drills a-d.

Drill a	Drill b	Drill c	Drill d
8,045	1,278	9,102	3,146
5,172	3,506	6,384	5,789
4,394	8,162	1,096	1,430
1,860	5,384	7,258	2,098
6,293	9,271	4,130	7,534
3,576	7,940	2,579	6,265

6c ● Skill Measurement

1. Take several 1-minute timings on Timed Copy A and B. Strike Enter twice after each group of three numbers.
2. If you finish the first column before time is called, go immediately to the second column. See if you can complete keying at least one column of numbers accurately in one minute.

Timed Copy A		Timed Copy B	
473.60	6,940	378.14	5,079
108.83	7,108	249.28	7,168
769.14	4,056	563.07	3,450
360.85	2,716	421.56	6,741
827.91	9,035	960.75	9,085
932.07	3,270	804.32	2,394
674.56	1,029	196.80	1,213
586.20	5,480	784.29	8,532
213.45	8,301	657.31	4,620

Electronic return

Electric return

think and
say each
letter

Computer return

Returning the Carrier

1. Reach the little finger of your right hand to the return key (No. 16).

2. Tap the return key quickly.

3. Return the finger at once to its home-key position.

Note: When using an electronic typewriter with automatic return or a microcomputer with word wrap, operate the return key at the end of each drill line.

1c ● Home-Key Practice

Directions: Key each line with your teacher at least once.

Technique Goal: Think and say each letter as you strike it.

home keys

```
1 ff jj ff jj ff jj ff jj ff jj fj fj fj fj fj fj fj

2 dd kk dd kk dd kk dd kk dd kk dk dk dk dk dk dk dk

3 ss ll ss ll ss ll ss ll ss ll sl sl sl sl sl sl sl

4 aa ;; aa ;; aa ;; aa ;; aa ;; a; a; a; a; a; a; a;

5 fj dk sl a; fj dk sl a; fj dk sl a; fj dk sl a; fj

6 fj dk sl a; fjdk sla; fjdk sla; fjdk sla; fj dk sl
```

1d ● Technique Builder: Stroking

use quick,
sharp strokes

Directions: Key each line once with your teacher. Repeat the lines a second time by yourself.

Technique Goal: Curve your fingers. Use quick, sharp strokes.

home keys

```
1 as ask as ask as ask all all lass lass as all lass

2 all fall all fall all all fall fall all fall falls

3 ad lad ad lad ad lad all a lad all a lad all a lad

4 a lad; a lad asks; a lass; a lass asks; ask a lass

5 a lass; as a lass; as a lass falls; as a lad falls

6 a lad asks; a lass asks; ask a lass; ask all lads;
```

1e ● Ending the Lesson

1. Pull the paper bail (No. 6) out from the cylinder (No. 5).

2. Pull the paper release lever forward (No. 7).

3. Remove paper with your free hand.

4. Return the paper bail and paper release lever to original positions.

Note: When using a microcomputer, turn off your equipment as directed in the user's manual.

Lesson 5 ■ . (decimal)

5a ● Number Review

Read down each column, keying the numbers as they appear. Strike Enter after the final number in each line.

Drill a	Drill b	Drill c	Drill d
474	682	790	731
585	140	986	204
696	537	512	685
414	960	894	347
525	245	170	956
636	301	423	810

5b ● Location of . (decimal)

Reach to . (decimal)
1. Find . on the chart.
2. Locate . on your keyboard.
3. Place your fingers over the home keys.
4. Reach to . with your second or third finger, whichever is more convenient on your machine.

> Technique hint:
> Sit erect in your chair; keep your fingers well curved.

5. Touch . lightly without moving the other fingers from home position.

6. Key the drill below, striking Enter after the final decimal in each line.

```
55..66..55..66..Enter
55..66..55..66..Enter
55..66..55..66..Enter
```

5c ● Location Drills: . (decimal)

1. Read down the column in Drill a, keying each number as it appears. Strike the Enter key after the final number in each line.

2. Key Drills b, c, d in the same manner.

Drill a	Drill b	Drill c	Drill d
5.56	1.06	38.50	947.35
6.65	2.54	14.69	331.46
6.55	3.10	25.70	893.28
5.60	4.76	65.18	165.10
5.50	5.21	46.02	742.79
6.60	6.59	55.76	480.91
5.05	7.83	86.30	254.52
6.06	8.23	75.49	620.36
5.06	9.47	96.05	517.84

LESSON 2

2a ● Keyboard Review

Review the Get Ready to Key Procedure explained on page 2.

explained on page 2.

Directions: Key each line once with your teacher.

Posture Goal: Place your feet flat on the floor for balance.

Spacing Guide:
Space once after a semi-colon (;) within a sentence.

think each key as you strike it

home keys

```
1 ff jj dd kk ss ll aa ;; ff jj dd kk ss ll aa ;; fj

2 fj dk sl a; fj dk sl a; fj dk sl a; fj dk sl a; fj

3 as as; ask a; ask a lass; ask a lad; ask all lads;

4 lad lad lads ask ask lass lass all all fall fall a

5 all lads fall; ask a lass; as a lass falls; a lass
```

2b ● Location of E and H

Plan for Learning New Keys

1. Find new key on keyboard chart.

2. Locate key on your keyboard.

3. Place fingers over home keys.

4. Know which finger strikes each key.

5. Watch your finger as you make the reach to the new key.

6. Key each short drill twice on the same line. Be sure to use the correct finger.

Reach to E

1. Find e on the chart.

2. Find it on your keyboard.

3. Place your fingers over the home keys.

4. Reach to e with the d finger.

5. Touch ed lightly without moving the other fingers from their home position.

6. Key the drill below twice on the same line.

```
ded ded ed ed ed led led
```

Reach to H

1. Find h on the chart.

2. Find it on your keyboard.

3. Place your fingers over the home keys.

4. Reach to h with the j finger.

5. Touch hj lightly without moving the other fingers from their home position.

6. Key the drill below twice on the same line.

```
jhj jhj hj hj ha had had
```

Lesson 4 ■ 1, 2, 3

4a ● Number Review

Read down each column, keying the numbers as they appear. Strike Enter after the final number in each line.

Drill a	Drill b	Drill c	Drill d
474	580	874	995
585	690	560	846
696	470	706	908
474	580	598	467
585	690	940	750
696	470	657	840

4b ● Location of 1, 2, 3

Reach to 1, 2, 3

1. Find 1, 2, 3 on the chart.

2. Locate 1, 2, 3 on your keypad.

3. Place your fingers over the home keys.

4. Reach to 1 with your first finger.

Reach to 2 with your second finger.

Reach to 3 with your third finger.

Technique hint:
Think and say the number to yourself as you tap the key with the tip of your finger.

5. Touch each new key (1, 2, 3) lightly without moving the other fingers from home position.

6. Key the drill below, striking Enter after the final number in each line.

```
111222333Enter
111222333Enter
111222333Enter
```

4c ● Location Drills: 1, 2, 3

1. Read down the column in Drill a, keying each number as it appears. Strike the Enter key after the final number in each line.

2. Key Drills b, c, d in the same manner.

Drill a	Drill b	Drill c	Drill d
41	414	140	412
41	411	401	523
41	141	410	639
52	525	250	578
52	522	502	629
52	252	520	481
63	636	360	168
63	633	603	793
63	363	630	547

2c ● Location Drills: E and H

Directions: Key each line once with your teacher. Repeat the lines a second time by yourself.

Technique Goal: Think and say each letter as you strike it.

Reach to e

Reach to h

```
        ded ded ded ded ed ed ed ed led led fled fled fled

    e   fee fee feed feeds feels feels less less else else

        sell sell sale sales deal deal desk desk jade jade


        jhj jhj jhj hj hj hj hj ha ha has has had had half

    h   has ash ash lash flash flash hall hall shall shall

        had a half; had a half; has a half; has had a half


        he heed heeds she shell shelf held head heads shed

  e/h   shed shells shade shale leash flesh flashed dashed

        hash hall; elf elk; he has shade; she held a leash
```

2d ● Technique Builder: Eyes on Copy

Directions: Set the line-space selector at "1" to single-space the drill. Key each line twice as shown.

Technique Goal: Keep your eyes on the book. Think each letter as you key it.

To double-space (DS), operate the return key twice.

single-space (SS) repeated lines

double-space (DS) when you start a new line

```
 1  fjdk sla; fjdk sla; ed hj ed hj ed hj he he she he
    fjdk sla; fjdk sla; ed hj ed hj ed hj he he she he
                                                     DS
 2  she she held held lad lad lass lass she head heads
    she she held held lad lad lass lass she head heads
                                                     DS
 3  as as has has lash lash; flash flash; flask flasks
    as as has has lash lash; flash flash; flask flasks
                                                     DS
 4  sale sale; a sale a sale; lake lake; a lake a lake
    sale sale; a sale a sale; lake lake; a lake a lake
                                                     DS
 5  sea sea sake sake; see see; see a leaf; see a leaf
    sea sea sake sake; see see; see a leaf; see a leaf
                                                     DS
 6  hall halls; sell sells; sells a desk; sells a desk
    hall halls; sell sells; sells a desk; sells a desk
                                                     DS
 7  ash ash; dash dash; he had a sled; she had a sled;
    ash ash; dash dash; he had a sled; she had a sled;
```

Lesson 3 ■ 7, 8, 9

3a ● Number Review

Read down each column, keying the numbers as they appear. Strike Enter after the final number in each line.

Drill a	Drill b	Drill c	Drill d
50	404	645	450
60	505	506	564
40	606	540	506
60	404	450	604
50	505	604	460
40	606	546	560

3b ● Location of 7, 8, 9

Reach to 7, 8, 9

1. Find 7, 8, 9 on the chart.

2. Locate 7, 8, 9 on your keypad.

3. Place your fingers over the home keys.

4. Reach to 7 with your first finger.

Reach to 8 with your second finger.

Reach to 9 with your third finger.

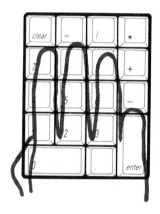

Technique hint: Key each number with a quick, sharp stroke.

5. Touch each new key (7, 8, 9) lightly without moving the other fingers from home position.

6. Key the drill below, striking Enter after the final number in each line.

777888999Enter
777888999Enter
777888999Enter

3c ● Location Drills: 7, 8, 9

1. Read down the column in Drill a, keying each number as it appears. Strike the Enter key after the final number in each line.

2. Key Drills b, c, d in the same manner.

Drill a	Drill b	Drill c	Drill d
47	474	740	478
47	477	407	589
47	747	470	690
58	585	850	584
58	588	508	670
58	858	580	477
69	696	960	659
69	699	609	508
69	969	690	746

2e ● Fluency Practice

Directions: Key each line twice SS. DS after each 2-line group.

Technique Goal: Use quick, sharp strokes. Release the keys instantly.

```
1 a lad; a lass; as a lad; as a lass; sell sell else

2 he he held held he held; he held; she has; as she;

3 all fall; all fall; a deal; a deal; a deal; a half

4 fee fee feel feel asked asked; he asked; she asked

5 as a; as a lad; as a lad falls; a lass; as a lass;

6 asked a fee; asked a fee; held a lead; held a sale

7 as he fell; as she fell; has a lease; had a lease;
```

LESSON 3

3a ● Keyboard Review

Spacing: Double
Margin: 50-space line
(Refer to page xii)

Directions: Key each line once with your teacher. Repeat the lines a second time by yourself.

Posture Goal: Sit erect. Hold elbows near the body. Keep wrists low and quiet and eyes on copy.

```
  e  ded ded ed ed see feel less see sale else desk see

  h  jhj jhj hj hj he held had has hall half dash shall

e/h  he heads shelf shake flesh she heeds leash flashed

all letters    add add ask ask less less head head fall fall feel
taught
     jell jell; she shall see; has a desk; held a sale;
```

3b ● Location of T and O

Reach to T
1. Find t on the chart.
2. Find it on your keyboard.
3. Place your fingers over the home keys.
4. Reach to t with the f finger.
5. Touch tf lightly without moving other fingers from their home position.

Reach to O
1. Find o on the chart.
2. Find it on your keyboard.
3. Place your fingers over the home keys.
4. Reach to o with the l finger.
5. Touch ol lightly without moving other fingers from their home position.

```
ftf ftf tf tf tf the the          Key twice on same line          lol lol ol ol ol old old
```

Lesson 2 ■ 0 (zero)

2a ● Number Review

Read down each column, keying the numbers as they appear. Strike Enter after the final number in each line.

Drill a	Drill b	Drill c	Drill d
44	44	546	664
55	45	656	454
66	46	454	556
44	65	564	454
55	54	465	646
66	46	654	565

2b ● Location of 0 (zero)

Reach to 0
1. Find 0 on the chart.
2. Locate 0 on your keypad.
3. Place your fingers over the home keys.
4. Reach to 0 with your right thumb.

Technique hint:
Strike 0 with the side of your right thumb. Release the key quickly.

5. Touch 0 lightly without moving the other fingers from home position.
6. Key the drill below, striking Enter after the final number in each line.

400500600Enter
400500600Enter
400500600Enter
400500600Enter

2c ● Location Drills: 0

1. Read down the column in Drill a, keying each number as it appears. Strike the Enter key after the final number in each line.
2. Key Drills b, c, and d in the same manner.

Drill a	Drill b	Drill c	Drill d
40	404	400	404
50	404	500	440
60	404	600	404
40	505	400	550
50	505	500	505
60	505	600	550
40	606	400	606
50	606	500	660
60	606	600	606

3c ● Location Drills: T and O

Directions: Key each line once with your teacher. Repeat a second time by yourself.

Technique Goal: Snap the finger toward the palm of the hand after each stroke.

Reach to t

Reach to o

t ftf ftf ftf ftf tf tf tf tf the the that that that
the that the that last let last let late late last
late take talk tell take talk tell these these set

o lol lol ol ol ol old old told told hold hold holds
of of of to to to those those too too took took of
do do does does so so; do so; do so; does so; does

t/o toe toes toss toss tot tot toast toast stood stood
dot dots soft soft jot jots hot hot lost lost lots
to jot; too soft; to those lots; to those lots too

3d ● Technique Builder: Finger Action Stroking

Directions: Set line-space selector at "1" to single space. Key each line twice.

Technique Goal: Move your fingers, not your arms or wrists.

double-space (DS) after second keying of line

1 fjdk sla; fjdk sla; ed hj tf tf ol ol late late at

2 to to of of too too took took hold hold holds does

3 at at late late look look food food off off let to

4 lot lot left left loss loss felt felt sold sold so

5 foot foot lost lost take take too too set set take

3e ● Fluency Practice

Directions: Key each line three times SS. DS between 3-line groups.

Technique Goal: Key without pauses.

Key each line three times

Key without pauses

1 she looks; she looks at; he took; he took the desk

2 she does; he does; she has; he has; she has a half

3 a joke; that jet; that lot; the shoe; the old shoe

4 he has a half; had a talk; had a loss; held a sale

1c ● Location of Home Keys (4, 5, 6) and Enter Key

1. Place the first three fingers of your right hand on 4, 5, 6.

2. Take your fingers off the home keys. Replace them. Say the keys as you touch them. Repeat several times to get the "feel" of these keys.

Technique hint:
Strike each key sharply with the tip of your finger; release quickly.

3. Curve your fingers, holding them lightly over the home keys. Think and say each number as you strike it.

4. At the end of each line, strike the Enter key with your little finger to move your cursor to the next line.

444555666Enter
444555666Enter
444555666Enter

1d ● Location Drills: 4, 5, 6, Enter

1. Read down the column in Drill a, keying each number as it appears. Strike the Enter key after the final number in each line. (In this drill and those that follow, strike Enter twice after keying each group of three numbers.)

2. Key Drills b, c, and d in the same manner.

Note: Your goal is to learn to key 4, 5, 6, and Enter by touch (without watching your fingers).

Drill a	Drill b	Drill c	Drill d
4	44	44	456
4	44	45	564
4	44	46	645
5	55	54	546
5	55	55	654
5	55	56	465
6	66	64	654
6	66	65	465
6	66	66	546
4	44	44	565
4	44	45	446
4	44	46	654
5	55	54	465
5	55	55	654
5	55	56	645
6	66	64	566
6	66	65	456
6	66	66	445

LESSON 4 REVIEW LESSON

Spacing: Double
Margins: 50-space line

4a ● Keyboard Review

Directions: Key each line once with your teacher. Repeat the lines again by yourself.

Posture Goal: Sit back in your chair with body centered opposite **h** key. Keep your eyes on the copy.

Finger-Action Stroking
When one of your fingers reaches from its home position to strike another key, keep the other fingers curved on the home keys. Make the reach without raising the wrist or moving your arm or elbow.

```
home    fj dk sl a; fj dk sl a; all all fall as ask ad add
row

   e    ded ded ed ed fed feed deed deal desk else see led

   h    jhj jhj hj hj he had has she shall held half heads

   t    ftf ftf tf tf at that late date let tell the these

   o    lol lol ol ol of off old told holds look took food
```

4b ● Basic Techniques Review

Directions: Key each line twice. Strive to achieve the specific goal provided for each set of five lines.

Posture Goal: Keep head turned toward book; wrists held low; elbows near body; fingers curved.

keep eyes on copy

```
1  adds adds fall falls dad dads fad fads asks flasks
2  sales shell asked fled deal sell deed jade lake he
3  had has she he shall held half dash head hall lash
4  take these test last date left fast tell felt talk
5  those look to told took hold loss looked food shoe
```

Technique Goal: Keep fingers deeply curved; use quick, sharp strokes.

use quick, sharp keystrokes

```
1  lass lass lads lads asks flask falls fads jak jaks
2  sales deals lease desks keel flake fled flesh safe
3  she shell shells shall flash flesh head heads half
4  state feet late staff health test sheet east steel
5  holds fold joke soft stood sold food told too took
```

Technique Goal: Strike space bar with quick down-and-in motion of thumb.

use quick down-and-in motion of thumb

```
1  a a as as as ask ask ad ad ads ads all all jak jak
2  see eke fee feel less she head he fell fed led she
3  ha had has half he she heads ah ash dash lash sash
4  the at let set jet that at let set jet the at that
5  of old off so do to too hold loss lot toe does oak
```

APPENDIX A

Learning to Operate the Ten-Key Numeric Keypad

Learning Goals:

1. To learn key locations on the ten-key numeric keypad.
2. To acquire proper techniques for stroking the keys.
3. To develop speed and accuracy in entering figures by touch.

Lesson 1 ■ 4, 5, 6, and Enter

1a ● Know Your Equipment

Located at the right side of the lettered keyboard is a special number keypad similar to those found on ten-key adding machines. Illustrations of this keypad on popular brands of computers are shown at the right.

These number keys are used primarily for doing mathematical calculations with certain types of software packages. They can also be used for keying numbers that occur within alphabetical data when no calculations are required.

Refer to the user's manual for instructions that apply to your particular equipment.

Apple IIc numeric keypad

IBM PC

Tandy 1000

1b ● Check Your Position

1. Place this book to the right of your machine.

2. Sit erect with your feet on the floor, elbows near your body, just as you would for operating the alphabetic keyboard.

3. Place the first three fingers of your right hand on the home keys (4, 5, 6) of the numeric keypad. Curve your fingers as you do for regular keying of letters.

       1st finger on 4
       2nd finger on 5
       3rd finger on 6

4c ● Fluency Practice

Directions: Key each line three times.

Technique Goal: Try to achieve fluency by cutting out pauses and wasted movements in your arms, elbows, and wrists.

```
1  she sold; she sold those; she sold those old shoes

2  eat the food; look at that desk; take these tests;

3  he asked; he asked to see the jet; she told a joke

4  he talks to; she talks to; she talks to the staff;

5  to the; to that; to do; do so; at the; at the sale

6  the the that that these these those those that the
```

LESSON 5

5a ● Keyboard Review

Spacing: Double
Margin: 50-space line

Directions: Key once; repeat.

Technique Goal: Use quick, sharp strokes. Release the keys instantly.

```
home    fjdk sla; fjdk sla; fj as ask all fall ad had jade
row

  t     ftf ftf tf tf to too took the these that take tell

  o     lol lol ol ol old of off do does hold look do food

        least staff jet dot test stood foot steel date oak
all letters
taught  she sold all the old shoes; he looked at the food;
```

5b ● Location of W and I

Reach to W

1. Find **w** on the chart.
2. Find it on your keyboard.
3. Place your fingers over the home keys.
4. Reach to **w** with the **s** finger.
5. Touch **ws** lightly without moving other fingers from their home position.

Reach to I

1. Find **i** on the chart.
2. Find it on your keyboard.
3. Place your fingers over the home keys.
4. Reach to **i** with the **k** finger.
5. Touch **ik** lightly without moving other fingers from their home position.

```
sws ws ws wish wish wish        Key twice on same line          kik kik ik ik id did did
```

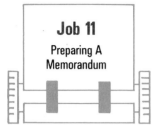

Job 11

Preparing A Memorandum

1. Key this memorandum.
2. Use a 60-space line.

TO: Robin LaCross, Editor | FROM: Dr. Mary Andreas, Principal
DATE: Current Date | SUBJECT: A JOB WELL DONE

(¶) On behalf of the students, faculty, and staff of Murray Middle School, I congratulate you and the staff of our school newspaper. You all have done an outstanding job of keeping us informed on what was happening here at the school.

(¶) Thank you for a Job Well Done! | xx

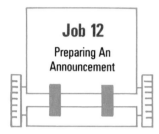

Job 12

Preparing An Announcement

1. Center this announcement on a full sheet of paper.
2. Space as directed on the illustration. Leave 10 spaces between columns.

EVERYONE'S WELCOME TO ATTEND
DS
ANNUAL FUN FAIR, MAY 12
DS

Free Juke Box Music	Dart Throwing Booth
Comedy Talent Contest	Paper Plane Race
Ring Toss Booth	Beat the Coach Ball Throw
Funny Photos Booth	Tank Dunk
Hot Dog Eating Contest	Teacher Slave Auction
Jazz Band Concert	Local DJs
Stage Show: "Anything Goes"	Dance: 8-11 p.m.

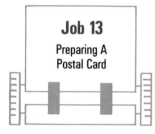

Job 13

Preparing A Postal Card

1. Key this postal card message.
2. Refer to p. 83.

Dr. Ramon Paulo | 2930 Kiel Avenue | Athens, OH 45703-3544 | Dear Dr. Paulo

(¶) Thank you for your recent ad in the Murray Middle School paper.

(¶) We would like you to attend our annual Appreciation Dinner in the school cafeteria on June 12, at 6:30 p.m.

Martha Graham | Coordinator of Student Activities

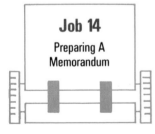

Job 14

Preparing A Memorandum

1. Key this memorandum.
2. Use a 60-space line.

TO: All Faculty | FROM: Martha Graham, Coordinator of Student Activities | DATE: Current date | SUBJECT: Outstanding Student Awards Program

(¶) Recently I sent you a list of student nominees for the Outstanding Student Awards.

(¶) Will you please check over this list carefully and rate each nominee with a 3 for high and a 1 for low. As you know, each year one to three student(s) on this list will be selected and recognized as the outstanding student(s) of the year at the annual Awards Program. Please let me have your selections by the end of the week.

(¶) Of course, you are invited to attend the Awards Program. Students really appreciate and look forward to your attendance at these events. | xx

Reach to w

Reach to i

5c ● Location Drills: W and I

Directions: Key each line once with your teacher. Repeat a second time by yourself.

Technique Goal: Reach to w and i without moving your hands forward. Hold the wrists low and quiet.

```
      sws sws sws sws ws ws ws ws we week week who whose
  w  wall wall walk walk well well how how law law laws
      west west show show few few week weeks was was low

      kik kik kik kik ik ik ik ik did did slid slid dike
  i  dike is is this this dish dish fish fish fill fill
      its its like likes list list still still life life

      with with wish wish wife wife will wills wide wide
 w/i wise wise waits waits wished wished with with will
      wait a while; a wise wish; he waits with his wife;
```

5d ● Technique Builder

Directions: Key each line twice.

Technique Goal: Quick, sharp keystrokes.

double-space (DS) when you start a new line

release the keys instantly

```
1 jfdk sla; ik ik ik ws ws ws did did dike dike wide
2 will will with with wait wait like likes it it its
3 we we well well side sides still was was wash wash
4 if if wife wife wide wide field fields while while
5 who who what what two two said said life life list
6 how how his his few few still still week week show
```

5e ● Fluency Practice

Directions: Key each line three times.

Technique Goal: Keep arms and wrists still.

key steadily

```
1 it was; it will; it will last; it will last a week
2 he was; she was; he said; she said; she saw a show
3 this file; these files; these weeks; all this week
4 at the side; at the west side; is at the east side
5 it is; it is wide; it is white; it is a white wall
6 she will wait; she will wait a few weeks; we will;
```

Lesson 5

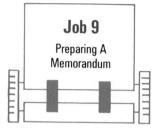

Job 9

Preparing A
Memorandum

1. Key this memorandum using a 60-space line.
2. Refer to p. 228 for proper format.

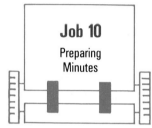

Job 10

Preparing
Minutes

1. Key these student council minutes in the form illustrated on p. 175.
2. Set your machine for a 1½" left margin and a 1" right margin.

TO: All Activity and Club Sponsors | FROM: Martha Graham, Student Activities Coordinator | DATE: April 5, 19-- | SUBJECT: Student Council and Class Officer Elections

(¶) Activity Guidelines are very clear. They state that elections for student council and class officers must take place not later than the third Friday in May in the year preceding the school year during which the officers will serve.

(¶) Please remind your advisory group that anyone wishing to be a candidate for any office must present a petition to the student council vice-president no later than May 3. This petition must have the signatures of ten members of the candidate's class. No person may sign more than one petition for the same student council or class office. | xx

MURRAY STUDENT COUNCIL MEETING

Minutes of Meeting

Date: Current date

Time: 3:30 p.m.

Place: Room 107, Murray Middle School

Present: All ten members; Ms. Martha Graham, Student Activities Coordinator; Dr. Mary Andreas, Principal

1. President of the student council, James Bly, opened the meeting by asking for approval and/or additions to the agenda.

2. Judy Moceri gave the Treasurer's report. The report was discussed and approved.

3. The chairperson of each of the special events committees presented an appraisal of the events for which he/she was responsible. All members agreed that this year's events were successful, with the exception of the field trip.

4. The Career Club presented a draft of its new constitution for Council approval. After some discussion, Ms. Graham suggested that the draft be sent back for some revisions.

5. The meeting was adjourned at 4:40 p.m.

LESSON 6

6a ● Keyboard Review

Directions: Key once; repeat.

Posture Goal: Sit erect; eyes on copy.

```
w  sws sws ws ws wish wise with was wall walk who how
i  kik kik ik ik did did slid slid dike dike hid hide
t o  of to the that let these so do those take last too
all letters  weeks date fast steel aid jail whole test fit like
taught  she held a safe lead; he looked at the white dish;
```

6b ● Location of R and N

Reach to R

1. Find r on the chart.
2. Find it on your keyboard.
3. Place your fingers over the home keys.
4. Reach to r with the f finger.
5. Touch rf lightly without moving other fingers from their home position.

Reach to N

1. Find n on the chart.
2. Find it on your keyboard.
3. Place your fingers over the home keys.
4. Reach to n with the j finger.
5. Touch nj lightly without moving other fingers from their home position.

```
frf frf rf rf fo for for    Key twice on same line    jnj jnj nj nj an and and
```

6c ● Location Drills: R and N

Directions: Key each line once with your teacher. Repeat a second time by yourself.

Technique Goal: Strike each key with a quick, sharp stroke; release quickly.

Reach to r

Reach to n

```
     frf frf frf frf rf rf rf rf for for her here there
r  are are here here their their real real work works
     were were world world three three first first fire

     jnj jnj jnj jnj nj nj nj nj an an and and sand end
n  land land ran ran end end lend lend than than then
     in in on on one one own owns send sends need needs

     near near friend friends nor nor north north learn
r/n  learn earn earn warn warn torn torn horn horn fern
     fern torn horn nor north friends learns earns warn
```

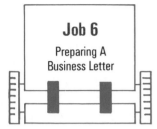

Job 6

Preparing A
Business Letter

1. Key this letter on a 50-space line.
2. Use modified block style, mixed punctuation.

Mrs. Ann Kramer | Advertising Manager | Burton Business Products | 28945 Roland Street | Athens, OH 45703-7865 | Dear Mrs. Kramer:

(¶) Our school newspaper is pleased to announce that it is currently seeking advertisers. Your company has been referred to us as a firm that makes outstanding business products that would be of interest to our readers.

(¶) The Murray Middle School paper has a circulation of over 300. In addition to being read by the students, it is read by many teachers and parents. Therefore, it would definitely be to your advantage to advertise in our paper.

(¶) If you are interested in having your products brought to the attention of our subscribers, please let us know as soon as possible.

Sincerely yours, | Eric Quesada | Business Manager | xx

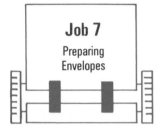

Job 7

Preparing
Envelopes

1. Address a large envelope to potential school newspaper advertisers shown on this list.
2. Refer to p. 90 for assistance in correct placement of an envelope address.

Mr. John Washington
Acme Sporting Goods Co.
17239 Porter Avenue
Athens, OH 45701-1222

Ms. Mary Krusinski
Arthur Yearbook Co.
4299 Yale Street
Athens, OH 45701-1064

Mrs. Betty Lawson
Lawson Novelty Co.
384 North Road
Athens, OH 45701-1235

Mr. Robert Digger
New Motor Sales
12 Bernard Boulevard
Athens, OH 45703-3202

Ms. Rhonda Kareem
P.O. Box 183
Athens, OH 45703-3600

Dr. Ramon Paulo
2930 Kiel Avenue
Athens, OH 45703-3544

Job 8

Preparing A
Business Letter

1. Key this letter using a 50-space line.
2. Use modified block style, mixed punctuation.

Dr. Paul Vanderlan | Allstate College | 521 Grand Avenue | Martinsville, OH 45146-1721 | Dear Dr. Vanderlan:

(¶) Enclosed is my registration form for the annual Student Activities conference to be held at your college on April 27-28. I understand that all conference attendees must make their own housing arrangements.

(¶) I am especially looking forward to the roundtable discussions on the legal implications of schools sponsoring student activities. This area is one of growing concern not only to school districts but also to sponsors of individual activities.

Sincerely yours, | Martha Graham | Student Activities Coordinator | xx | Enclosure

Working in a School Office (Simulation)

6d ● Technique Builder

Directions: Key each line twice SS. DS between each 2-line group.

Technique Goal: Use quick, sharp keystrokes.

```
1 nj nj rf rf an and and hand hands than than thanks

2 in in kind kind one one done done far far her hers

3 here here there there first first air air red read

4 no no not not note notes think thinks thank thanks

5 near near own own down down front front word words

6 were were their theirs where where free free rates

7 now now know knows known when when fine fine finds

8 trend trends rain rain train trains worn worn rind
```

6e ● Fluency Practice

Directions: Key each line twice SS. DS between each 2-line group.

Technique Goal: Key steadily without pauses between strokes.

```
1 if he is; if he is here; if she is; if she is here

2 we went; we went to the store; it was; it was fine

3 on the land; on the road; in the air; in the world

4 two or three; two or three lines; one or two words

5 it is; it is on the north side; it was for her son

6 on the trains; in their hands; near the front door

7 there were ten art shows; read all this final news

8 she wrote her two friends; he ran down that street
```

LESSON 7

7a ● Keyboard Review

Spacing: Double
Margin: 50-space line

Directions: Key once; then repeat.

Posture Goal: Curve fingers over keys.

```
r  frf frf rf rf for far nor nor hear hard fire start

n  jnj jnj nj nj an an and land need need new new now

all letters   when know send want line free join sent rate shown
taught        needs a loan; wrote his friend; sent her the news;
```

Job 3

Preparing A Table

1. Center this list of school paper staff members on a half sheet of paper.
2. DS after the heading; DS between items.
3. Leave 10 spaces between columns.

SCHOOL PAPER STAFF

Editor	Robin LaCross
Assistant Editor	Mary Lizardo
Business Manager	Eric Quesada
Reporter	Cynthia Schultz
Reporter	Mickey Miyaki
Reporter	Debbie Harley
Photographer	Martin Kruski
Sponsor	Gordon Gardner

Job 4

Preparing a Business Letter

1. Key this letter for the school paper editor on a 50-space line.
2. Use block style, open punctuation.

Miss Loretta Espuda | Editor | Jackson Middle School | 1400 South Rutgers Avenue | Athens, OH 45703-1224 | Dear Loretta

(¶) On behalf of the school paper staff and the students at Murray Middle School, I want to thank you for your cooperation in helping us develop a school newspaper at our school.

(¶) Our school paper has been a real success with both students and faculty. It has encouraged our students to get involved in school activities.

(¶) We look forward to working together again with your staff and hope that joint activities can be carried out in the future involving both our schools.

Sincerely yours | Robin LaCross | Editor | xx

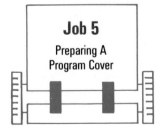

Job 5

Preparing A Program Cover

1. Format/key the program cover centering the copy vertically and horizontally on a half sheet of paper.
2. DS each line with a QS before and after the design.

```
         LUNCHEON MEETING
         STUDENT COUNCIL

              xx
            x    x
          x        x
         x   SC    x
          x        x
            x    x
              xx

      Special Events Dining Room
        Murray Middle School
         November 15, 19--
             1:00 p.m.
```

7b ● Location of C and . (period)

Reach to C

1. Find c on the chart.
2. Find it on your keyboard.
3. Place your fingers over the home keys.
4. Reach to c with the d finger.
5. Touch cd lightly without moving other fingers from their home position.

Reach to . (period)

1. Find . on the chart.
2. Find it on your keyboard.
3. Place your fingers over the home keys.
4. Reach to . with the l finger.
5. Touch .l lightly without moving other fingers from their home position.

```
dcd  dcd  cd  cd  ca  car  car        Key twice on same line        l.l  .l  .l  .l  fell.  fell.
```

Reach to c

Reach to . (period)

Spacing Guide

Space twice after a period that ends a sentence.

When the period comes at the end of a line, return without spacing. Space only once after a period following an initial or abbreviation.

Reach to left shift key

7c ● Location Drills: C and . (period)

Directions: Key each line once with your teacher. Repeat the lines a second time by yourself.

Technique Goal: Reach to the new keys without moving your hands out of position.

```
       dcd  dcd  dcd  dcd  cd  cd  cd  cd  car  car  cars  call  call
  c    can  can  care  care  cards  cards  call  calls  cost  cost
       each  each  class  class  act  acts  force  force  car  car

          l.l  l.l  l.l  .l  .l  .l  fill.  fell.  sell.  call.  hall.
(period) .  ill.  ail.  all.  wall.  well.  hail.  fail.  real.  seal.
          tell.  will.  fall.  feel.  deal.  cool.  shell.  school.
```

7d ● Shifting for Capitals: Left Shift Key

1. The left shift key (No. 21) is used to key capital letters with the right hand.
2. Use a one-two count.

One Depress the shift key with the a finger. Hold it down.

Two Strike the capital letter; then quickly release the shift key and return the a finger to its home position.

Directions: Change to single spacing. Key each line two times. DS between each set of two lines.

Posture Goal: Hold shoulders erect with body leaning slightly forward.

```
1  Ha  Ha  Hal  Hall  La  La  Lane  Ja  Ja  Jan  Jan  Ka  Ka  Karl
2  Lee  ran.   Lee  ran  here.   I  see  it.   I  can  see  Kit.
3  H.  J.  Hill  had  a  hat.   Jo  will  write  ft.  for  feet.
```

Unit 18 ■ Working in a School Office (Simulation)

Learning Goals:
1. To format/key job activities that would likely be encountered in beginning office jobs.
2. To become aware of the necessity for accuracy in office work.
3. To become aware of and use desirable work habits and attitudes.

General Directions

Unit 18 is designed to give you an opportunity to apply your basic skills and knowledge in a simulated office situation. You will be performing the types of jobs often found in offices. General instructions are given in the "Guide for Office Employees" in Job 1 below. Specific instructions are included with each job.

You will be working as a clerical assistant for one period each day in the office of Ms. Martha Graham, Student Activities Coordinator at Murray Middle School, 1729 Winston Avenue, Athens, OH 45701-2979. In addition you may be asked to do office work for faculty members and students on school-related matters. Accuracy is a trait that is valued highly in an office worker. Proofread your work carefully and correct all errors. Make certain you understand the instructions for each job before you begin; then work as efficiently as you can to produce quality work.

Job 1

Preparing A Report

1. Key this report on a 60-space line.
2. Center the heading on line 13.
3. SS the numbered items; DS between them. Carryovers (second lines of enumeration) are keyed using a second tab stop or the tab indent feature; the carryover line may also be keyed flush with enumeration.

GUIDE FOR OFFICE EMPLOYEES

QS

1. Report for work at the time that you have been assigned. Please sign the attendance sheets each day.

2. If you are going to be absent, phone the activities office between 7:30 and 8:00 a.m.

3. Specific instructions will be included with each job requiring formatting of letters. Key the current date on line 18.

4. Refer to your textbook whenever you need help in placing material attractively on the page.

5. Proofread each job and correct all errors before you remove the paper from your machine.

6. Leave all completed jobs on my assistant's desk. You will be told whether you are to keep unfinished jobs for the next day or to leave them for someone else.

Job 2

Preparing a Business Letter

1. Using a 60-space line, key this letter for Ms. Graham's signature.
2. Use modified block style, mixed punctuation.

Mr. John Truski | Marketing Representative | United Fundraisers | 1305 Oakman Avenue | Athens, OH 45701-1376 | Dear Mr. Truski:

(¶) Thank you for sending me your new catalog of items that could be used by the clubs at Murray Middle School to raise funds for school activities and encourage school pride.

(¶) As we discussed at our meeting of September 26, it will be primarily up to our student leaders to decide which items will be offered for sale through our student activities. Also, I am assuming that your artist will work with our students in developing a new school logo to be placed on all items that we purchase.

(¶) As soon as we select the items for this year's fundraisers, I will contact you with our total order. We at Murray Middle School look forward to working with you again this school year.

Sincerely yours, | Martha Graham | Student Activities Coordinator | xx

7e ● Technique Builder: Shift Key Control

Directions: Key each line two times SS. DS between 2-line groups.

Technique Goal: Hold the shift key down until you strike the capital letter; then release it quickly.

space twice after period at end of a sentence

```
1 It is here.  Nan hit it.  Jeff can see it.  I ran.

2 He can sell it.  I can take it.  Jo will tell her.

3 I ran fast.  I ran to school.  Lane ran to school.

4 Joan went there.  Joe called.  Nan called for her.

5 Jake has a friend.  He is her friend.  He is late.

6 I like to work.  Jo works hard.  He needs to work.
```

LESSON 8   REVIEW LESSON

8a ● Keyboard Review

Directions: Key once, then repeat.

Posture Goal: Wrists held low; elbows near body.

Spacing: Double
Margin: 50-space line

hold wrists low

keep elbows near body

```
w sws sws ws ws who whose how laws week was what few

i kik kik ik ik it its with this side file fill life

r frf frf rf rf for are were there three works world

n jnj jnj nj nj in fine fan one soon known when than

c dcd dcd cd cd costs close clean chief child chance

. l.l l.l .l .l .l ill. fill. will. all. call. fall.

Shift Hi Hi Hill Lil Lil; Lil Kine; Kate Kate; Kate Kane
```

8b ● Basic Techniques Review

Directions: Key each line twice; concentrate on the technique goal.

Technique Goal: Keep fingers curved; make quick, sharp strokes.

quick, sharp strokes

```
1 we week well west who what was how few two law low

2 is this it with will his if its like life said did

3 for are were here there where their her first work

4 and in on one not an than thank then when own need

5 can call case card cost check which each since act
```

70-space line

140a ● Keyboard Review

5 minutes

Directions: Key each sentence three times SS. DS between 3-line groups.

alphabet   With more fighting, a boxer jabs a quick volley into a dazed opponent.

figure   The race on May 3, 1989, was won by a No. 5 car at 178 miles per hour.

shift   Robin J. Valdes from the Center For Music in San Juan spoke on Monday.

easy   People should not blame others for a problem they bring on themselves.

---

12 minutes

140b ● Timed Writings

Directions: 1. Take a 1' control writing on each ¶ in 136d, page 235. Circle errors. Figure *gwam*.

2. Take a 5' control writing on all five ¶ s combined. Circle errors and figure *gwam*.

---

28 minutes

do not pause between words

140c ● Formatting Problems

Directions: Problem 1   Interoffice Memorandum

Key the following memorandum in simplified style using approximately 1" side margins or the default margins on your equipment.

Current date | J. Murray Morris | COMPANY DINNER DANCE

(¶) The annual company dinner dance will be held on the third Saturday of next month. This event will be held at Red Run Country Club beginning with light refreshments at 7:30 p.m. Dinner will be served at 8:30, followed by a gala evening of dancing.

(¶) We are expecting more than 150 of our current and past employees to attend this event. If you are not planning to attend, will you please inform your department manager by the end of next week. Ms. Roberts, our president, and the entire planning committee are looking forward to seeing you at this special annual company celebration.

Robert J. Birmingham | xx

Directions: Problem 2   Invoice

Key the invoice below. Set left margin and tab stops for each column. Refer to 133c, page 231, if necessary. Compute total and enter under amount.

SOLD TO Murray Middle School | 1729 Winston Avenue | Athens, OH 45701-2979 | DATE July 25, 19-- | OUR ORDER NO. 7068 | CUSTOMER ORDER NO. 343 | SHIPPED VIA United Truck | SALESPERSON Bernie Lincoln | TERMS 2/10, n/30

Quantity	Description	Unit Price	Amount
4	GTE Overhead Projectors	119.50	478.00
1	FM Broadcast PA	947.75	947.75
3	Cordless FM Microphones	49.00	147.00

140d ● Extra-Credit Activity: Composing a Short Report

Directions: Compose a short report using the information given in 136d, page 235. Use the title, The Census and You. Cite in your report at least one new use for census data. Refer to 53c, page 99, if necessary.

140e ● Enrichment Activity: Composing and Reformatting a Short Report

Following the directions in 140d above, compose a report. After printing your composed report, use the block and move feature of your computer and rearrange the paragraphs in the report. Print the new report.

8b Continued

Directions: Key each line twice. Concentrate on the technique goal.

Technique Goal: Depress shift key with the a finger. Strike the capital letter; quickly release shift key.

Reach to left shift key

1 Jane Noakes and Karl Hicks; Lane Katt and Nan Hale

2 Jill North and Keith Halls; Jo Lind and Kent Hart;

3 John called Lil Nolan. He called Joan Noakes too.

4 Jon wrote to Joan Lands. Jeff wrote to Kate Haak.

Technique Goal: Tap return key quickly with ; finger.

Electronic return

Computer return

1 I said she
2 ran there.

3 Jan took a ride
4 in the new jet.

5 He went to the lakes
6 in her fine old car.

7 I will walk to that store
8 if I need dark red shoes.

9 Kent starts to work there as a
10 clerk at the end of this week.

Computing Gross Words a Minute (*gwam*)

Five characters/spaces are counted as one word. Each line in 8c has 50 strokes, or 10 words. For each full line keyed, give yourself 10 *gwam*. For a partially keyed line, note the scale under the sentences. Add the figure below the last character or space keyed to your complete sentence score. This total is your gross words a minute (*gwam*).

8c ● Sentence Skill Builder

Directions: Key a 1-minute writing on each line below. Compute your gross words a minute (*gwam*).

Technique Goal: Use quick, crisp, short strokes.

1 I was asked to look at the north side of the door.

2 Jan wants to trade her old car for a nice new one.

3 One word in the line was too hard for her to read.

4 He saw lots of fine artwork at the fair this week.

5 Lil said that she was not late to her first class.

| 1 | 2 | 3 | 4 | 5 | 6 | 7 | 8 | 9 | 10 |

139b ● Building Skill

Directions: Key each sentence three times SS. DS between 3-line groups.

The booklet entitled <u>Great Software Packages</u> is on sale for only $.95.
Spence Wilson (a first-year runner) came in first in the 100-yard run.
Bert's <u>Sports Bloopers</u> will be shown next week at 9 p.m. on channel 2.
Almost 32% of the employed students at school averaged $5.50 per hour.
The old Abbott and Costello tapes can be rented for around $3.00 each.

| 1 | 2 | 3 | 4 | 5 | 6 | 7 | 8 | 9 | 10 | 11 | 12 | 13 | 14 |

---

30 minutes

139c ● Formatting Problems

Directions: Problem 1   Business Letter from Script
1. Key the letter shown in block style with open punctuation. Set margins for a 50-space line; place today's date on line 18.
2. Address a large envelope.

Mr. Loren Logan/45 Lincoln Way/Chicago, IL 60645-2038/Dear Mr. Logan

¶ Enclosed is your $10 rebate check for purchasing three special metallic cassette recording tapes.
¶ We know you will find the quality of the tapes to exceed by far any others that you have used in the past. We hope you agree.
Sincerely yours/Mary Durant/Customer Services/xx/Enclosure

Directions: Problem 2   Interoffice Memorandum
Key the following memorandum on a 60-space line. Key the heading information flush left with the margin. Space twice after the colon and key the information following each heading. Set the right margin 60 spaces to the right of the left margin.

TO: All Department Heads | FROM: Juanita Bryant, Manager | DATE: March 2, 19-- | SUBJECT: Management Team Meeting
(¶) The next meeting of our Management Team will be held on Friday, March 17. We will meet in the Conference Room at 2:30 p.m. The meeting should end at approximately 4:30 p.m.
(¶) The primary agenda item will be a discussion of the new employee benefit program and its effects on all employees. As you know, this program allows employees to choose how they want their benefits packaged. They will be given a base dollar amount and asked how they want their dollars allocated to vacation, health and life insurance, training, etc. Please be prepared to discuss all options of the program as they relate to your department.
(¶) As I have requested in the past, please submit any items that you feel should be added to our March 17 agenda. As time permits, all additional items will be discussed. These suggested agenda items should reach my office no later than March 9. | xx

Directions: Problem 3   Business Letter from Script
Rekey the letter in Problem 1 above. Make the following changes: **1.** Address the letter to Ms. Merle Olsen, 14 Dover Road, Erie, PA 18018-7615.
2. Change the amount of the check to $12.50.

LESSON 9

9a ● Keyboard Review

Directions: Key once, then repeat.

Posture Goal: Sit erect; eyes on copy.

keep eyes
on copy

c cd cd check checks card cards face face cost costs

. l.l l.l .l .l .l .l. ill. ital. kil. dal. Lt. Ill.

shift Lance Jones and Jane Keel; Jack Halls and Nan Ides

all letters
taught He asked her if she knew where to send the checks.

Jets will take off at the rate of three each week.

| 1 | 2 | 3 | 4 | 5 | 6 | 7 | 8 | 9 | 10 |

9b ● Location of G and U

Reach to G

1. Find g on the chart.
2. Find it on your keyboard.
3. Place your fingers over the home keys.
4. Reach to g with the f finger.
5. Touch gf lightly without moving other fingers from their home position.

Reach to U

1. Find u on the chart.
2. Find it on your keyboard.
3. Place your fingers over the home keys.
4. Reach to u with the j finger.
5. Touch uj lightly without moving other fingers from their home position.

fgf fgf gf gf go got got

Key twice on same line

juj juj uj uj us use use

Reach to g

Reach to u

9c ● Location Drills: G and U

Directions: Key once with your teacher, a second time by yourself.

Technique Goal: Reach your fingers, not your hands, to the new keys.

fgf fgf fgf fgf gf gf gf gf go good good gone gone

g got got sign sign light light right right get gets

eight eight age age girl girls green green gas gas

juj juj juj juj uj uj uj uj us use used hour hours

u out out our our could could should should due dues

just just such such full full four four hour hours

138c ● Formatting Problems

Directions: Problem 1 Simplified Style Letter in Rough Draft

1. Key/format the letter shown below in simplified style. Set margins for a 50- space line; begin the dateline on line 15.

2. Address a small envelope.

June 30, 19--

~~Miss~~ Mrs. Elizabeth Bradford East
219 Jefferson Street, ~~West~~
Springfield, IL 62702-1949

MICROWAVE REFUND

We recieved your letter dated June 15 providing the information ~~that~~ we requested regarding the microwave purchase from
our store. The copies of your sales receipt and correspondence
regarding this appliance have been very helpful.

I personally checked out the problems you have been having
getting your microwave repaired properly by our service staff.
We have decided the best way to rectify this situation is for
our store to replace your current unit. If this solution meets
with your approval, please let me know. I can be reached at
555-2153.

Thank you, Mrs. bradford, for your patience in this matter.
We look forward to serving you again ~~soon.~~ in the very near future

Paula Cooper, Customer Services Manager — ALL CAPS

xx

Directions: Problem 2 Table

Key the table below on a half sheet of paper in exact vertical center. Leave 6 spaces between columns; DS items.

STUDENT SUCCESS SEMINARS

Topic	Date	Chairperson
Improving Study Skills	October 11	Mary Flores
Speed Reading	December 5	Max Cutler
Effective Library Use	February 3	Jeff Walters
Choosing a Career	April 16	Lynn Broderick

LESSON 139

70-space line

5 minutes

139a ● Keyboard Review

Directions: Key each sentence three times SS. DS between 3-line groups.

alphabet A just, quick, but exact mind will help you develop a zest for living.

figure In the period 1951-1974, Lucille Ball starred in 495 television shows.

3d finger Unless we allow the millions of local goods to be sold, you will lose.

easy You must have a goal in mind if you want to profit from your practice.

| 1 | 2 | 3 | 4 | 5 | 6 | 7 | 8 | 9 | 10 | 11 | 12 | 13 | 14 |

9d ● Technique Builder: Wrists Low and Steady

Directions: Key each line two times SS. DS between 2-line groups.

Technique Goal: Curve your fingers. Hold your wrists low and steady.

curve your
fingers

keep wrists and
elbows still

```
1 uj gf uj gf such such glad glad long long run runs

2 four four though though thought thought turn turns

3 just just would would sound sounds through through

4 to do; to do the; to go; to go to the; to go there

5 if he; if she; if he can; if she can; if we do the

6 I can go.  He will go there.  He can go there too.

7 He will need four hours.  He will go in two hours.

8 One of their goals is to hold the wrists down low.
  |  1  |  2  |  3  |  4  |  5  |  6  |  7  |  8  |  9  |  10  |
```

Keep wrists low.

Position of Wrists

Keep your wrists low, but do not allow them to touch the machine. Keep forearms parallel to the slant of the keyboard.

Forearms parallel to slant of keyboard.

9e ● Sentence Skill Builder

Directions: Key two 1' writings on each sentence. Figure your *gwam*.

Posture Goal: Keep the wrists low.

```
 1 I can do the work if I find the tools that I need.
 2 He will learn the rules that she has on the cards.
 3 I know that he and she can gain a good high skill.
 4 Kate thought that the chair was not right for her.
 5 Jack said he likes to eat fast food for his lunch.
 6 Ned told us a good joke that he heard at the show.
 7 Lu will walk to that new store with all the girls.
 8 Half of the words on the last test were hard ones.
 9 It was the sort of chance we knew she had to take.
10 One thing he needs to do is take care of his cars.
   |  1  |  2  |  3  |  4  |  5  |  6  |  7  |  8  |  9  |  10  |
```

LESSON 138   70-space line

5 minutes   **138a ● Keyboard Review**

Directions: Key each sentence three times SS. DS between 3-line groups.

keep arms and   alphabet   We made the very best quality kegs for all our expensive frozen juice.
wrists quiet

figure   Charles Lindbergh crossed the Atlantic in 33 hours 39 minutes in 1927.

long words   Nevertheless, their scientists discovered it overwhelmingly difficult.

easy   We thought it was a very good plan to change paper in the new printer.

| 1 | 2 | 3 | 4 | 5 | 6 | 7 | 8 | 9 | 10 | 11 | 12 | 13 | 14 |

10 minutes   **138b ● Speed Builder**

Directions: Take two 1' writings on each ¶; try to increase speed on the second writing. Figure *gwam*.

Alternate Procedure: Work for speed as you take one 5' writing on all four ¶s combined. Figure *gwam*.

all letters used   1.4 si   5.3 awl   85% hfw

	gwam 1'	5'
The school year is almost ended for pupils all over the nation.	13	3	51
Most have worked to get ready for more education and future entry-level	27	5	53
employment. In the next four weeks these pupils will have to make a	41	8	56
choice on how to spend the summer.	48	10	58
Many thousands of teenagers every summer search for jobs in which	13	12	60
they can earn some money for a trip, new sports equipment, or simply	27	15	63
to help out with the family budget. Getting a paycheck of your very own	42	18	66
can be fun, but there are several points that should be kept in mind in	56	21	69
obtaining summer employment.	62	22	70
Work to get employment that is in line with your career plans. In	13	25	73
that way you can gather first-hand information about your chosen career.	28	28	76
You will be able to decide whether or not you and your career make a	42	30	78
good team. It's quite important that you learn this about yourself.	56	33	81
This is not the only principle to keep in mind, however.	67	35	83
A summer job gives you a chance to learn how to work. Capitalize	13	38	86
on the opportunity to interact with other workers, to take directions,	27	41	89
and put what you presently know to an acid test. This is the payoff for	42	44	92
summer work—a golden opportunity to learn just what is expected, plus	56	47	95
a chance to see how well you can fill the bill.	66	48	96

gwam 1' | 1 | 2 | 3 | 4 | 5 | 6 | 7 | 8 | 9 | 10 | 11 | 12 | 13 | 14 |
      5' | 1 | 2 | 3 |

LESSON 10

Spacing: Double
Margin: 50-space line

10a ● Keyboard Review

Directions: Key once; repeat.　　　　　　**Posture Goal:** Keep eyes on copy.

use quick,
sharp strokes

g `great great light lights large large charge charge`

u `would would south south course course thing things`

all letters
taught

`I will join their staff as soon as I get a chance.`

`Kids who work here are out of class for that hour.`

` | 1 | 2 | 3 | 4 | 5 | 6 | 7 | 8 | 9 | 10 | `

10b ● Location of V, Y, and Shift

Reach to V

1. Find v on the chart.
2. Find it on your keyboard.
3. Place your fingers over the home keys.
4. Reach to v with the f finger.
5. Touch vf lightly without moving other fingers from their home position.

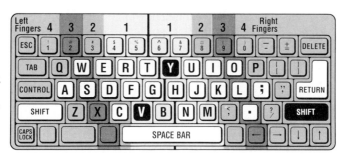

Reach to Y

1. Find y on the chart.
2. Find it on your keyboard.
3. Place your fingers over the home keys.
4. Reach to y with the j finger.
5. Touch yj lightly without moving other fingers from their home position.

`fvf  fvf  vf  fiv  five  five`　　　Key twice on same line　　　`jyj  jyj  yj  yj  ja  jay  jay`

10c ● Location Drills: V and Y

Reach to v

Reach to y

Directions: Key each line once with your teacher. Repeat by yourself.

Technique Goal: Think the letters as you key. Use quick, sharp strokes.

　`fvf fvf fvf fvf vf vf vf vf five fives lives lives`

v `have have five five give give dive dive hive hives`

　`save saves gave gave wave waved raves leave leaves`

　`jyj jyj jyj jyj yj yj yj yj jay jays lay lays slay`

y `sly sly fly fly try try jay jay ray ray stay stays`

　`the they eye eyes try tray fry fray lay lays yells`

　`very very every every vinyl vinyl navy navy vanity`

v/y `vainly vainly vaguely vaguely convey convey savory`

　`valley valley verify verify varsity varsity vanity`

LESSON 137

5 minutes

137a ● Keyboard Review

Directions: Key each sentence three time SS. DS between 3-line groups.

alphabet   Everyone expects to enjoy a warm fire quickly blazing in the new dorm.

figure   If they want the 23 books, the cost of the set has gone up to $149.50.

weak fingers   I will oppose the plan to supply it. We saw the weakness and laxness.

easy   They kept their goals before them during the time they were in charge.

| 1 | 2 | 3 | 4 | 5 | 6 | 7 | 8 | 9 | 10 | 11 | 12 | 13 | 14 |

10 minutes

137b ● Building Skill: Figures and Symbols

Directions: Key each sentence once SS.   Work at your control level.
Take two 1′ writings on each sentence.

1   On March 7, 1990, a team of 5 trapeze artists worked 101 stories high.

2   The Great Pyramid, 755 feet across and 481 feet high, covers 13 acres.

3   I paid invoice #76 (dated June 4) with Check #32 in the amount of $84.

| 1 | 2 | 3 | 4 | 5 | 6 | 7 | 8 | 9 | 10 | 11 | 12 | 13 | 14 |

30 minutes

137c ● Formatting Problems: Business Letters

Directions: Problem 1   Modified Block Style Letter

1. Key/format the letter shown below in modified block style with mixed punctuation. Set margins for a 60-space line; begin the dateline on line 18.

2. Address a small envelope.

The opening and closing lines of this letter are in problem form. Capitalize and punctuate them correctly.

January 22, 19-- | mr bernard o carter | 50 regis drive | detroit mi 48202-1587 | dear mr carter

(¶) Thank you very much for stopping at our exhibit booth at the Autorama Show this last month. I agree with you that the show was a great exhibit of outstanding custom cars.

(¶) It was a real pleasure for us to explain to you how our company can help you develop and market custom design cars at realistic prices. As we explained at the time, our firm makes a variety of kit cars that can be easily assembled. These kits can be ordered with a variety of body parts and engines to provide a truly one-of-a-kind automobile. If you will call us at 555-1555, I will be pleased to supply more detailed information.

(¶) Thank you again, Mr. Carter, for your interest in Custom Designs.

sincerely yours | betty burke | marketing representative | xx

Directions: Problem 2   Business Letter with Subject Line

Key the letter above as you did in Problem 1. Add this subject line:

SUBJECT: Custom Cars Marketing Potential

Directions: Problem 3   Business Letter with Attention Line

Key the letter above as you did in Problem 1. Address the letter to Attention Ms. Helen B. Hudson | R & D

Specialty Shops | 735 Oakman Lane | Dearborn, MI 48129-1524 | Ladies and Gentlemen

10d ● Shifting for Capitals: Right Shift Key

Spacing Guide:
Remember to space twice after a period that ends a sentence (except at the end of a line).

1. The right shift key (No. 18) is used to key capital letters with the left hand.
2. Use a one-two count.

One Depress the shift key with the ; finger. Hold it down.
Two Strike the capital letter; then quickly release the shift key and return the ; finger to its home position.

Reach to right shift key

Directions: Key each line twice. Use single spacing.

Posture Goal: Use a quick, firm reach to the shift key.

```
1  Ted Ted Fran Fran; Ted and Fran; Fran and I; Frank

2  Ted is here.  Fran can see Ted.  She can see Fran.

3  Frank is ill.  I need Art here.  She and I see it.
```

10e ● Technique Builder: Shift Key Control

Directions: Key each line three times SS. DS after the third line.

Technique Goal: Hold the shift key down until you strike the capital letter; then release quickly.

return without spacing after . at end of line

```
1  vf yj vf yj day day dry dry say say stay stay days

2  yes yet hear the they ray gray tray sly slay style

3  She can.  She can have her turn.  I can give five.

4  Jan and I can stay.  Jan can stay there five days.

5  Ann and Karl are here.  Jan left her friend there.

6  I can learn.  She can get all the funds she needs.
```

LESSON 11

Spacing: Double
Margin: 50-space line

11a ● Keyboard Review

Directions: Key once; repeat.

Posture Goal: Sit back in chair. Keep eyes on copy.

```
    v  give give live live gave gave view views save save
    y  you you years years way way ways says says why why
shift  Fred Sills and Ann Shields; Rick Weld and Sue Todd
all letters  You will have to judge the facts in each new case.
  taught  Kris needs to work hard if she wants a good grade.
```

return quickly

```
  I  1  I  2  I  3  I  4  I  5  I  6  I  7  I  8  I  9  I  10  I
```

20 minutes

Alternate Procedure: Work on control as you take a 1' writing on ¶ 1. Move to succeeding ¶s when you complete each one within the error limit specified by your teacher. If time allows, repeat any ¶s in which you exceeded the error limit.

136d ● Speed Ladder Paragraphs

Directions: Take a 1' writing on ¶ 1 DS. Repeat procedure on succeeding ¶s. Take three 1' writings on any ¶ you do not finish in the time given.

all letters used   1.4 si

	gwam 5'
Every ten years a very important count takes place. That count	3 | 56
is the census that occurs at the start of each decade. To conduct an	5 | 58
accurate tally of the entire nation requires a great deal of planning	8 | 61
and a lot of effort.	9 | 62
There are a great many reasons to take a very correct count. One	12 | 65
of the most crucial to our local, state, and federal governmental agen-	14 | 67
cies is the fact that billions of tax dollars are given out based on	17 | 70
the number of people who live in a given area.	19 | 72
Census figures are used to decide how many seats each state is	22 | 75
to have in the House of Representatives. The numbers are also used to	24 | 77
draw up the boundary lines of voting districts, not only for the House but	27 | 80
also for many of the state and other local bodies.	29 | 82
One more very important use of census data is that it acts as a	32 | 85
guide to shape new laws and policies. In every branch of government,	35 | 88
lawmakers look to the census data to help them plan public policies.	38 | 91
Data on age, income, family size, etc. are used to help form policy.	40 | 93
It is easy to see that it is quite important to get an exact count	43 | 96
of all the residents of our country and every related area. Many things	46 | 99
that we consider to be just everyday items are often decided by govern-	49 |102
ment, based to great extent on census data. The count which is taken	51 |104
each decade plays a key role in our daily lives.	53 |106

gwam 5' | 1 | 2 | 3 |

---

10 minutes

136e ● Language Arts Skills: Creative Keying

Directions: Key a short unbound report on ways you plan to use your keying   skills. Refer to page 100 if necessary.

11b ● Location of B, M, and Tab

Reach to B

1. Find b on the chart.
2. Find it on your keyboard.
3. Place your fingers over the home keys.
4. Reach to b with the f finger.
5. Touch bf lightly without moving other fingers from their home position.

Reach to M

1. Find m on the chart.
2. Find it on your keyboard.
3. Place your fingers over the home keys.
4. Reach to m with the j finger.
5. Touch mj lightly without moving other fingers from their home position.

fbf fbf bf bf ib fib fib   Key twice on same line   jmj jmj mj mj ja jam jam

Reach to b

Reach to m

11c ● Location Drills: B and M

Directions: Key each line once with your teacher. Repeat a second time by yourself.

Technique Goal: Use finger, not hand, motions as you reach for these keys.

```
      fbf  fbf  fbf  fbf  bf  bf  bf  bf  buff  buff  job  job  jobs
  b   big  big  both  both  boy  boy  boys  blue  blue  ball  ball
      bus  bus  by  by  buy  buy  but  but  hub  hub  lab  lab  burn

      jmj  jmj  jmj  jmj  mj  mj  mj  mj  jam  jam  make  make  made
  m   men  men  mean  mean  them  them  come  come  much  much  am
      same  same  game  games  more  more  most  most  from  from

      boom  boom  bomb  bombs  comb  combs  brim  brim  blossoms
 b/m  beam  beam  blame  blame  broom  broom  bloom  bloom  balm
      become  become  became  became  member  member  basement
```

Electronic Tabulation

11d ● Indenting for Paragraphs

1. Clear all tab stops. Move the carrier so that the point of keying is at the right margin of your paper. Depress the tab clear key (No. 27) and hold it down as you return the carrier so that the point of keying is at the left margin of your paper. You have cleared all tab stops.

2. Set a tab stop. Space in 5 spaces from the left margin. Depress the tab set key (No. 28). You have set a tab stop at paragraph point.

3. Tab to paragraph point. Return the carrier so that the point of keying is at the left margin. Find the tab key (No. 24) on your machine. Touch lightly the tab key using the closest little finger. You are now at paragraph point.

Computer Tabulation

Note: Tabs are preset on a microcomputer. Touch the tab key with your little finger to indent for paragraphs.

Unit 17 ■ Improving Your Basic Skills—Measurement

(Lessons 136–140)

Learning Goal:

To evaluate the understanding and skills gained by keying a variety of business problems using new copy with limited directions.

As your teacher directs, prepare the problems on special forms provided in the workbook or on plain paper.

General Directions

Use a 70-space line (center – 35; center + 35 + 5) unless otherwise directed. SS sentences and drill lines. DS paragraphs.

This unit includes measurement of straight-copy and problem keying skills. You will be expected to format/key the lessons with less directional material by applying what you have learned in previous lessons.

LESSON 136

5 minutes

136a ● Keyboard Review

Directions: Key each sentence three times SS. DS between 3-line groups.

alphabet To move enough zinc for export would require buying trucks and a jeep.

figure The use of electronics in the 1991 cars has increased 129% since 1983.

direct reaches The executive was aware that exemptions were awarded, then taken away.

easy Eight of the new men felt so tired they slept right through the night.

| 1 | 2 | 3 | 4 | 5 | 6 | 7 | 8 | 9 | 10 | 11 | 12 | 13 | 14 |

5 minutes

136b ● Control Builder

Directions: Take four 1' writings on the ¶ below at the control level.

Goal: 2 or fewer errors per writing.

all letters used   1.4 si

One computer expert has been quoted as saying that some people have actually tried to get even with computers. The units have been kicked, stabbed, and bombed by users who went crazy with frustration. They have been electrically damaged with a metal key and in at least one case jumped on and wrecked by the heel of a shoe.

5 minutes

136c ● Language Arts Skills: Capitalization Guides

Directions: The following are capitalization guides for *business letter parts* followed by lines to illustrate those guides.

Study each guide; then key the line that illustrates the guide. Key each line three times SS; DS between 3-line groups.

Capitalize the first word, titles, and proper names used in the salutation.
Dear Floyd: Dear Sir: Gentlemen: Dear Dr. Franklin: Dear Ms. Door:

Capitalize only the first word of the complimentary close.
Sincerely yours, Cordially yours, Yours truly, Very truly yours, Truly

Capitalize all titles appearing in the address.
Ms. Ellen Hill, Legal Chief; Ben Burns, Manager; Mr. R. Hicks, Manager

If a title follows the name of the writer in the closing line, it must be capitalized.
Yoko Tukodo, Coordinator; Jon Brinski, Vice President; Mary Tull, Dean

11e ● Paragraph Keying

Directions: Clear all tab stops. Set your machine for a 5-space paragraph indention. Key the paragraphs twice DS. Repeat if time permits.

Note: If you are using an electronic typewriter with an automatic return or a microcomputer with word wrap, your teacher will explain how you are to handle the right margin.

all letters learned   *gwam* 1'

tab ⟶ Kids who want to have good health try to stay   9
fit. They like to walk a lot or jog in the fresh   19
air. Most of them ride bikes too.   26
tab ⟶ Yet these same boys and girls may find it hard   36
to eat what is good for them. A few will buy much 46
more junk food than they should.   52

| 1 | 2 | 3 | 4 | 5 | 6 | 7 | 8 | 9 | 10 |

Computing Gross Words a Minute (gwam).

To figure *gwam* on paragraph copy, note the figure at the end of the last complete line keyed in the column at the right. For a partially keyed line, note (in the scale at the bottom of the paragraphs) the last stroke keyed. Add this figure to the figure at the end of the last complete line keyed. The total is your *gwam*.

LESSON 12   REVIEW LESSON

12a ● Keyboard Review

Directions: Key once; repeat.

Posture Goal: Elbows in; wrists low.

Spacing: Double
Margin: 50-space line

```
g  fgf  fgf  gf  gf  get  great  glad  gone  long  light  right
u  juj  juj  uj  uj  out  our  hour  four  would  should  could
v  fvf  fvf  vf  vf  five  give  have  save  gave  leave  drive
y  jyj  jyj  yj  yj  yes  yet  you  yours  years  days  way  say
b  fbf  fbf  bf  bf  be  been  back  best  bill  both  board  by
m  jmj  jmj  mj  mj  more  most  much  means  mind  some  homes
```

12b ● Basic Technique Review

Directions: Key each line twice. Concentrate on the technique goal.

Posture Goal: Shoulders erect with body leaning slightly forward.

Technique Goal: Keep the fingers deeply curved; make quick, sharp strokes.

```
1  sign  large  length  charge  change  eight  wrong  strong
2  source  just  due  such  thus  thought  runs  found  house
3  view  voice  have  gives  five  serve  gave  leave  drives
4  style  young  years  yet  eyes  stays  try  why  ways  gray
5  brought  bank  book  club  blue  big  doubt  job  base  buy
6  farm  whom  make  made  film  from  times  them  same  name
```

135b ● Timed Writings

Directions: 1. Take a 1' controlled writing on each paragraph in 131d, page 227. Circle errors. Figure *gwam*.

2. Take one 5' controlled writing on all five ¶s combined. Circle errors and figure *gwam*.

---

30 minutes

keep your feet flat on the floor

135c ● Formatting Problem

Directions: Problem 1   Memorandum with Table

Key the formal interoffice memorandum below in the form shown in 132c, page 228. Use a 60-space line. Leave 6 spaces between columns in the table. DS above and below the table.

TO: Paula Peterson FROM: Kent Farmer DATE: June 4, 19-- SUBJECT: Directory Update

(¶) The new Office Directory failed to list four of our new office employees. It is important for you to update your directory to include them. Listed below are their names and telephone numbers:

Black, Donald	557-2410
Jensen, Diana	556-2361
Larsen, Marianna	557-2289
Mitsui, Emi	556-2294

(¶) A new directory will be printed in the near future that will include all the new employees. If you have any questions regarding room assignments and telephone lines, please do not hesitate to call.

Directions: Problem 2   Table

Key the following table centered vertically on a full sheet. DS between the heading and the first item: DS the items. Leave 6 spaces between columns.

BOARD OF TRUSTEES MAILING LIST

Mrs. Judith Ball	6521 Griffith Way	Chico, CA 95926-4335
Ms. Ann Blackstone	2351 Gearhardt	Phoenix, AZ 86001-5467
Dr. Laurie Growth	14 Chickadee Lane	Seattle, WA 98118-1254
Ms. Rebecca Falk	29 Main Street	Boise, ID 83705-2121
Mr. Jerry Kilpatrick	12 Viola Drive	Baker, CA 33612-1788
Ms. Marilyn Martinio	539 Otis Avenue	Redding, CA 96001-3210
Mrs. Carol Rameriz	15 Carrol Drive	Logan, UT 84321-3625
Dr. Hans Schultz	822 Cedar Street	Butte, MT 59701-8945
Mr. T. Hillman Wills	41 Grove Circle	Spokane, WA 99216-6378

135d ● Extra-Credit Activities

Directions: Problem 1

Key the memorandum in 132c, Problem 1, page 228. Key in the heading as follows: TO: J. T. Armour FROM: Jerry B. Kilbert DATE: May 15, 19-- SUBJECT: (same)

Directions: Problem 2

Key the table in 135c, page 233, Problem 2, on a full sheet of paper. Center in reading position. DS after the heading; SS the items. Leave 4 spaces between columns.

Technique Goal:
Depress right shift key with the ; finger. Strike the capital letter; quickly release the shift key.

1 Dee Smith and Ray Brown; Deb Green and Frank Sands

2 Sue Thoms and Bob Arndt; Barb Vance and Thane Eads

3 Ana saw Don Reese. Rosa Ramos rode with Sam Weld.

Technique Goal: Tap return key quickly with ; finger.

1 Both girls
2 came late.

3 Their class met
4 once each week.

5 Each girl will bring
6 a gift for her date.

7 We thought our team would
8 lose the game that night.

9 They can all stay at school so
10 no one will have to walk home.

Tabulation steps

1. Clear all tab stops.

2. Set a 5-space paragraph (¶) indention.

3. Tab to begin a ¶.

12c ● Paragraph Skill Builder

Directions: Five-space paragraph indention DS. Key the paragraph (¶) once for practice; then take three 1' writings on it. Figure your *gwam* on the best writing.

gwam 1'

tab ⟶ Set your goals if you want to make the best   9
use of your time. This is true for your work at   19
home as well as what you do at your school. You   29
will get more work done when you know what it is   40
you want to do.   43

| 1 | 2 | 3 | 4 | 5 | 6 | 7 | 8 | 9 | 10 |

LESSON 13

13a ● Keyboard Review

Spacing: Double
Margin: 50-space line

Directions: Key once; repeat.

Posture Goal: Keep feet flat on the floor, one ahead of the other.

use quick, sharp strokes

b fbf fbf bf bf board board doubt doubts bring bring

m jmj jmj mj mj him him room room my my month months

v y yj vf yj vf voice voice leave leave you your young

in in fine find kind line mine thin think thing since

all letters taught June is the best month to hold the race this year.

We gave them the names of the four books he needs.

| 1 | 2 | 3 | 4 | 5 | 6 | 7 | 8 | 9 | 10 |

134b ● Language Arts Skills: Titles of Published Works

Directions: **1.** The first sentence gives the rule for the sentences following.

2. Key each sentence three times.
3. Take a 1' writing on each sentence.

1 The title of a short poem, article, or song is set in quotation marks.
2 Poet Joyce Kilmer wrote that quite famous short poem entitled "Trees."
3 The article, "The Future of Large Cities," appeared in the Daily News.
4 Everyone at the outdoor concert listened to the great hit, "Rhapsody."

| 1 | 2 | 3 | 4 | 5 | 6 | 7 | 8 | 9 | 10 | 11 | 12 | 13 | 14 |

30 minutes

134c ● Formatting Problems

Directions: Problem 1 Interoffice Memorandum

Format/key the formal memorandum below on a 60-space line. Refer to 132c, page 228 if necessary.

TO: All Personnel FROM: A. J. Lama, Human Resource Manager
DATE: May 12, 19-- SUBJECT: Revised Policy Manual

(¶) In the next few days you will be receiving the revised company Policies and Procedures Manual. This manual is being provided to all the hourly and salaried employees.

(¶) Please read the manual very carefully, paying particular attention to the changes that have been made in the section that discusses wage and fringe benefits. Description of the company's new tuition reimbursement program should be of particular interest.

(¶) After you have read the manual, please sign the acknowledgement page and send it to your immediate supervisor.

Directions: Problem 2 Invoice

Key the invoice below. Set left margin and tab stops. Figure total and enter under amount. Refer to 133c, page 231, if necessary.

SOLD TO Russell and Coe, 538 Indian Hills Drive, Fort Wayne, IN 46809-6723
DATE December 12, 19-- OUR ORDER NO. 98736 CUSTOMER ORDER NO. 3749
SHIPPED VIA Union Freight SALESPERSON D. L. Bastady TERMS 2/10, n/30

Quantity	Description	Unit Price	Amount
2	M53 C-2594 Hand Mixers	15.95 ea	31.90
10 pr	FM-79Z Wire Cutters	4.45 pr	44.50
8 gal	23-60 White House Paint	8.95 gal	71.60

LESSON 135

70-space line

5 minutes

135a ● Keyboard Review

Directions: Key each sentence three times SS. DS between 3-line groups.

alphabet Your jams quite luckily won five prizes at today's big market exhibit.
figure The first ferris wheel was built in 1893 and was over 20 stories high.
4th finger The page appeared in the bazaar paper after the artist approached him.
easy The key to the future is knowing how to plan the right goals for work.

| 1 | 2 | 3 | 4 | 5 | 6 | 7 | 8 | 9 | 10 | 11 | 12 | 13 | 14 |

Reach to X

1. Find x on the chart.
2. Find it on your keyboard.
3. Place your fingers over the home keys.
4. Reach to x with the s finger.
5. Touch xs lightly without moving other fingers from their home position.

Reach to P

1. Find p on the chart.
2. Find it on your keyboard.
3. Place your fingers over the home keys.
4. Reach to p with the ; finger.
5. Touch p; lightly without moving other fingers from their home position.

sxs sxs xs xs ix six six   Key twice on same line   ;p; ;p; p; p; pa par par

Reach to x

Reach to p

13c ● Location Drills: X and P

Directions: Key each line once with your teacher. Repeat a second time by yourself.

Technique Goal: Reach to the new keys with your fingers. Keep your wrists low.

```
     sxs  sxs  sxs  sxs  xs  xs  xs  xs  six  six  fix  fix  ox  box
  x  lax  lax  flax  flax  flex  flex  next  next  fox  fox  hoax
     excel  excel  flux  flux  hex  hex  relax  relax  axe  axes

     ;p;  ;p;  ;p;  ;p;  p;  p;  p;  p;  par  par  part  pass  pass
  p  past  past  page  page  pay  pay  put  put  trip  trip  kept
     flip  flip  slip  slip  pile  pile  play  play  spar  spare

       expect  expect  expand  expands  expert  experts  extent
 x/p   explain  explains  expense  expenses  explore  explores
```

13d ● Technique Builder: Down-and-in Motion of Right Thumb

Directions: Key each line twice SS. DS between 2-line groups.

Technique Goal: Strike space bar with quick down-and-in motion.

curve right thumb over space bar

use quick down-and-in motion of thumb

```
1  xs p;  sx p;  sx p;  flax  flax  help  help  cap  caps  six
2  fox  tax  fox  lax  six  jinx  box  hex  coax  hoax  vex  axe
3  top  stop  lot  lay  play  plan  plus  post  nap  hope  ship
4  fix  the  step;  keep  the  box;  pay  the  tax;  six  steps
5  I can pay it.  He can pay for it.  She can pay it.
6  I paid six of the girls for the good job they did.
   |  1  |  2  |  3  |  4  |  5  |  6  |  7  |  8  |  9  |  10  |
```

133c ● Formatting Problems: Invoices

Directions: Problem 1

Key the invoice as shown below. Clear all tabs stops; set your margin and tab stops as indicated. Use the tab key to key across each line. After you key the last amount, underline and DS to key total.

VIDEORAMA
922 Oliva Rd.
San Diego, CA
92128-7836
(619) 372-8456

Invoice

Date February 12, 19--

City Appliance Center
1583 Bellanger Drive
Green Bay, WI 54301-7896

Our Order No. 2983

Cust. Order No. 2710-60

Shipped Via Allstate Freight

Terms 2/10, n/30

Salesperson Brooks Patterson

Quantity	Description	Unit Price	Total
	DS		
6	118CD Rex CD Player	289.95	1,739.70
1	Z9035 35" Direct View TV Set	2,690.00	2,690.00
3	Z9019 19" TV Set W/Remote SS	229.50	688.50
			5,118.20
left margin	1st tab	2d tab	3d tab
(Approx. center)	(2 spaces)	(Approx. center)	(Approx. center)

Directions: Problem 2

Key the invoice below as directed in Problem 1.

SOLD TO Electronic City | 441 West Gratiot Street | Lowell, MA 01649-2389
DATE April 2, 19-- OUR ORDER NO. 1640 CUST. ORDER NO. 3298-70 SHIPPED
VIA Southwest SALESPERSON T. Shields TERMS 2/10, n/30

Quantity	Description	Unit Price	Amount
3	SX12 Video Arcade w/Joystick	99.95	299.85
4	All-Sports Video Cartridges	59.75	239.00
1	WW15 Set 15" Triaxial Speakers	249.50	249.50
			788.35

LESSON 134

5 minutes

134a ● Keyboard Review

Directions: Key each sentence three times SS. DS between 3-line groups.

alphabet To know the fall gym party and major banquets are exclusive amazed us.

figure You can buy the model 432 set for $156 or pay 12 payments of $13 each.

e,i Their dividend increased each nine periods with a credit being issued.

easy The foreman wants each of his men to work with him for the next month.

| 1 | 2 | 3 | 4 | 5 | 6 | 7 | 8 | 9 | 10 | 11 | 12 | 13 | 14 |

13e ● Paragraph Keying

Directions: Set machine for a 5-space paragraph indention. Key the ¶ twice DS. Repeat if time permits.

Technique Goal: Reach to the tab key; release and quickly return to home key position.

all letters learned

gwam 1'

keep wrists and elbows still

tab——→ We know that those who hit the most home runs   9
in a ball game strike out a great deal too.   Keep   19
this fact in mind the next time you do not do a job   30
as well as you should have.   35

| 1 | 2 | 3 | 4 | 5 | 6 | 7 | 8 | 9 | 10 |

LESSON 14

14a ● Keyboard Review

Spacing: Double
Margin: 50-space line

Directions: Key once; repeat.

Posture Goal: Keep fingers deeply curved.

x   sxs sxs xs xs six six lax flax next next flex flex
p   ;p; ;p; p; p; par part pal pail plan pain tip trip
b m bf mj bf mj mail mail best best name names bad bad
an   an and can man change chance plan plant stand want

all letters taught

Their next big job is to pave all the new streets.
He could key the words on the form at a high rate.

| 1 | 2 | 3 | 4 | 5 | 6 | 7 | 8 | 9 | 10 |

14b ● Location of Q and , (comma)

Reach to Q
1. Find q on the chart.
2. Find it on your keyboard.
3. Place your fingers over the home keys.
4. Reach to q with the a finger.
5. Touch qa lightly without moving other fingers from their home position.

Reach to , (comma)
1. Find , on the chart.
2. Find it on your keyboard.
3. Place your fingers over the home keys.
4. Reach to , with the k finger.
5. Touch ,k lightly without moving other fingers from their home position.

aqa qa qa quit quit quit   Key twice on same line   k,k k,k ,k rk, irk, irk,

132c, continued

Directions: Problem 2

Key the following memorandum in simplified style using the directions given on page 228. Review the model on page 229 for additional help.

The memorandum is being sent to Robert Funaro, Academic Dean, by J.A. Mendola, President, and dated July 15, 19--. The subject is Paralegal Program.

(¶) The next meeting of the Paralegal Program Committee will be held on Monday, July 29, at 2:00. We will be meeting in the library conference room, and light refreshments will be served.

(¶) It is my plan at this meeting to finalize all components of this program so that we may begin scheduling students for our winter quarter. I hope you and the other members of the academic committee will be prepared to present the final course outlines. With your help I believe that we should be able to complete the meeting by 5:00. J. A. Mendola xx

LESSON 133

70-space line

5 minutes | **133a ● Keyboard Review**

Directions: Key each sentence three times SS. DS between 3-line groups.

alphabet | The plain fire hazards of the extra job were quickly given to the men.

figure | On December 25, 1989, more than 23 inches of snow fell on 11 counties.

4th finger | Paul requested a quote from his area plumbing store for copper piping.

easy | The problems of authority of those in power are not always understood.

| 1 | 2 | 3 | 4 | 5 | 6 | 7 | 8 | 9 | 10 | 11 | 12 | 13 | 14 |

10 minutes | **133b ● Speed Builder**

Directions: Take a 1′ writing on each ¶; try to increase speed on the second writing. Figure *gwam*.

Work for speed as you take one 5′ writing on all three ¶s combined. Figure *gwam*.

all letters used
1.4 si   5.4 awl
85% hfw

	gwam 1′	5′
Successful employment is the major goal of all students today as	13	3	46
it has always been in the past. Recognized, it is often difficult for	27	5	48
young persons to find jobs. The ratio of unemployment of young students	42	8	51
of high school age to the complex total unemployment base is the highest	56	11	54
and during the last ten years ranged up to one-fourth. School dropouts	71	14	57
have one of the highest rates.	77	15	58
Leaving a school program before completion has a major effect on	13	18	61
whether a person is likely to be unemployed. The great majority of	27	21	64
dropouts were below seventeen years of age when they decided to quit	40	23	66
school. It does seem that most drop out in the tenth grade. Almost one	55	26	69
third of all dropouts do so in this grade.	64	28	71
When you examine the kinds of entry level jobs held by young job	13	31	74
seekers, you will find that almost one-half of them are in the clerical	27	34	77
or distribution areas. In 1989, it was found that a third of a group	41	36	89
interviewed were hired because of their ability to key at fifty words	55	39	82
per minute. As a result, it is suggested that all students take a year	70	42	85
of keyboarding.	73	43	86

gwam 1′	1	2	3	4	5	6	7	8	9	10	11	12	13	14
5′		1			2			3	

14c ● Location Drills: Q and , (comma)

Directions: Key each line once with your teacher. Repeat the lines again by yourself.

Spacing Guide: Space once after a comma within a sentence.

Reach to q

Reach to , (comma)

```
        aqa  aqa  aqa  qa  quit  quite  quiet  quills  quips  equip
      q pique  quilt  square  quench  queen  quart  quote  quotes
        quaint  quake  quick  queue  squid  squeak  equal  plaque

        k,k  k,k  k,k  ,k  ,k  work,  rock,  broke,  trick,  truck,
, (comma) fork,  forks,  sock,  socks,  dock,  dike,  lock,  clock,
        kick,  choke,  steak,  rake,  kale,  king,  chock,  soak,

     q/, quack,  quad,  quell,  quest,  lacquer,  opaque,  qualm,
```

14d ● Technique Builder

Directions: Key each line twice SS; then key 1-minute writings on the last three lines.

Technique Goal: Do not look from the copy to the keyboard and back again. Keep eyes on copy at all times.

> space once after a comma within a sentence

```
1 qa ,k qa ,k qa ,k quit, qualm, quip, quite, squeal
2 quick, quill, queen, quotes, qualms, quilt, quench
3 to quote, to quit, the quick, the queen, the quilt
4 I was quick to quote the girls with the red quilt.
5 Drive right, as the life you save may be your own.
6 As you type, use quick, short, firm, sure strokes.
7 We can gain the high skills we need for this work.
  |  1  |  2  |  3  |  4  |  5  |  6  |  7  |  8  |  9  |  10  |
```

14e ● Paragraph Skill Builder

Directions: Set tab for a 5-space indention. Key the ¶ DS once for practice; then take three 1-minute writings on it. Figure *gwam* on the best writing.

all letters learned   *gwam* 1′

```
tab ──→ Do not punch or mash the keys when you type.   9
        Just hit them with a quick stroke and then get off.  20
        Be sure to give this plan a try the next time you  30
        sit down at your desk or in front of a screen.  39
  |  1  |  2  |  3  |  4  |  5  |  6  |  7  |  8  |  9  |  10  |
```

GRIFFFIN PUBLISHING CO.

302 Valleycrest Rd. / Rochester, NY 14616-5039

INTEROFFICE MEMORANDUM

all major lines
begin at left
margin

December 12, 19--
QS

salutation

Linda Stockbridge
DS

subject line
in all caps

SIMPLIFIED MEMORANDUM FORMAT
DS

At the last meeting of the Management Committee, company correspondence was discussed in detail. At this meeting the group
reviewed in detail the need to further streamline company correspondence. As a result of this review, we now recommend that
all memorandums be formatted using the simplified style.
DS

1" left
margin

The simplified style, a basic format that conveniently contains
essential information, can be completed in a minimum amount of
time. This time savings is a definite plus in efforts to improve communication.

1" right
margin

DS

The subject line in the simplified memorandum is keyed in capital letters. The use of all capitals eases reading and makes
the subject line stand out, although the subject can be keyed
in capitals and lowercase letters without reducing the effec-
tiveness of the format. The memorandum is signed by the sender
above the keyed signature.
DS

In your role as office manager, I know you will take the necessary steps to see that the simplified memorandum style is used
in all our future company internal correspondence.
QS

keyed name on
the fourth line
below memorandum
body

Lauri Havens
DS

reference initials

xx

Interoffice Memorandum/Simplified Style

LESSON 15

15a ● Keyboard Review

Directions: Key once; repeat.

Technique Goal: Wrists low and still.

q | aqa aqa qa qa quit quits quote quotes quart quarts

(comma) | k,k k,k ,k ,k work, all, fork, fill, dark, squall,

x p | xs p; xs p; tax tax box box up up group group keep

he | he he she she held held the them these their there

all letters taught | She was quick to point out the tax we have to pay.
My friends would like to play big jokes on me too.

| 1 | 2 | 3 | 4 | 5 | 6 | 7 | 8 | 9 | 10 |

15b ● Location of Z and ? (question mark)

Reach to Z

1. Find z on the chart.
2. Find it on your keyboard.
3. Place your fingers over the home keys.
4. Reach to z with the a finger.
5. Touch za lightly without moving other fingers from their home position.

Reach to ? (question mark)

1. Find ? on the chart.
2. Find it on your keyboard.
3. Place your fingers over the home keys.
4. Reach to ? with the ; finger.
5. Hold down left shift key as you reach your right little finger to the question mark.

aza za za zone zone zone   Key twice on same line   ;?; ?; ;?; ?;? Why? Why?

15c ● Location Drills: Z and ? (question mark)

Reach to z

Reach to ? (question mark)

Directions: Key once with your teacher. Repeat again by yourself.

Technique Goal: Reach to the shift key without moving your arms or wrists.

	aza aza aza za za za zone zones zero zip zeal zinc
z	zoo size maze maze gaze graze doze quiz quiz froze
	haze haze lazy prize prize raze raze razing dozing
	;?; ;?; ;?; ?; ?; ?; Is it? Can they go? Why go?
?	Where is my pen? Why did we pay? Were you there?
	Can he tell them how? or why? Whom will she take?

space once ⟶   ⟵ space twice

	Did it buzz? Is this a quiz? Who won that prize?
z/?	Did they freeze? Was I in a daze? Had she dozed?
	Which is your size? Have they put out that blaze?

132a ● Keyboard Review

5 minutes

Directions: Key each sentence three times SS. DS between 3-line groups.

alphabet A dozen more even now expect to qualify for those kinds of great jobs.

figure The 1,365 runners ran 2.6 miles with 4,780 fans watching and cheering.

weak fingers Paul watched the pleasant haze go away near the loop's play zone area.

easy They sent us many old ornaments from the ancient foreign temple ruins.

| 1 | 2 | 3 | 4 | 5 | 6 | 7 | 8 | 9 | 10 | 11 | 12 | 13 | 14 |

132b ● Technique Builder: Stroking

10 minutes

keep your eyes
on the copy

Directions: Take two 1' writings on each line SS. DS between 2-line groups.

1 wax please quiz zero size ease pop palm set ooze zipper case sloop axe

2 craze taxes flaw zoo zone lamp square play plow hazy police quick upon

3 The pupils can do the jobs, although their actions appeared otherwise.

4 The lazy pupils did not tax themselves and promptly failed their quiz.

| 1 | 2 | 3 | 4 | 5 | 6 | 7 | 8 | 9 | 10 | 11 | 12 | 13 | 14 |

132c ● Formatting Problems: Interoffice Memorandum

30 minutes

Formal Memorandum

If a form is not available, set the left margin approximately 1½" from the left edge of the paper. Beginning 2" from the top of paper (line 12), key the TO:, FROM:, DATE:, SUBJECT: in ALL CAPS flush left with the margin. Set the right margin 60 spaces to the right of the left margin.

Simplified Memorandum

A simplified memorandum may be keyed on printed company letterhead or on plain paper. In this format all parts of the document begin at the left margin. The dateline is keyed 1½" (line 10) from the top of a plain sheet (or a DS below a company's letterhead) and followed by a QS. A QS also separates the body and the sender's name. All other parts of this memorandum are separated by a DS. Use approximately 1" side margins or use the default margins on your equipment. See model on page 229.

Directions: Problem 1

Key the formal memorandum below on a 60-space line. Key the heading information flush left with the margin. Space twice after the colon and key the information following each heading. Set the right margin 60 spaces to the right of the left margin.

TO: All Office Employees
                              DS
FROM: James LaPorte, Office Manager
                              DS
DATE: August 15, 19--
                              DS
SUBJECT: Errors in Office Directory
                              DS
The new Office Directory failed to list many of our new office employees. It is important for you to update your directory to include them. Please request from your unit head the supplemental listing that has been prepared.

                              DS
A new directory will be printed in the near future that will include all the new employees. If you have any questions regarding the room assignments, please do not hesitate to call.

                              DS

xx

(continued on page 230)

15d ● Technique Builder

Directions: Key each line one time. Take three 1' writings on the ¶s below.

Technique Goal: Hold shift key down; release it quickly. Try to keep a steady, even pace.

Spacing Guide
Space twice after a question mark at the end of a sentence; space once after a question mark within a sentence.

home row	Ada has a flask; Dad has a salad; lads shall fall;
e/h	Jake had a desk. She had a sale. He asked a fee.
t/o	Take these foods too. He told jokes to the staff.
w/i	This is what we did with the saws while we waited.
r/n	Rhonda and her friends ran down there in the rain.
c/.	Face facts. Carl can choose. Each school closed.
g/u	Our group thought all the ground was rough though.
v/y	On your drive you will have views of every valley.
b/m	Both members seemed to blame them for the bad job.
x/p	I expect to pay a tax on the six extra parts next.
q/,	Quinn, not one to quit, quickly drew a new square.
z/?	Was Zane amazed? What size is their frozen pizza?
left shift	Hired were P. O. Yang, Lee Isaac, and N. K. Jones.
right shift	Beth and Ron Eads live on Gem Avenue in San Diego.
all letters	Have Jack quit buying sox; Pam will find a blazer.
all letters	Danny Flammon saw Bix give the prize a quick jerk.

```
| 1 | 2 | 3 | 4 | 5 | 6 | 7 | 8 | 9 | 10 |
```

all letters learned   *gwam 1'*

Now that you know where to find each of the   9
keys, your job is to work hard and learn to type   18
well. This is a goal that all of you can reach.   28
There is no quiz you can take that will prove   37
your skill. You must do more than read your text. 48
If you try, you are bound to gain a high speed.   57

```
| 1 | 2 | 3 | 4 | 5 | 6 | 7 | 8 | 9 | 10 |
```

131d ● Speed Ladder Paragraphs

Directions: 1. Take 1' writings on ¶ 1 DS until you complete the ¶ in 1'.
2. When you complete ¶ 1 in 1', continue on to ¶ 2. Repeat this procedure as you try to complete each of the five ¶ s in the time given.
3. Take three 1' writings on any ¶ you cannot finish in the given time.

all letters used   1.4 si

reach with your fingers; keep hands and wrists quiet

	gwam 5'

To run an automobile, no other alternative fuel seems to offer — 3 | 55
as much as hydrogen. It is quite plentiful, it is cheap, and it burns — 5 | 57
so cleanly that its exhaust is just a puff of steam with slight traces — 8 | 60
of nitrogen oxides. — 9 | 61

Energy experts around the world are now looking very closely at — 12 | 64
all aspects of using hydrogen as a fuel. At this time there are two — 14 | 66
multi-million dollar studies being done to see if there is a chance this — 17 | 69
fuel could power whole bus fleets. — 19 | 71

One country is trying to fly airplanes powered by hydrogen. An — 21 | 73
automaker and a builder of power plants are getting together to build — 24 | 76
a pilot plant to make hydrogen from solar energy. One firm has gone — 27 | 79
so far as to build a car that runs on this fuel. — 29 | 81

There are many problems that researchers must zero in on and solve — 31 | 83
if hydrogen is to become a future fuel replacement for autos. One of — 34 | 86
these is the fuel's power compared to gas. At the present time, in the — 37 | 89
models tested, it takes a large tank of hydrogen to go just a few miles. — 40 | 92

No one knows for sure whether hydrogen, or some other fuel, will — 43 | 95
be the best answer to solving our environmental problems. Two things — 45 | 97
we know for sure are that we cannot go on polluting the very air we — 48 | 100
all breathe, and that auto exhaust emissions are known to be one of — 51 | 103
the biggest offenders. — 52 | 104

gwam 5' | 1 | 2 | 3 |

131e ● Skill Comparison

Directions: Take four 1' writings on the ¶ in 131b, page 226. Compare rates.

Unit 2 ■ Improving Your Keying Techniques (Lessons 16–20)

Learning Goals:

1. To reinforce proper stroking techniques, using the goals stressed in the text.

2. To stroke difficult, awkward, and long reaches smoothly with a minimum of hand, wrist, and arm movements.

3. To key short, common, balanced-hand words by word response; that is, by thinking and keying whole words rather than individual letters.

4. To key one-hand words by letter response, and to combine word response with letter response into a flowing rhythmic pattern.

5. To identify keying errors.

6. To increase the keying rate on sentences and short paragraphs by approximately one word each lesson.

General Directions

Use a 50-space line for all lessons in this unit (center − 25; center + 25 + 5). SS sentences and drill lines. DS between repeated groups of lines. DS paragraph copy. Set machine for a 5-space paragraph indention.

Practice time is given for each section of a lesson in this unit. If it seems best to vary the schedule, do so with the approval of your teacher.

LESSON 16

7 minutes **16a ● Keyboard Review**

Directions: Key each line twice SS. DS between 2-line groups.

sit erect;
feet flat
on floor

```
  z  aza aza za za zeal zones doze quiz maze graze zest
  ?  ;?; ;?; ?; ?; Who?  When?  How many?  Is she here?
 ou  our four found house south though course out doubt
       Chris asked me what my grade was on the math quiz.
alphabet  Rick plans to move to Texas if he finds a new job.
       |  1  |  2  |  3  |  4  |  5  |  6  |  7  |  8  |  9  | 10  |
```

8 minutes **16b ● Technique Builder: Keying Whole Words**

Directions: Key each line as your teacher dictates SS. DS between 2-line groups.

Do not key the lines
between words.

```
1 if|if|it|it|is|is|if it|if it|it is|it is|if it is
2 to|to|do|do|so|so|to do|to do|do so|do so|to do so
3 he|he|is|is|he is|he is|she|she|is|is|she is|he is
4 if|if|he|he|if he|if he|if he is|she|she|if she is
5 it|it|is|is|it is she|it is she|if|if|if it is she
```

think and
key whole
words

Lesson 16   **29**

Unit 16 ■ Learning to Key Business Forms (Lessons 131–135)

Learning Goals:

1. To format formal and simplified memorandums.
2. To format business invoices.
3. To gain a better understanding of the use of memos and invoices in business.

General Directions

Use a 70-space line (center – 35; center + 35 + 5) for drills and timed writings in this unit. SS sentences and drill lines. DS paragraph copy. As your teacher directs, prepare the problems on special forms provided in the workbook or on plain paper.

LESSON 131

5 minutes | **131a ● Keyboard Review**

Directions: Key each sentence three times SS. DS between 3-line groups.

alphabet | Nine of the judges were baffled as five boys quickly mixed the prizes.

figure | The population of Alaska grew from 400,481 in 1980 to 501,790 in 1990.

direct reach | The fourth group needed to develop enough funds to replace the floors.

easy | Almost always a light touch is best tried to build good keying skills.

| 1 | 2 | 3 | 4 | 5 | 6 | 7 | 8 | 9 | 10 | 11 | 12 | 13 | 14 |

5 minutes | **131b ● Control Builder**

Directions: Take four 1' writings on the ¶ below at the control level.

Goal: 2 or fewer errors per writing.

all letters used   1.4 si

    Not many foods are more American than the hot dog. The billions that are sold each year prove it. Yet, there are two other sandwiches that rate above the famous dog and bun. Can you believe that peanut butter and jelly is the unequaled champ, and the hamburger ranks next? Because of this, the vendors who capitalize by selling hot dogs will have to work harder.

10 minutes | **131c ● Speed Ladder Sentences**

Directions: Key each sentence for 1'. Your teacher will call the guide at 15", 12", or 10" intervals. As time permits, repeat sentences on which you were not able to complete a line with the call of the guide.

		15"	12"	10"
1	Be sure to sit up straight in the chair.	32	40	48
2	One foot should be placed ahead of the other.	36	45	54
3	Keep the wrists low and the elbows near your body.	40	50	60
4	Your fingers should be slightly curved above your keys.	44	55	66
5	Keep your copy at the right of the machine for easy reading.	48	60	72
6	Your table should be clear of unneeded books and other materials.	52	65	78
7	Strike and release a key quickly; then strike a next one the same way.	56	70	84

| 1 | 2 | 3 | 4 | 5 | 6 | 7 | 8 | 9 | 10 | 11 | 12 | 13 | 14 |

16c ● Sentence Skill Builder

Directions: Key each sentence two times; then take a 1' timed writing on each sentence. Figure your *gwam.*

Key short easy words as a whole

```
1 She asked me to strike each key as if it were hot.

2 You should keep your eyes on the book as you work.

3 I hope he can key the whole word some of the time.

4 They can store a great deal more on the hard disk.

5 Check all words on the screen; then you can print.
    |  1  |  2  |  3  |  4  |  5  |  6  |  7  |  8  |  9  |  10  |
```

7 minutes

16d ● Proofreading Your Work

Directions: Some common keying errors are listed below to help you locate and mark each of your own errors.

As you read each error description, note the circled examples.

1. A wrong letter or a strikeover.

2. An incorrect or omitted punctuation mark.

3. Failure to space between words.

4. Failure to capitalize a letter.

5. An omitted or added word.

6. A repeated or missing stroke.

```
    Now (thar) you (know) where all
can watch your speed (climb,)  If
one once in a while, (donot) let it
    (be) sure to keep your mind on
type(or) as you key words on (on) your
to get (llax) in (you) quest for a hi
```

10 minutes

16e ● Continuity Practice

Directions: Key the copy below one time DS; circle your errors. Take a 1' writing on each ¶. Try to make fewer errors.

The syllable intensity (si) is given for the ¶s below. It is a guide to the difficulty of the material. Copy of average difficulty has an si of 1.5. The material in these ¶s is rated easy.

key without pauses

all letters used   1.0 si

	gwam 1'	total words
Now that you know where all the keys are, you	9	9
can watch your speed climb. If you hit the wrong	19	19
one once in a while, do not let it faze you.	28	28
Be sure to keep your mind on the job as you	9	37
type or as you key words on your screen. Vow not	19	47
to get lax in your quest for a high rate.	29	57

```
    |  1  |  2  |  3  |  4  |  5  |  6  |  7  |  8  |  9  |  10  |
```

130b ● Timed Writings

Directions: Take a 1' writing on each paragraph of 126c, page 220 *or* take a 5' writing on all paragraphs combined. Circle errors; figure *gwam*.

130c ● Formatting Problems: Business Letters with Enclosures

Directions: Problem 1

1. Key in modified block style, mixed punctuation. Set 60-space line; begin dateline on line 18.

2. Use today's date; address a large envelope.

> When multiple enclosures are referred to in the letter, follow the word Enclosures with a colon and two spaces and list each enclosure.
>
> xx
> DS
> Enclosures: Catalog Pages
>   Order Form

Ms. Dorothy Jacobs | 2271 Ridgewood Drive | Grand Rapids, MI 49506-4590 |

Dear Ms. Jacobs:

(¶) I am returning your check for the amount of $298.75 that you sent our company on September 5. So that we may process your order for a monitor, please send us more information about the model and make of the unit you are requesting. As you know, our firm carries a large variety of monitors to meet each customer's specific needs.

(¶) I am enclosing the pages from our current catalog that illustrate all the monitors we carry. These pages provide specific order information for you to use. Also enclosed is our order form, which when completed will provide us the information necessary to fill your order properly.

(¶) Thank you for understanding this necessary delay, Ms. Jacobs. I look forward to your order.

Sincerely, | James Cortez | Order Manager | xx | Enclosures: Catalog Pages | Order Form

Directions: Problem 2

1. Key in block style, open punctuation.

Set 60-space line; begin on line 18.

2. Address a large envelope.

October 5, 19-- | Mrs. Wilma Kerr | 642 St. Charles Place | New York, NY 10038-7345 | Dear Mrs. Kerr

(¶) We regret that as of September 30 we can no longer accept orders for our Model 17B electronic typewriter. This model has been discontinued by the manufacturer, and no units are available.

(¶) We are, however, pleased to announce that a new model to replace the 17B unit is available. We believe that once you review the enclosed brochure, you will find the new Model 18B far superior to the one you originally requested.

(¶) I am also enclosing a listing of current users of the Model 18B unit that you may want to contact regarding their experience with the new unit. Please do not hesitate to call me on our toll free number if you wish any additional information.

Sincerely yours | SUPERIOR OFFICE EQUIPMENT | Ms. May Wong | President | xx | Enclosures: Brochure | Listing

---

130d ● Extra-Credit Activities

Directions: Problem 1

Compose and key an answer to the letter in Problem 1 of 130c. Tell Mr. Cortez you completed the order form and are sending it with a check. Thank him for the catalog and tell him that you look forward to receiving your monitor. Use the letter style you prefer and your own return address.

Directions: Problem 2

Prepare Problem 1, 124d, page 218, in block style with open punctuation.

Directions: Problem 3

Prepare Problem 2, 129c, page 224, in modified block style with mixed punctuation. Add a subject line.

LESSON 17

7 minutes

17a ● Keyboard Review

Directions: Key each line twice SS. DS between 2-line groups.

keep eyes
on copy;
sit erect

n	jnj jnj nj nj no noon none note one once nine nice
t	ftf ftf tf tf fit fight tune tunes then thin think
er	hers here there were where ever every other serves

alphabet

Juan did not expect to win first prize so quickly.
Beth told him to give more help to those who lost.

| 1 | 2 | 3 | 4 | 5 | 6 | 7 | 8 | 9 | 10 |

14 minutes

17b ● Technique Builder: Keying Whole Words

Directions: Key each line three times SS. DS between 3-line groups.

key short
words as
a whole

1 He told us how to hold our forks in the right way.
2 At least half of them knew she had paid the bills.
3 Write all of their names on the front of the form.
4 Most girls will want to ride the bus to the games.
5 The name of that town was shown right on the sign.
6 It was their turn to lend us a hand with our work.
7 Both men did lay their pens down at the same time.

| 1 | 2 | 3 | 4 | 5 | 6 | 7 | 8 | 9 | 10 |

10 minutes

17c ● Continuity Practice

Directions: Key the copy below DS; circle all errors. Repeat.

Use the 1' column at
right and the 1' scale
underneath the ¶s to
figure your 1' rate. Use
the 2' column and scale
to figure your 2' rate.

all letters used   1.0 si   *gwam* 1'   2'

A small car may not have quite as much zip   9 | 4

as you would like, and you know that it will not   18 | 9

have room for six or eight of your friends.   27 | 14

It will do some good things, though. It will   9 | 18

use just half as much gas as a great big car, and   19 | 23

you will not need to look so far to find a spot to   29 | 28

park it.   31 | 29

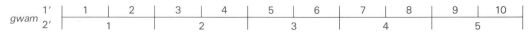

gwam 1' | 1 | 2 | 3 | 4 | 5 | 6 | 7 | 8 | 9 | 10 |
2' | 1 | 2 | 3 | 4 | 5 |

129c ● Formatting Problems: Business Letters with Special Features

Directions: Problem 1   Business Letter with Enumerated Items

1. Key in modified block style, mixed punctuation. Set 60-space line; begin on line 18.

2. Use today's date; address a large envelope.

Mrs. Rachel Jones | 7929 Monica Road | Flint, MI 48108-4005 | Dear Mrs. Jones:

(¶) Thank you for joining the Marathon Video Club. Your membership card is enclosed. As a member you are eligible for the following advantages:

1. Your membership is honored by all 13 Marathon Club stores.

2. You will receive a $2 discount on all tape rentals.

3. You may keep all rented tapes for two days and pay only the one-day rate.

(¶) Beginning next month, you will have the option of charging your rentals and your membership on our special charge card. We believe you will agree that membership in the Marathon Video Club is a great deal.

Sincerely, | James Wingfoot | Regional Manager | xx | Enclosure

Directions: Problem 2   Business Letter in Rough-Draft Form

1. Key in block style, open punctuation. Set 50-space line; begin on line 18.

2. Address a large envelope.

April 13, 19--

```
Mr. Kenneth Mitchell
239 Cody (Ave.) spell out
Billings, mt  59105-6483
```
← —————————————— *Dear Mr. Mitchell*

```
                                letter              in
I am pleased to enclose with this a calendar outling the activities of
Black History Week at Martin Luther King School.  The week of January
9 (-13) has been set a side for this purpose.
                                            activities
You will note from the calendar that special have been planned for
both the day and even ing at the school.  Outstanding speakers and
films have been selected.

       if you have any sugescscions that would add to the program please
let me know soon as you can.

Sincerely yours
Mrs. Delores Delaney /Program Coordinator
xx
```
Enclosure

LESSON 130

70-space line

5 minutes

130a ● Keyboard Review

Directions: Key each sentence 3 times SS. DS between 3-line groups.

stroke smoothly, without pauses

alphabet Making a good showing on this next quiz is plainly my first objective.

figure On April 15, 1985, tornadoes struck the Middle West at least 37 times.

e, i Neither niece received notice of their vacancies in the science field.

easy During the time they were asked to make the new light, they were busy.

| 1 | 2 | 3 | 4 | 5 | 6 | 7 | 8 | 9 | 10 | 11 | 12 | 13 | 14 |

17d ● Sustained Skill Building

Directions: 1. Key two 1′ writings on each ¶ in 17c DS. Circle errors. Figure *gwam.*

2. Take two 2′ writings on both ¶ s combined. Circle errors. Figure *gwam.* Compare rates on 1′ and 2′ writings.

LESSON 18

50-space line

18a ● Keyboard Review

7 minutes

Directions: Key each line twice SS. DS between 2-line groups.

keep eyes on copy

```
b   bfb  bfb  bf  bf  bad  back  be  been  big  bill  both  books
p   ;p;  ;p;  p;  p;  page  part  plan  plant  play  post  point
re  red  real  rest  reach  are  care  great  green  sure  free
alphabet  Six  big  rocks  jut  out  right  there  beside  the  pier.
          Van  said  they  were  quite  hard  to  film  in  the  haze.
```

```
|   1   |   2   |   3   |   4   |   5   |   6   |   7   |   8   |   9   |   10   |
```

10 minutes

Do not key the lines between words.

think and key whole words

18b ● Technique Builder: Keying Whole Words

Directions: Key lines 1–5 twice SS as your teacher dictates the words. DS between 2-line groups. Then take two 1′ writings on the paragraphs that follow.

```
1  for | for | the | the | for  the | and | and | this | this | and  this
2  as | as | you | your | as  you | as  your | she | she | is | is | she  is
3  I | I | have | have | I  have | they | they | will | will | they  will
4  at | at | their | their | at  their | are | are | not | not | are  not
5  this | this | did  this | you | you | are | are | you  are | you  are
```

gwam 1′

```
     A  lot  of  the  time  you  will  find  that  you  can    9
think  and  key  whole  words.  This  means  you  will  not   19
key  all  of  them  at  the  same  rate.                       26

     If  a  word  is  long  or  hard,  of  course,  you  can    9
slow  down  a  bit.  Your  speed  is  bound  to  go  up  if   19
you  learn  to  key  in  this  way.                            25
```

```
|   1   |   2   |   3   |   4   |   5   |   6   |   7   |   8   |   9   |   10   |
```

128c ● Formatting Problems: Business Letters with Tables

Directions: Problem 1

1. Key/format the letter below in simplified letter style. Set margins for a 60-space line; begin dateline on line 18.
2. Center the table horizontally, leaving

6 spaces between columns. SS tabular material; DS before and after the table.
3. Address a small envelope.

April 22, 19-- | Ms. Gloria Riveria | Service Manager | Johnson Motors, Inc. | 7898 Grand Avenue | Detroit, MI 48202-2147 | AUTOMOTIVE MANUALS

(¶) Thank you for your request for information on our automotive manuals. The Wilcox Company has for many years published the latest in manuals for all makes and models of cars and trucks. The new information you requested is listed below:

Light Duty Trucks	Catalog #689
Early Convertibles	Catalog #489
Foreign Cars-British	Catalog #358

(¶) All our manuals provide complete chassis as well as motor information. Included are well-illustrated diagnostic procedures for making repairs.

(¶) We sincerely hope that the information you requested has been provided, and we look forward to hearing from you again in the near future.

Robert Bains | Managing Editor

Directions: Problem 2

1. Key/format the letter in Problem 1 in modified block style with mixed punctuation. Margin and date placement remain the same. Remember to key the subject, Automotive Manuals, and include a salutation and complimentary close,

Sincerely yours. Address the letter to:
Mr. Al Davis, Service Manager
State Auto Service Center
3820 College Avenue
Muncie, IN 47303-1750

LESSON 129

5 minutes

129a ● Keyboard Review

Directions: Key each sentence 3 times SS. DS between 3-line groups.

keep your feet flat on the floor

alphabet Julia got very few dark boxes of any size in the shipment from Quincy.

figure The invoice was not due until October 6, 1991, and it came to $645.10.

4th finger Pat appeared puzzled but happy when the pizza appeared at their place.

easy Quick typists always keep both their eyes on their copy when they key.

| 1 | 2 | 3 | 4 | 5 | 6 | 7 | 8 | 9 | 10 | 11 | 12 | 13 | 14 |

10 minutes

129b ● Skill Builder

Directions: 1. Take a 1' writing on the ¶ in 127b, page 221. The last word keyed will be your goal word.
2. Take a 5' writing with the return

called after each minute. When the return is called, start the paragraph over again. Try to reach your goal each minute as the return is called.

10 minutes | **18c ● Sentence Guided Writings**

Directions: 1. Take a 1' writing with the call of the guide each 20''. Try to complete each sentence as the guide is called. (Your teacher will tell you how the guide will be called.) **2.** Take two 1' writings on the last sentence without the call of the guide.

	words	in line	gwam 20''

keep arms and wrists quiet

		words	gwam 20''
1	Listen to the guide call.	5	15
2	Sit up straight in your chair.	6	18
3	Do not take your eyes off the book.	7	21
4	Hold your thumb close to your space bar.	8	24
5	Try to raise your rate by one word each line.	9	27
6	Be sure to keep your mind on your work as you key.	10	30

| 1 | 2 | 3 | 4 | 5 | 6 | 7 | 8 | 9 | 10 |

---

8 minutes | **18d ● Continuity Practice**

Directions: Key both ¶s DS. Circle all errors. Repeat.

all letters used   1.1 si

	gwam 1'	2'
All of us ought to take better care of our	9	5
earth than we have in the past. Unless we do so,	19	10
it will no longer be such a good place to live.	28	14
Trash piles up so fast that soon there may be	9	19
no more places to put it. Maybe we should hire a	19	24
waste czar whose job would be to make us quit being	30	29
so lax in our trash habits.	35	31

1	2	3	4	5	6	7	8	9	10
1		2		3		4		5	

---

10 minutes | **18e ● Sustained Skill Building**

Directions: Key a 1' writing on each ¶ in 18d. Figure *gwam.* Try to equal your 1' rate as you take two 2' writings on both ¶s combined.

fingers deeply curved

hands upright over keys

Lesson 18

33

127c, continued

Directions: Problem 2   Compose a Business Letter

1. Compose a letter in reply to the letter in Problem 1 in modified block style with mixed punctuation. Use today's date; address the letter to Mr. Morris Scott, President | Administrative Assistants Association | 1331 Birch Road | Kansas City, MO 64129-5432 | Dr. Sue Rigby will be the signer of the letter. In this letter, thank Mr. Scott for his kind remarks about the keynote address and tell him how much you enjoyed the conference. Also, tell him to forward the names of the vendors who wanted you to speak.

2. Address a small envelope.

LESSON 128

70-space line

5 minutes

128a ● Keyboard Review

Directions: Key each sentence three times SS. DS between 3-line groups.

strike keys with quick, sharp strokes

alphabet	Both executives will question and itemize key profit figures for July.
figure	The 1987 national snowmobile race attracted 13,570 cold weather fans.
double letters	Their official annual meeting accommodations committee appeared happy.
easy	The man on the bike did not turn into the lane as you had said he did.

| 1 | 2 | 3 | 4 | 5 | 6 | 7 | 8 | 9 | 10 | 11 | 12 | 13 | 14 |

10 minutes

128b ● Speed Builder

Directions: Take two 1' writings on each ¶; try to increase speed on the second writing. Figure *gwam.*

Alternative Procedure: Work for speed as you take one 5' writing on all four ¶s combined. Figure *gwam.*

all letters used   1.4 si   5.3 awl   85% hfw

	gwam 1'	5'
Ultimately, all of us have to face the question about the kind of	13	3	50
career that we will choose. You may have already been advised to choose	28	6	53
a career while you are still in school so that you can get ready for it.	43	9	56
Almost all jobs require some special training. Hopefully, you will	56	11	58
realize this fact before it's too late.	64	13	60
Just lazily dreaming about a career is not sufficient. Examine your	14	16	63
thinking carefully. What can you do best? What do you enjoy doing?	28	18	65
Your parents and teachers have urged you to make a careful choice	42	21	68
and then resolve to be the best in your field. This is sound advice. If you	57	24	71
are good enough, there is room in any area.	65	26	73
As a general rule, you will be right to avoid the trap that often	13	28	75
awaits those who know a little bit about a lot of things but not much	27	31	78
about anything in particular. The world has enough persons like that.	41	34	81
Most students who wish to enter a career find thousands available	13	37	84
to them. The problem is to discover the job that you can do well and	27	40	87
that you enjoy doing. If you cannot do it well, you'll fail. If you	41	42	89
dislike it, you will miss one of the thrills life holds for us. You	55	45	92
certainly must select your career with care.	64	47	94

gwam 1' | 1 | 2 | 3 | 4 | 5 | 6 | 7 | 8 | 9 | 10 | 11 | 12 | 13 | 14 |
     5' | 1 | 2 | 3 |

LESSON 19

7 minutes

19a ● Keyboard Review

Directions: Key each line twice SS. DS between 2-line groups.

keep fingers
deeply curved

y   jyj jyj yj yj you your yes yet year eye cycle city

q   aqa aqa qa qa quit quiet quart quote squire square

nd   end send find found friend land hand window second

alphabet   Please wake me if I doze past six on that morning.
            Joy now lives in a quaint house near a good beach.

| 1 | 2 | 3 | 4 | 5 | 6 | 7 | 8 | 9 | 10 |

15 minutes

19b ● Sentence Guided Writings

Directions: 1. Use lines 1–12 for 1′ writings with the call of the guide each 20″.   **2.** Use lines 13–16 for 1′ writings without the call of the guide.

words | in line | gwam 20″

return quickly;
do not pause

1 Read your theme in class.   5 | 15

2 *Speak up so all can hear.*   5 | 15

3 I plan to work out in the gym.   6 | 18

4 *It is a great way to keep fit.*   6 | 18

5 My new phone can record your voice.   7 | 21

6 *Please tell me to return your call.*   7 | 21

7 These drills will help you learn to key.   8 | 24

8 *Use the new skill each day in your work.*   8 | 24

9 We joined the drive to keep our street clean.   9 | 27

10 *Our club wants to find ways to aid the group.*   9 | 27

11 Kathy left her bike in the stand next to our room.   10 | 30

12 *When she came back after class, one tire was flat.* 10 | 30

13 One thing they had to learn was how to read a map.   10 | 30

14 *He told us to work all three of the math problems.* 10 | 30

15 The lunch break seems way too short to most of us.   10 | 30

16 *Chris thought he would be late for class that day.* 10 | 30

LESSON 127

5 minutes

127a ● Keyboard Review

Directions: Key each sentence three times SS. DS between 3-line groups.

reach to keys
with fingers

alphabet The new juggler's quick force and dexterity amazed the viewing public.

figure Lake Superior is over 31,820 square miles or 51 323 square kilometers.

double letters The matter of getting good foods soon assured immediate staff success.

easy No person can make you feel inferior without your consent or approval.

| 1 | 2 | 3 | 4 | 5 | 6 | 7 | 8 | 9 | 10 | 11 | 12 | 13 | 14 |

10 minutes

127b ● Paragraph Guided Writings

Directions: 1. Set goals of 40, 50, and 60 words a minute. Take two 1' writings at each rate. Try to reach your goal word as time is called.

2. Your teacher may call the quarter or half minutes to guide you.

3. Key additional writings at the 50- and 60-word rates as time permits.

1.4 si

The fast food industry has really been in high gear in the last
decade. There have been fast food franchises for more than forty years;
however, a greater number of choices are being offered to the public.
You now can add yogurts, sub sandwiches, tacos, ribs, egg rolls, and a
whole lot more than hamburgers to the list.

30 minutes

127c ● Formatting Problems: Business Letters with Special Features

Directions: Problem 1   Business Letter with Postscript

1. Key/format the letter below in modified block style with mixed punctuation. Set margins for a 50-space line; begin dateline on line 18.

2. Address a small envelope.

A postscript is the last item in a letter. The postscript appears a DS below the enclosure notation (if used) or the reference initials if an enclosure notation is not used. The postscript need not be preceded by the letters *P.S.*

```
xx
 ←—DS
A video tape of your
```

December 9, 19— | Dr. Sue Rigby | 1817 Wentworth Drive | Topeka, KS 66603-1811 | Dear Dr. Rigby: | SUBJECT: Keynote Address

(¶) On behalf of the Administrative Assistants Association, I am very pleased to congratulate and thank you for the outstanding keynote address that you delivered to our annual conference earlier this month. It was exciting and gave all of us a lot to think about.

(¶) Since several of our vendors at this conference would like to contact you, they have asked me to supply your address. Should I give this information to them, or would you rather that I give you their names and telephone numbers so you may make the call? Please let me know your wishes in this matter.

Sincerely yours, | Morris Scott | President | xx | A video tape of your presentation will be sent to you.

(continued on next page)

19c ● Continuity Practice

Directions: Key the ¶s below DS. Circle all errors.

all letters used   1.1 si

		gwam 2′	3′

A few surveys have found that students do not · 5 3 21

learn as much as they should in school these days. 10 7 24

At least one study of this kind showed that some 15 10 27

could not find major bodies of water on a world 19 13 30

map, for example, or get the right answers on a 24 16 34

simple math quiz. 26 17 35

You could claim, though, that this practice 5 3 22

of pointing out what kids don't know is not new. 9 6 25

It seems that each generation is quick to tell what 15 10 28

is wrong with the next one. Chances are good that 20 13 32

in a few years those in school now will be the ones 25 17 35

making these kinds of comments. 28 19 37

gwam 2′ | 1 | 2 | 3 | 4 | 5 |
3′ | 1 | 2 | 3 | 4 |

19d ● Sustained Skill Building

Directions: 1. Take one 1′ writing on each paragraph in 19c DS. Circle all errors; figure *gwam*.
2. Use these paragraphs for 2′ and 3′ writings as time permits.

To figure *gwam* on the 1′ writing, use the nearest figure above the copy. For the 2′ and 3′ writings, use the columns and scales to figure *gwam*.

LESSON 20

50-space line

20a ● Keyboard Review

Directions: Key each line twice SS. DS between 2-line groups.

curve fingers; not wrists

x   sxs sxs xs xs tax tax mix mix fix fix box axe axle

p   ;p; ;p; p; p; plan plan plant plant play play pray

to   to too took top told town toward touch total today

alphabet   Quite a few boys just came back from the zoo trip.

Dawn wants all of us to go in their van next time.

| 1 | 2 | 3 | 4 | 5 | 6 | 7 | 8 | 9 | 10 |

126c ● Speed Ladder Paragraphs

Directions: **1.** Take 1' writings on ¶ 1 DS until you complete the ¶ in 1'. **2.** When you complete ¶ 1 in 1', continue on to ¶ 2. Repeat this procedure as you try to complete each of the five ¶ s in the given time.

all letters used   1.4 si

gwam 5'

We do not need to be experts on the rules and procedures of proper | 3 | 55
etiquette to treat others with courtesy at all times. We simply must | 5 | 58
apply some standard rules of courtesy. These rules just mean treating | 8 | 61
people fairly. | 9 | 61

When you are not quite sure of all the rules of good conduct in a | 12 | 64
certain situation, just think about the other person's feelings. Act | 14 | 67
in a way that will make others feel very comfortable. You will not go | 17 | 69
far wrong if you heed this advice. | 19 | 71

Good manners are only ways of showing your consideration for the | 21 | 74
other person. You do not say unkind things about another person in | 24 | 76
public, because you do not want to hurt that person even when you think | 27 | 79
those unkind things could be true or even partially true. | 29 | 81

When you use good manners, you merely put another person's comfort | 32 | 84
ahead of your own. That is the acid test of good manners. Do you make | 35 | 87
the people with whom you associate feel at ease? Do they prize your | 37 | 90
friendship? Let these questions be your guide in relations with others. | 40 | 93

In any relationship with others the use of good manners appears to | 43 | 95
involve the Golden Rule. A person is as likely to return kindness for | 46 | 98
kindness as to return insult for insult. It is quite unusual to find | 49 | 101
an individual who will never respond kindly to good manners. Try it | 51 | 104
and see if you don't agree. | 52 | 105

gwam 5' | 1 | 2 | 3 |

---

10 minutes

126d ● Language Arts Skills: Composing at Your Machine

Directions: Compose a paragraph, telling what the following quotation means to you.

"The more we study, the more we discover how little we know."

Lesson 126

220

20b ● Technique Builder: Keying Whole Words

Directions: Key each line twice SS. DS between 2-line groups. Take a 1' writing on each sentence. Figure *gwam*.

key each word as a unit, not letter by letter

```
1  in | in | our | our | in our | for | for | an | an | and for | and for

2  will | will | be | be | will be | of | of | of | that | that | of that

3  with | with | us | us | with us | has | has | been | been | has been

4  we | we | can | can | we can | on | on | the | on the | that | on that

5  for the | and the | did the | in their | for their | at this

6  Go with us to their game if you can find the time.

7  They will all be there by the first of this month.

8  I think he will have to wait for the rest of them.

9  She wants to send notes to those who are not here.
   |  1  |  2  |  3  |  4  |  5  |  6  |  7  |  8  |  9  |  10  |
```

20c ● Continuity Practice

Directions: Key both ¶s twice DS. Repeat if time permits.

all letters used   1.1 si

use quick, sharp strokes

		gwam 2'	3'
We now know quite a lot about which jobs in	4	3	27
life are apt to cause the most stress. As a rule,	9	6	30
those which require one to meet and deal with the	14	10	33
public each day head the list.	18	12	36
You need to give some extra thought to how you	22	15	39
may want to spend your working years. As you will	27	18	42
soon learn, the size of your paycheck each month	32	21	45
is not the only thing to think about.	36	24	48

```
gwam 2' |    1    |    2    |    3    |    4    |    5    |
     3' |      1      |      2      |      3      |      4      |
```

20d ● Sustained Skill Building

Directions: 1. Take a 1' writing on each ¶ in 20c DS. Circle errors and figure *gwam* on each writing.

2. Take a 2' writing and a 3' writing on the combined ¶s. Circle errors and figure *gwam* on each writing. Try to equal your 1' rate on these writings.

30 minutes

125c ● Formatting Problems: Business Letters with Special Features

Directions: Problem 1 Business Letter with Attention Line

1. Key/format the letter below in block style with mixed punctuation. Set margins for a 60-space line; begin the dateline on line 18.

2. Address a large envelope.

An attention line is used to direct a letter to a particular person. The attention line appears as the first line of the letter address. Key the attention line immediately above the company name on the envelope.

```
Attention Miss Carol Key
Largo & Key, Inc.
2573 Winsome Drive
Charleston, WV  25312-1078
```

May 10, 19-- | Attention Miss Carol Key | Largo & Key, Inc. | 2573 Winsome Drive | Charleston, WV 25312-1078 | Ladies and Gentlemen:

(¶) Our company is very interested in obtaining information about recent automation procedures being used in today's modern office. We particularly are interested in word processing and fax equipment.

(¶) We have not made any real changes in our equipment or practices in the last ten years. It is my understanding that your company specializes in the design of office systems that take advantage of all latest techniques and equipment.

(¶) I am enclosing a list of our current equipment. Please send me any information that you may have regarding automating the office.

Sincerely, | Mrs. Jane Roberts | Administrative Support Department | xx | Enclosure

Directions: Problem 2 Business Letter with Subject Line

1. Key/format the letter below in modified block style with open punctuation. Set margins for a 50-space line; begin

the dateline on line 18.

2. Address a small envelope.

When a subject line is used in a letter, it appears on the second line below the salutation. It may be centered on the line, or it may be keyed at the left margin as shown.

```
Mr. Rodger Avion
361 Oakman Avenue
Lynn, MA  01905-1206
            ←──DS
Dear Mr. Avion
            ←──DS
SUBJECT:  Accounting Software
```

June 1, 19-- | Mr. Rodger Avion | 361 Oakman Avenue | Lynn, MA 01905-1206 | Dear Mr. Avion | SUBJECT: Accounting Software

(¶) Thank you for your software request.

(¶) Yes, we do have the latest software in the accounting area and will be pleased to send you the complete information about our products and our guaranteed services. Of course, there will be no fee for this information or, if you request, the services of one of our representatives.

(¶) Please review the product information when you receive it, and let us know how we may be of further assistance. All of our software specialists stand ready to assist you in designing an accounting system that provides you with necessary data.

Sincerely yours | AUTOMATED ACCOUNTING | Antonio J. Espino | Director | xx

LESSON 126

70-space line

5 minutes

126a ● Keyboard Review

Directions: Key each sentence three times SS. DS between 3-line groups.

think as you
key each
drill line

alphabet To organize and make plans for an exquisite display was the objective.

figure Each wing on the X13A, which was built in 1989, has over 6,500 rivets.

left hand Few water excesses were decreased as wave after wave faced a new crew.

easy If you want to learn from your practice, you must have goals in sight.

| 1 | 2 | 3 | 4 | 5 | 6 | 7 | 8 | 9 | 10 | 11 | 12 | 13 | 14 |

10 minutes

126b ● Skill Comparison

Directions: Take three 1' writings each on 102c, page 181, and 124c, page 216. Figure *gwam;* compare your script and rough-draft copy rates.

Unit 3 ■ Learning the Figure Keys (Lessons 21–25)

Learning Goals:

1. To strike the figure keys by touch, using the correct fingers.
2. To increase basic skill by refining stroking and operating techniques and by keying a variety of drills and timed writings.

General Directions

Use a 50-space line for all lessons in this unit (center − 25; center + 25 + 5). SS sentences and drill lines. DS between repeated groups of lines. DS paragraph copy. Set machine for a 5-space paragraph indention.

LESSON 21

7 minutes

21a ● Keyboard Review

Directions: Key each sentence twice SS. DS between 2-line groups.

quick down-and-in motion as you strike the space bar

alphabet

Place your new video camera in the giant size box.

I took quite a long time to find the eject button.

easy

He held both of his hands at just the right slant.

Lay all the keys there when she is done with them.

| 1 | 2 | 3 | 4 | 5 | 6 | 7 | 8 | 9 | 10 |

8 minutes

21b ● Location of 1 and 7

Plan for Learning New Keys

1. Find new key on keyboard chart.
2. Locate key on your keyboard.
3. Place fingers over home keys.
4. Know what finger strikes each key.
5. Watch your finger as you make the reach to the new key.
6. Key each short drill twice on the same line. Be sure to use the correct finger.

Reach to 1

1. Find **1** on the chart.
2. Find it on your keyboard.
3. Place your fingers over the home keys.
4. Reach to **1** with the **a** finger.
5. Touch **1a** lightly without moving other fingers from their home position.

Reach to 7

1. Find **7** on the chart.
2. Find it on your keyboard.
3. Place your fingers over the home keys.
4. Reach to **7** with the **j** finger.
5. Touch **7j** lightly without moving other fingers from their home position.

Key twice on same line

ala ala ala 1a 1a 1a ala   j7j j7j j7j 7j 7j 7j j7j

30 minutes

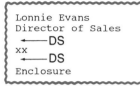

```
Lonnie Evans
Director of Sales
  ←——DS
xx
  ←——DS
Enclosure
```

An enclosure notation is used when some item (or items) is sent with a letter. The notation appears at the left margin a DS below the reference initials.

If necessary, see directions for addressing large envelopes on page 93.

124d ● Formatting Problems: Business Letters with Enclosure Notations

Directions: Problem 1

1. Key/format the letter below in modified block style with mixed punctuation. Set margins for a 50-space line; begin dateline on line 18.

2. Address a large envelope.

December 1, 19-- | Mrs. Marian Kraft | 4801 Sunset Road | Portland, OR 97203-1234 | Dear Mrs. Kraft:

(¶) Thank you for requesting information about our new club, CD Only. This club was organized primarily to provide services to owners of compact disc players.

(¶) We are equipped to provide repair service for all makes and models of compact disc players and accessories. In addition, our members receive our monthly magazine, which outlines what is happening in the music world. Membership in our club entitles you to special discounts on the purchase of CD discs and equipment.

(¶) Please complete the enclosed application form so that you can start enjoying the benefits of club membership.

Sincerely yours, | Lonnie Evans | Director of Sales | xx | Enclosure

Directions: Problem 2

1. Prepare a copy of the model letter shown on page 217.

2. Prepare the letter in simplified

block style. Set the margins for a 50-space line; begin dateline on line 18.

3. Address a large envelope.

LESSON 125

70-space line

5 minutes

125a ● Keyboard Review

Directions: Key each line three times SS. DS between 3-line groups.

return carrier quickly

alphabet The banquet speaker excited and amazed a large crowd of jovial youths.

figure The 351 turbo engine car can go over 140 MPH and do 0-60 in 5 seconds.

adjacent key We hope to develop quickly a joint guide to reviewing the weekly news.

easy They may make the six men go to the playing field to finish the games.

| 1 | 2 | 3 | 4 | 5 | 6 | 7 | 8 | 9 | 10 | 11 | 12 | 13 | 14 |

---

10 minutes

125b ● Timed Writings

Directions: 1. Take a 1' writing on each paragraph of 121b, page 209, *or* take a

5' writing on all paragraphs combined. Circle errors; figure *gwam*.

21c ● Location Drills 1 and 7

Directions: Key each line twice SS. DS between 2-line groups.

Reach to 1

Reach to 7

```
1   a1a a1a a1a 1a 1a 1a 11 aims, 11 aides, 11 and 111
    Kay drove 111.1 miles.  Hire 11 boys and 11 girls.

7   j7j j7j j7j 7j 7j 7j 77 jobs, 777 jars, 77 and 777
    I bought 77 books.  See page 777.  All 7,777 came.

number    After 17 days at sea they docked on June 17, 1777.
fluency   Our firm sold 1,717 new cars and 1,177 new trucks.
      |  1  |  2  |  3  |  4  |  5  |  6  |  7  |  8  |  9  | 10 |
```

21d ● Technique Builder   6 minutes

Directions: Key each line twice SS. DS between 2-line groups.

key with
flowing rhythm

```
1  and I | and go | and look | and grade | and limp | and right
2  to jump | to show | to start | to save | to have | to regard
3  the fee | the boy | the man | the date | the rest | the time
4  of their | of this | of that | of them | of facts | of great
5  did do | did go | did draw | did join | did extra | did link
```

12 minutes

21e ● Continuity Practice

Directions: Key both ¶s DS. Circle all errors. Repeat each exercise. Try to make no more than four errors per writing.

keep your eyes
on the copy

all letters used 1.1 si	gwam 1'	3'
Each time that you sit down to key, take a	9	3	33
second or so to decide just what it is you want	18	6	36
to do. Your goal may be to improve your stroking	28	9	39
speed, or it may be to make fewer errors than you	38	13	43
made the last time.	42	14	44
One thing we know for sure is that you will do	9	17	47
your best if you work on only one skill at a time.	20	21	51
It is quite hard to make your fingers fly and still	30	24	54
have all the words come out right. When you zip	40	27	57
along, you can expect to make a few mistakes.	49	30	60

```
gwam  1' |  1  |  2  |  3  |  4  |  5  |  6  |  7  |  8  |  9  | 10 |
      3' |       1       |        2        |       3       |
```

//////hendrix consultants, inc.

115 Gateway Drive
Seattle, WA 98168-4301
(206) 559-0182

Business letter in simplified style   50-space line; open punctuation

	words
All Major lines begin at left margin — April 17, 19-- ← begin on line 18 / return 4 times	3

Address in all caps with no punctuation begins on the fourth line below date

```
MISS MARIA GARCIA
DIRECTOR OF WORD PROCESSING
CLAY & SMITH LEGAL SERVICES
146 ACCESS DRIVE
SPOKANE WA   99216-6792
```

	words
MISS MARIA GARCIA	7
DIRECTOR OF WORD PROCESSING	12
CLAY & SMITH LEGAL SERVICES	18
146 ACCESS DRIVE	21
SPOKANE WA 99216-6792	26

Omit salutation
                                   DS

Subject line in all caps; double-space above and below it

```
FORMATTING THE SIMPLIFIED LETTER                          32
                   DS
Our consulting firm has found the simplified letter       43
to be the most efficient in terms of production time.     54
It is formatted as follows:                               59
```

Begin enumerated items at left margin

```
1.  Use a block format.                                   64

2.  Begin the address (in ALL CAPS with no punc-          74
tuation) on the fourth line below the date.               83

3.  Do not use a salutation or complimentary close.       93

4.  Always use a subject heading keyed in all caps, a     104
double space below the address.  The body of the          114
letter begins a double space below the subject line.      124

5.  Begin enumerated items at the left margin.            134

6.  Indicate the writer's name and title in all caps      144
on the fourth line below the body of the letter.          154

7.  Key only the operator's reference initials in         164
lower case a double space below the writer's name.        174
```

Omit complimentary close

```
Firms using this letter format like its efficiency.       185
                                        return 4 times
```

Writer's name and title in all caps on the fourth line below letter body

```
PHILIP WANG, SUPPORT SERVICES MANAGER                     192
                   DS
ez                                                        193
```

LESSON 22

7 minutes

22a ● Keyboard Review

Directions: Key each line twice SS. DS between 2-line groups.

keep arms and
wrists quiet

alphabet

You see best if you tilt the screen exactly right.
Pat vowed to make her quota for that zone by June.

1   a1a a1a 1a 1a 1a 11 and 111, add 11 and 11, age 11

7   j7j j7j 7j 7j 717 units, 77 jobs, 77 and 77 and 17

easy   Make sure you sign your name on both of the forms.

| 1 | 2 | 3 | 4 | 5 | 6 | 7 | 8 | 9 | 10 |

---

5 minutes

22b ● Location of 5 and 9

Reach to 5
1. Find 5 on the chart.
2. Find it on your keyboard.
3. Place your fingers over the home keys.
4. Reach to 5 with the f finger.
5. Touch 5f lightly without moving other fingers from their home position.

Reach to 9
1. Find 9 on the chart.
2. Find it on your keyboard.
3. Place your fingers over the home keys.
4. Reach to 9 with the l finger.
5. Touch 9l lightly without moving other fingers from their home position.

f5f f5f f5f 5f 5f 5f f5f   Key twice on same line   191 191 191 91 91 91 191

---

6 minutes

22c ● Location Drills 5 and 9

Directions: Key each line twice SS. DS between 2-line groups.

Reach to 5

5   f5f f5f f5f 5f 5f 5f 551 feet, 55 firms, 55 and 55
Send 555 pens. We won 155 games. Build 515 sets.

9   191 191 191 91 91 91 99 lines, 919 lots, 99 and 99
Use all 99. I fell 19 feet. He sold 919 in 1991.

22d ● Continuity Practice   6 minutes

Directions: Key the ¶ as many times as you can in the time allotted.   words

Reach to 9

The world of high tech has great news for those   10

who do not spell as well as they should. Software   20

can now be used to help them catch words they miss.   30

| 1 | 2 | 3 | 4 | 5 | 6 | 7 | 8 | 9 | 10 |

123c, continued

Directions: Problem 3

1. Key/format the letter shown below in block style with open punctuation. Set margins for a 50-space line; begin the dateline on line 18.

2. Address a small envelope.

February 10, 19-- | Mr. Jonathon Bridge | 583 Low Bridge Road | Monroe, LA 71203-1714 | Dear Mr. Bridge

(¶) Thank you for opening a Money Market checking account with our bank. We are sure that you will find this the best account in terms of economy and in terms of meeting your checking needs.

(¶) As you get to know Chemical Bank even better, you will find we offer a complete line of banking services. These services include high interest savings accounts that are time flexible and a variety of personal and home equity loans designed to meet your borrowing needs.

(¶) Please drop in to see us again soon. We look forward to serving you.

Sincerely | CHEMICAL BANK | Lori Cummings, Manager | xx

LESSON 124

70-space line

124a ● Keyboard Review

5 minutes

keep wrists and
arms quiet

Directions: Key each line 3 times SS. DS between 3-line groups.

alphabet   Kip was very excited to qualify for the bronze medal in the high jump.

figure   A total of 2,819,246 immigrants entered the country between 1955–1964.

combination   Send a copy of this statement report information to their new address.

easy   To key right, you will be hitting those keys as if they were very hot.

| 1 | 2 | 3 | 4 | 5 | 6 | 7 | 8 | 9 | 10 | 11 | 12 | 13 | 14 |

124b ● Language Arts Skills: Number Expression Guides

5 minutes

Directions: Key each sentence 3 times. The first sentence gives the rule; the remaining sentences apply the rule.

1 Amounts of money, either dollars or cents, should be keyed in figures.

2 The cost of this year's automobile has gone up from $9,197 to $12,500.

3 We got four tapes at $6.50, three tapes at $7.50 and six tapes at $12.

124c ● Skill Builder from Rough Draft Copy

5 minutes

Directions: Take four 1' writings on the paragraph; key for control.

1.4 si   words

We all agree that a changes in our auto safety are key if the ac- 13

cident related deaths are going to be reduced. Yet the debate as to 27

whether riders
~~weather drivers~~ should have too use seat belts or ~~weather~~ *whether* auto makers 41

a decade
should install airbags, that has gone on for more than ~~ten years~~, has 55

been anwsered. car makers must put auto matic belts or air bags in all 69

new cars. 71

(continued on page 218)

22e ● Sentence Guided Writings

Directions: 1. Take a 1' writing on each sentence with the call of the guide each 20''. Try to complete each sentence as the guide is called.

2. Take two 1' writings on the last sentence without the call of the guide.

	words in line	gwam 20''
1 Our roads can be safe for all.	6	18
2 *If you drive, learn the rules.*	6	18
3 Be sure your car is in good repair.	7	21
4 *Have your brakes and tires checked.*	7	21
5 Keep to your right and pass on the left.	8	24
6 *Slow down a bit when you drive at night.*	8	24
7 Wear a seatbelt when you are in a moving car.	9	27
8 *Never use your brakes when you are in a skid.*	9	27
9 Glance in your rear view mirror every ten seconds.	10	30
10 *Turn on the headlights so you can see and be seen.*	10	30
11 If you do not drive a car, pass these rules along.	10	30
12 *They can help others make our roads a safer place.*	10	30

8 minutes

22f ● Sustained Skill Building

Directions: 1. Take one 1' writing on each ¶ in 21e, page 38.
2. Take one 2' writing and one 3' writing on both ¶s combined. Figure *gwam.*

3. For the 2' rate, use the 1' column and scale to get total words; divide by 2.
4. Try to equal your 1' rate on the longer writings.

LESSON 23

50-space line

7 minutes

23a ● Keyboard Review

Directions: Key each line twice SS. DS between 2-line groups.

keep eyes on copy

alphabet Most all kids love to spend time down at the mall.
Jacques bought pizza mix for that party last week.

1,7 Amy will be 17 on May 17. She lives at 7177 Pine.

easy Turn right when you come to the end of that block.

| 1 | 2 | 3 | 4 | 5 | 6 | 7 | 8 | 9 | 10 |

2119 DEL RIO DR., SAN JOSE, CA 95119-3348 (408) 272-8327

50-space line; open punctuation

words

March 5, 19-- ←——— begin on line 18   3
      return 4 times

letter address Mrs. Pamela Davidson   7
Advanced Video Services   12
754 Timberline Street   16
Chula Vista, CA 92011-5097   22
              DS

salutation Dear Mrs. Davidson   26
       DS

body I am pleased to have this opportunity to respond to   36
your questions regarding the charges for consulting   46
services at Creative Consulting.   53

Our fees for researching and analyzing the staffing   64
and training needs of your firm are billed at $90 per   74
hour plus expenses. Our training seminars are billed   85
on a daily basis of $500 per day plus the costs of   95
materials.   98

We will be happy to provide you a free appraisal of   108
your needs and to identify all our charges.   117

Please contact me if I may be of further assistance.   128
              DS

complimentary
close Sincerely yours   131
     DS

company name in CREATIVE CONSULTING   135
closing lines
(all CAPS)   return 4 times

keyed name Preston Price   138
official title Assistant Manager   141
     DS
reference initials rs   142

Business letter in block style

23b ● Technique Builder

Directions: Key each line three times from dictation SS. DS between 3-line groups.

1 of this | of this | of these | of these | of your | of their

2 to be | to be | to have | to have | to them | to them | to our

3 for the | for this | for that | for them | for your | for it

4 are in | are in | are for | are for | are on | are on | are at

5 in our | in our | in his | in his | in her | in her | in which

6 and it | and it | and it will | and it will | and it would

7 is not | is not | is not the | is not the | is not the one

8 minutes

23c ● Location of 4, 8 and : (colon)

Reach to 4
1. Find 4 on the chart.
2. Find it on your keyboard.
3. Place your fingers over the home keys.
4. Reach to 4 with the f finger.
5. Touch 4f lightly without moving other fingers from their home position.

Reach to 8
1. Find 8 on the chart.
2. Find it on your keyboard.
3. Place your fingers over the home keys.
4. Reach to 8 with the k finger.
5. Touch 8k lightly without moving other fingers from their home position.

f4f f4f f4f 4f 4f 4f f4f   Key twice on same line   k8k k8k k8k 8k 8k 8k k8k

> The : is the shift of the ;. Touch ;:;
> three times. Space twice after : used
> as punctuation.

12 minutes

23d ● Location Drills 4, 8 and : (colon)

Directions: Key each line twice SS. DS between 2-line groups.

Reach to 4

Reach to 8

4
f4f f4f f4f 4f 4f 4f 44 fans, 414 fins, 4,414 feet
We saw 44 ships. Divide by 414. I sold 144 more.

8
k8k k8k k8k 8k 8k 8k 88 keys, 18 kites, 8,188 ties
They ran 818 yards. Ask for 88. Leave on May 18.

:
;:; ;:; :; :; Note: To: From: Dear Mrs. Browne:
She said: I want these four: Send the following:

number
fluency
It read as follows: Ship all 418 to 159th Street.
On June 18, 1989, we drew 45,179 fans to the game.

| 1 | 2 | 3 | 4 | 5 | 6 | 7 | 8 | 9 | 10 |

Lesson 23

123b ● Speed Builder

Directions: Take two 1′ writings on each ¶; try to increase speed on the second writing. Figure *gwam*.

Alternate Procedure: Work for speed as you take one 5′ writing on all four ¶s combined. Figure *gwam*.

all letters used   1.4 si   5.3 awl   85% hfw   *gwam* 1′   5′

	1′	5′	
Try this little test. First, key your name in full; then key it	13	3	54
again. The second time, however, skip every other letter. Which was	27	5	56
easier and faster—the first or the second keying? The first one was	41	8	59
likely a bit easier and quicker, even though you keyed twice as many	55	11	62
letters. Why was this true? What did the test prove?	66	13	64
When you keyed your full name the first time, you keyed it from	13	16	67
habit. This, however, did not help you on your second keying. You had	27	19	70
to concentrate on each letter separately as you keyed it. As a result,	42	21	72
you keyed slowly. Good habits are a valuable aid in keying words as	55	24	75
they are in almost everything else you do. They often save you time.	69	27	78
Have you ever attempted to break a bad habit? Everyone says the	13	30	81
job is not easy. Although it might not seem like it, good habits are	27	32	83
no easier to change than bad ones. Once you learn to keyboard correctly,	42	35	86
you are on the way because your good habits will take over for you.	55	38	89
There are only two things to remember about building good habits.	13	41	92
First, when you key, key correctly. If you realize that the right way	28	44	95
is the easy way, this rule will not be too hard to follow. Next, do	41	46	97
practice with zeal! You certainly cannot expect to key well if you	55	49	100
waste part of the practice session every day.	64	51	102

gwam 1′ | 1 | 2 | 3 | 4 | 5 | 6 | 7 | 8 | 9 | 10 | 11 | 12 | 13 | 14 |
  5′ | | 1 | | 2 | | 3 |

123c ● Formatting Problems: Business Letters in Block Style

Directions: Problem 1

1. Prepare a copy of the model letter shown on page 215.

2. Prepare the letter in block style with open punctuation. Set margins for a 50-space line; begin the dateline on line 18.

3. Address a small envelope. If a workbook is not available, use a small envelope or paper cut to size (6½ × 3⅝″).

Directions: Problem 2

Rekey the letter in problem 1, but address the letter to:

Supply an appropriate salutation. Address a small envelope.

Mrs. Mary Jo Happley
1308 Pine Bluff Drive
Fremont, NE 68025-2567

(continued on page 216)

23e ● Paragraph Skill Builder

Directions: Key the ¶ once for practice; then take three 1' writings on it.

Figure *gwam* on the best writing.

all letters used   1.1 si

```
                           .              4                 .              8
     When you see a new word in print, try to guess
                     12             .              16                .
     what it means. The way it is used in the sentence
       20                  .              24             .              28
     should give you a quick hint. To find the exact
              .              32             .              36                .
     meaning, though, you will need to look it up. Then
       40             .              44             .              48             .
     seize the chance to put your new word to work on the
              52             .              56
     job when you speak or write.
```

LESSON 24

50-space line

7 minutes   **24a ● Keyboard Review**

Directions: Key each line twice SS. DS between 2-line groups.

sit erect;
keep your eyes
on the copy

alphabet   A fine text can equip you with good verbal skills.
           Jud seized the chance to show me what he could do.

: colon   Use the colon to show time: 7:15, 8:15, and 9:15.

easy   The girls are just the right height for the chair.

```
| 1 | 2 | 3 | 4 | 5 | 6 | 7 | 8 | 9 | 10 |
```

---

5 minutes   **24b ● Location of 2 and 0 (zero)**

Reach to 2
1. Find 2 on the chart.
2. Find it on your keyboard.
3. Place your fingers over the home keys.
4. Reach to 2 with the s finger.
5. Touch 2s lightly without moving other fingers from their home position.

Reach to 0 (zero)
1. Find 0 on the chart.
2. Find it on your keyboard.
3. Place your fingers over the home keys.
4. Reach to 0 with the ; finger.
5. Touch 0; lightly without moving other fingers from their home position.

s2s s2s s2s 2s 2s 2s s2s   Key twice on same line   ;0; ;0; ;0; 0; ;0 0; ;0;

122c, continued

Directions: Problem 1

1. Prepare a copy of the model letter shown on page 212.

2. Prepare the letter in modified block style with mixed punctuation. Set margins for a 50-space line; begin the dateline on line 18.

3. Address a small envelope. Envelopes are printed on the back of the letterhead paper in the workbook. If a workbook is not available, use a small envelope or paper cut to small envelope size (6 ½ ″ × 3⅝ ″).

Directions: Problem 2

1. Key/format the letter shown below in modified block style with mixed punctuation. Set margins for a 50-space

line; begin the dateline on line 18.

2. Address a small envelope.

words

June 13, 19--   3

Mr. George Burns   6
Training Director   9
Rex International, Inc.   14
197 Appian Avenue   17
Houston, TX 77024-6583   22

Dear Mr. Burns: 25

At a recent convention of training professionals,   35
I came in contact with a firm that offers a complete   46
software program designed to assist all sizes of   55
businesses with their staff training needs.   64

I believe that their products would be just what   74
you could use in solving the training needs of   83
your company. Their approach is very practical.   93

I will send you in the next few days an up-to-date   103
listing of their training software along with the   113
pricing of these products.   118

Sincerely yours,   121

Note: In this letter and the remaining letters in the book, use your initials for the *xx* shown in the problem copy.

XX

Mrs. Ellen Hadley   125
Training Coordinator   129

LESSON 123

70-space line

5 minutes

123a ● Keyboard Review

Directions: Key each sentence three times SS. DS between 3-line groups.

keep your eyes on the copy as you return each line

alphabet   One excited gazelle quickly raced away and jumped the river before us.

figure   The world's largest lemon, discovered May 4, 1974, weighed over 5 lbs.

weak fingers   Prior approval was quickly acquired for requesting solution inquiries.

easy   At the present time of the audit, their profit picture is very dismal.

| 1 | 2 | 3 | 4 | 5 | 6 | 7 | 8 | 9 | 10 | 11 | 12 | 13 | 14 |

24c ● Location Drills: 2 and 0 (zero) 7 minutes

Directions: Key each line twice SS. DS between 2-line groups.

2 s2s s2s s2s 2s 2s 2s 22 sales, 212 sets, 122 steps
  He is 22. I am 21. On May 22 we drove 212 miles.

0 ;0; ;0; ;0; 0; 0; 0; 200 pets, 100 pens, 900 tons.
  Each number ends with a zero: 10, 20, 40, and 50.

Reach to 2

Reach to 0

24d ● Technique Builder 5 minutes

Directions: Key each line three times from dictation SS.

DS between 3-line groups. Do not pause between phrases.

1 and the sets | and the seats | and the ink | and the oil
2 if they were | if they look | if they bet | if they give
3 for the rest | for the inn | for the cats | for the pups

11 minutes

24e ● Script Builder

Directions: 1. Practice the ¶ twice DS. Take two 1' writings. Figure *gwam*.

2. Take two 1' writings on 23e, page 42. Compare rates on the two ¶s.

all letters used 1.2 si

gwam 1'

Do you realize that not all firms require one 9
to go to work five days a week? Some of them will 19
let people put in extra hours so they can finish 29
their jobs in only four days. 35

10 minutes

24f ● Continuity Practice

Directions: Key both ¶s DS. Circle all errors. Repeat the exercise. Try to make no more than four errors per writing.

all letters used 1.2 si

	gwam 1'	3'	

keep elbows in; feet flat on floor

The ways in which quite a few men and women   9 | 3 | 27
work have changed in the past ten years. Hours are   19 | 6 | 31
getting shorter. Use of flextime has increased.   29 | 10 | 34
Job sharing does not seem to occur often.   37 | 12 | 37

More and more of our citizens are now working   9 | 15 | 40
at home. In a large number of cases, two persons   19 | 19 | 43
from the same household do this. With an office   29 | 22 | 46
at home, they don't face the stress of commuting.   37 | 25 | 49

gwam 1' | 1 | 2 | 3 | 4 | 5 | 6 | 7 | 8 | 9 | 10
     3' | 1 | | 2 | | 3

2119 DEL RIO DR., SAN JOSE, CA 95119-3348 (408) 272-8327

50-space line; mixed punctuation

center point

	words
begin on line 18 ——►April 17, 19--	3

return 4 times

letter address	Mr. Jay Kaczmarski	7
	Modern Shipping, Inc.	11
	4756 W. State Street	15
	San Diego, CA 92110-1374	20
	DS	
salutation	Dear Mr. Kaczmarski:	24
	DS	
body	Thank you for inquiring about the services that we	35
	provide at Creative Consulting.	41
	DS	
	Creative Consulting is a firm totally dedicated to	51
	analyzing the staffing and the training needs of all	62
	sizes of business firms. In addition, we provide	72
	suggested solutions to help firms meet those needs.	83
	DS	
	Our staff is highly trained to provide confidential	93
	consulting services. We often can do in days what	103
	otherwise might take an in-house staff months.	113
	DS	
	If you need more information, please give me a call.	123
	DS	
complimentary close	center point ——►Sincerely yours,	127

return 4 times

keyed name and official title	Ms. Roxanne Ray, Manager	131
	DS	
reference initials	db	132

Business letter in modified block style

LESSON 25

7 minutes

25a ● Keyboard Review

Directions: Key each line twice SS. DS between 2-line groups.

alphabet She quizzed me on the value of certain junk bonds.
          Be sure to put the wax on your skis before you go.

2 s2s s2s 2s 2s 22 sets, 221 slides, 22 or 222 suits

0 ;0; ;0; 0; 0; 10 pans, 101 plans, 10 or 100 plants

easy More than half of the men here paid their own way.

| 1 | 2 | 3 | 4 | 5 | 6 | 7 | 8 | 9 | 10 |

---

5 minutes

25b ● Location of 3 and 6

Reach to 3

1. Find **3** on the chart.
2. Find it on your keyboard.
3. Place your fingers over the home keys.
4. Reach to **3** with the **d** finger.
5. Touch **3d** lightly without moving other fingers from their home position.

Reach to 6

1. Find **6** on the chart.
2. Find it on your keyboard.
3. Place your fingers over the home keys.
4. Reach to **6** with the **j** finger.
5. Touch **6j** lightly without moving other fingers from their home position.

d3d d3d d3d 3d 3d 3d d3d   Key twice on same line   j6j j6j j6j 6j 6j 6j j6j

---

9 minutes

25c ● Location Drills: 3 and 6

Directions: Key each line twice SS. DS between 2-line groups.

Reach to 3

Reach to 6

3 d3d d3d d3d 3d 3d 3d 33 days, 333 hours, 33 and 33
   Give us 333 feet. Take 3,333 gallons. I have 33.

6 j6j j6j j6j 6j 6j 6j 66 jolts, 66,666 jets, 6 or 6
   I weigh 66 pounds. Send 666 now. Collect 66 now.

number
fluency

   We won our games 57 to 46, 48 to 39, and 31 to 20.
   Flight 7658 landed at 12:49, just 30 minutes late.

   In 1987 she sold 452 cans of pop and 396 hot dogs.
   He called three new numbers: 823, 946, and 1,705.

| 1 | 2 | 3 | 4 | 5 | 6 | 7 | 8 | 9 | 10 |

122b ● Skill Builder

Directions: 1. Take a 1' writing on the ¶ below. The last word keyed will be your goal word.
2. Take a 5' writing with the return called after each minute. When the return is called, start the paragraph over again. Try to reach your goal each minute as the return is called.

1.3 si

It has required many long hours of practice for you to reach your present level of keying skill. If you neglect to maintain your practice, this skill may gradually slip away from you. You now have a skill that can be of very great assistance to you in the future. Make good use of it in all your classes and daily life.

122c ● Formatting Problems: Business Letters

30 minutes

General Information

Letter Styles: Business basically uses three letter styles. The modified block style shown on page 212 is the most commonly used. The block style shown on page 215 and the simplified block letter shown on page 217 are growing in usage.

Punctuation Styles: Two commonly used punctuation styles are open and mixed. In *open* punctuation, no punctuation marks are used after the salutation or the complimentary close. In *mixed* punctuation, a colon is placed after the salutation and a comma after the complimentary close.

Vertical Placement of Dateline: Vertical placement of the date varies with the length of the letter. However, for short to average business letters the date is placed on line 18. The address begins on the 4th line space (3 blank spaces) below the date.

Margins: The line length used for business letters varies according to the number of words in the letter. A 50-space line works well for most short letters; a 60-space line works well for most average-length letters. Or, if you prefer, set 2" side margins for a short letter, 1½" side margins for an average-length letter, or 1" side margins for a long letter.

Title in Addresses: As a mark of courtesy to the person to whom a letter is addressed, you may use a personal or professional title on a letter, envelope, or card: *Mr. Robert Wertz, Dr. Ann Hendricks.* When a woman's preferred title is unknown, use *Ms.* as the personal title.

Abbreviations: Excessive abbreviations should be avoided. It is preferred, however, to use the two-letter state abbreviation in an address when using a ZIP Code. Leave two spaces between the state abbreviation and the ZIP Code.

Reference Initials: Reference initials of the typist should always be placed two line spaces below the keyed name of the writer of the letter at the left margin.

Stationery: Most business letters are prepared on 8½" × 11" stationery that has a letterhead which includes the name and address of the company.

Envelopes: Either large or small envelopes may be used for one-page letters. Large envelopes should be used for two-page letters and in instances where materials are enclosed with the letters.

(continued on page 212)

25d ● Paragraph Skill Builder

Directions: Key the ¶ once for practice; then take three 1' writings on it.   Figure *gwam* on the best writing.

all letters used   1.2 si

```
                .            4            .            8
        One of the big jobs that faces all of us as
     .            12           .           16           .
citizens is how to take good care of our present
      20            .           24           .           28
energy sources.  There is a lot of air, sun, and
           .           32           .           36           .
water, for example, but their quality is now at
         40            .           44           .
risk.  What we need to do is make better use of
    48            .
what we have.
```

25e ● Sentence Guided Writings

Directions: Key each sentence for a 1'   20''. Try to complete each sentence as
writing with the call of the guide each   the guide is called.

		words in line	gwam 20''
1	Alex will be 17 on October 17.	6	18
2	We had 17 copies of Volume 71.	6	18
3	See pages 59 to 95 for more advice.	7	21
4	Mark ran for only 59 yards, not 95.	7	21
5	Notice: do not confuse items 48 and 84.	8	24
6	Two groups of 48 add up to more than 84.	8	24
7	Their last trip took 20 hours and 20 minutes.	9	27
8	Jo put down .20 when it should have been .02 .	9	27
9	Martha is just 36 years old, but her mother is 63.	10	30
10	If you have two sets of 33, your total will be 66.	10	30

25f ● Extra Credit: Sustained Skill Building

Directions: 1. Take two 1' writings on each ¶ in 24f, page 43. Figure *gwam*.
2. Take two 3' writings on both ¶s

combined. Circle errors. Figure *gwam* on the better writing.
3. Compare your 3' rate with your 1' rate.

121c ● Speed Ladder Sentences

Directions: Take two 1' writings on each sentence. Your teacher will call the guide at 15", 12", or 10" intervals. As time permits, repeat sentences on which you were not able to complete a line with the call of the guide.

		guide 15"	12"	10"
1	Set skill goals that you want to reach as you practice.	44	55	66
2	Work hard to reach the skill goal you have set for yourself.	48	60	72
3	Keep these goals fixed in your mind during each practice session.	52	65	78
4	If you follow these suggestions, your keyboarding skills will improve.	56	70	84

| 1 | 2 | 3 | 4 | 5 | 6 | 7 | 8 | 9 | 10 | 11 | 12 | 13 | 14 |

---

10 minutes

121d ● Language Arts Skills: Composing at Your Machine

Directions: Compose a paragraph telling what the following quotation means to you.

"I will prepare myself, and someday my chance will come."

LESSON 122

70-space line

5 minutes

122a ● Keyboard Review

Directions: Key each sentence three times SS. DS between 3-line groups.

reach with fingers; keep hands and wrists quiet

alphabet The last prizes were quickly won by Mickey for just diving excitement.

figure Almost 7,500 persons attended between March 1, 1980 and June 30, 1985.

long reach Once the council was formed, Bob observed very many new legal changes.

easy Try not to hurry to finish their job until the plan is all done by me.

| 1 | 2 | 3 | 4 | 5 | 6 | 7 | 8 | 9 | 10 | 11 | 12 | 13 | 14 |

Unit 4 ■ Improving Your Basic Skills (Lessons 26–30)

Learning Goals:

1. To continue refining stroking skills and operating techniques.
2. To reinforce the learning of the figure keys.
3. To operate the tab, margin release key, and shift lock.
4. To return the carrier with the end-of-line signal.
5. To key at about the same rate from script copy as from typescript.

General Directions

Use a 50-space line for all lessons in this unit (center – 25; center + 25 + 5). SS sentences and drill lines. DS between repeated groups of lines. DS paragraph copy. Set machine for a 5-space paragraph indention.

LESSON 26

7 minutes

26a ● Keyboard Review

Directions: Key each sentence twice SS. DS between 2-line groups.

sit erect;
keep arms and
wrists quiet

alphabet	I have a good ink jet printer and a laser one too.
	He was amazed how quickly copy can be sent by fax.
1, 7	Sandra did problems 11 through 77. Add 17 and 71.
at	at great water rather matter attend nation station
easy	Their goal is to make a high profit with no risks.

| 1 | 2 | 3 | 4 | 5 | 6 | 7 | 8 | 9 | 10 |

15 minutes

26b ● Sentence Guided Writings

Directions: **1.** Take a 1′ writing on each sentence with the call of the guide each 20″.

2. Try to complete each sentence as the guide is called.

3. Take two 1′ writings on the last two sentences without the call of the guide.

words in line / gwam 20″

return quickly;
no pauses

1 He made sure the job was well done.   7 | 21

2 *Leave the papers lying on the desk.*   7 | 21

3 Their group left today for a field trip.   8 | 24

4 *They asked how much a ticket would cost.*   8 | 24

5 The speed of the new computer will amaze you.   9 | 27

6 *She plans to ride her new bike in the parade.*   9 | 27

7 Some of them spent their time playing video games. 10 | 30

8 *We hurried to the library after our morning break.* 10 | 30

20 minutes   **121b ● Speed Ladder Paragraphs**

Directions: 1. Take 1′ writings on ¶ 1 DS until you complete the ¶ in 1′. **2.** When you complete ¶ 1 in 1′, continue on to ¶ 2. Repeat this procedure as you try to complete each of the five ¶ s in the time given.

all letters used   1.4 si

	gwam 5′

Summer camps have been around for a very long time. The primary   3 | 55
purposes for these camps were to give young men and women a chance to   5 | 57
get outdoors, enjoy nature, and participate in most sports and hobby   8 | 60
activities.   9 | 61

Things have changed at summer camps. They have now become quite   11 | 63
specialized. There are now even camps for those who are really into   14 | 66
computers. These camps have only one special purpose. They offer the   17 | 69
chance to learn more about computers.   18 | 70

Yes, there are now quite a few summer and vacation programs all   21 | 73
over the country that offer the chance not only to learn more about the   24 | 76
world of computers, but still take time for such things as sports, arts   27 | 79
and crafts, swimming, and learning to avoid poison ivy.   29 | 81

These camps are not limited to computer junkies either. You don't   31 | 83
have to be a whiz kid to attend. Some even cater to the whole family,   34 | 86
where toddlers are turned over to a sitter. At the present time boys   37 | 89
have been outnumbering the girls by two to one. This trend will change.   40 | 92

Most of the time campers are divided into groups by experience or   43 | 95
age and allowed to learn at their own pace. Those who are new at this   45 | 97
sort of thing often start out by playing programmed games. Some will   48 | 100
learn computer music, which could mean that songs around the campfire   51 | 103
will never be the same.   52 | 104

gwam 5′ | 1 | 2 | 3 |

26c ● Tab Control

Directions: 1. Clear all tab stops. (Refer to page 21 for instructions.)
2. Set five tab stops at 5-space intervals from left margin.

3. Key each sentence once as shown DS. Strike tab key sharply and return finger to home position as you tab for the sentences.

On the microcomputer these stops may be preset for you.

return quickly
without pauses

You should learn to operate your tab key by touch.

tab once   5 ⟶ Just complete each line without slowing down.

tab twice 10 ⟶ Move your hand to home position quickly.

tab 3 times 15 ⟶ Indent when starting each new line.

tab 4 times 20 ⟶ Do not look back at your keys.

tab 5 times 25 ⟶ Tap your tab key sharply.

26d ● Paragraph Guided Writings

Directions: 1. Take a 1' writing on ¶ 1 below. Figure *gwam.* Add four words to your *gwam* for a new goal.

2. Take two more 1' writings on ¶ 1. Strive to reach your goal on each writing.
3. Repeat Directions 1 and 2 on ¶ 2.

all letters used

¶ 1 1.1 si

No one should say that a mule lacks good sense. In a burning barn, a horse will freeze and have to be led out with a blindfold over its eyes. A cow will walk out quietly with a little help. A mule, on the other hand, will just kick the door down to make an exit.

¶ 2 1.2 si

When you stop and think about it, most of us could learn a good lesson here. Too often we count on other people to solve our problems for us. Like that mule in the barn, we could take care of things ourselves just by using a little more common sense now and then.

Lesson 26

The lessons in Cycle 4 introduce you to some of the keying/formatting duties performed in a typical business office. Cycle 4 also provides material to help you improve your basic keying skills.

Business Letters: The two basic letter styles introduced in Cycle 2 (block style and modified block style) are again presented in Cycle 4, this time as they are commonly used in business correspondence. In addition, the simplified block letter style will be presented in this cycle. You will learn to format letters of different lengths so that they are placed properly on the page.

Business Forms: Interoffice memorandums and invoices are introduced in Unit 16.

Improving Basic Skills: By this time you have acquired considerable keying speed and control. Increases in speed do not come so rapidly now as they did early in the year. The skill-building material provided in this cycle will put the finishing touches on your keying skill.

Extra-Credit Activities and Enrichment Activities: Problems are given at the end of units for students who finish early and wish extra credit.

Unit 15 ■ Learning to Format Business Letters (Lessons 121–130)

Learning Goals:

1. To learn to format business letters in three basic styles: block, modified block, and simplified block.

2. To learn proper placement of enclosure notations, attention lines, subject lines, postscripts, and enumerated items in business letters.

General Directions

Use a 70-space line (center − 35; center + 35 + 5) for drills and timed writings in this unit. SS sentences and drill lines. DS paragraph copy. Much of the problem copy that you will key will be set in lines either longer or shorter than those for which your margins are set. It will be necessary for you to pay attention to the end-of-line signal and use the margin release on the typewriter.

Note: If you are using a computer, your keyed copy will wrap to the next line automatically.

Your teacher will tell you whether or not to correct errors when formatting problems. As your teacher directs, prepare the problems on special forms provided in the workbook or on plain paper.

LESSON 121

5 minutes

121a ● Keyboard Review

Directions: Key each sentence three times SS. DS between 3-line groups.

begin slowly; increase speed as you repeat the sentences

alphabet The six jet airliners flew by very quickly overhead at amazing speeds.

figure All attendance at our away games between 1988 and 1990 increased 120%.

s/w I saw flaws from the last rows as the swimmers swam in the swim shows.

easy It is easier to do it right in the beginning than need to do it again.

| 1 | 2 | 3 | 4 | 5 | 6 | 7 | 8 | 9 | 10 | 11 | 12 | 13 | 14 |

LESSON 27

7 minutes

27a ● Keyboard Review

Directions: Key each line twice SS. DS between 2-line groups.

key with a
steady rhythm

alphabet	Our store stocks frozen orange juice by the quart.
	Do not expect her to move more than one mile away.
5,9	Avenue 99 is only 55 more miles. Divide 95 by 59.
ha	has had hand hard have chance change happy perhaps
easy	Sit down right there when the chief says to do so.

| 1 | 2 | 3 | 4 | 5 | 6 | 7 | 8 | 9 | 10 |

To key all-cap items, depress the shift lock with the left little finger (No. 23) and key.

To release the shift lock, depress either the right or left shift key.

Note: On microcomputers check operator's manual.

27b ● Keying in All Capital Letters   7 minutes

Directions: Key the sentences below two times SS.

She wrote her report on THE SWISS FAMILY ROBINSON.

Read their DAILY BULLETIN during the FIRST period.

16 minutes

27c ● Paragraph Guided Writings

Your instructor may call the ½' guide on the 1' writings to aid you in checking your rate.

Directions: 1. Take a 1' writing on ¶1. Figure *gwam*. Add four words to your *gwam* for a new goal.
2. Take two 1' writings on the same ¶ as you strive to reach your new goal.

3. Repeat Steps 1 and 2 for ¶ 2.
4. Take a 3' writing on both ¶s combined. Figure *gwam*. Compare your new rate to your 1' writing.

all letters used   *gwam 3'*

		gwam 3'
¶1 1.2 si	More than you are aware, you are likely to	3 | 31
	judge people by the way they shake your hand. The	6 | 34
	same thing happens the other way around, of course.	10 | 38
	They tend to size you up that way too.	12 | 41
¶2 1.2 si	As those kinds of special treatment which are	16 | 44
	based on gender have now gone out of style, the	19 | 47
	rules for shaking hands apply equally to both sexes.	22 | 50
	No more is it proper for women to stay in their	26 | 54
	seats when others stand to shake hands.	28 | 56

gwam 3' | 1 | 2 | 3 | 4 |

27d ● Technique Builder: Stroking

strike keys with quick, sharp strokes

Directions: Take a 1′ writing on each sentence SS.

1 Send some boys and girls to the north gym at noon.

2 One needs good sight to see his or her own faults.

3 That was the day on which he hit the big home run.

4 Ships do come in, but they must first be sent out.

5 Be sure to take good care when you ride your bike.

6 If you pull on the oars, you do not rock the boat.

7 The nurse told us to drink less pop and more milk.

8 Vote for those you know will do the best they can.

9 They say that a slim mind may have a broad tongue.

10 Luck is the one thing you can be sure will change.

LESSON 28

50-space line

7 minutes

28a ● Keyboard Review

Directions: Key each line twice SS. DS between 2-line groups.

alphabet
The woman spoke on the subject of the ozone layer.
Sixth and seventh graders were required to attend.

4, 8 They knew half of 88 was 44. Count from 48 to 84.

is is his list miss wish visit discuss furnish island

easy They did not spend their time working at the firm.

| 1 | 2 | 3 | 4 | 5 | 6 | 7 | 8 | 9 | 10 |

12 minutes

28b ● Keying Outside the Right and Left Margins

The position of the backspace key varies from machine to machine. On some, it is on the right side of the keyboard. On others, it is on the left side. Reach for the backspace key with the little finger.

Directions: 1. Right margin. Using an exact 50-space line (center – 25; center + 25), key the first sentence.
2. Find the margin release key (No. 31) on your machine. When the carrier locks, use the correct little finger to depress the margin release key and complete the sentence. Repeat.

3. Left Margin. Return the carrier to the left margin.
4. Depress the margin release key; backspace five spaces into the left margin, and key the second sentence. Repeat.

 This exercise can't be performed on a microcomputer.

right margin
    Learn to use the special keys that your typewriter has.

left margin
Learn to use the special keys that your typewriter has.

30 minutes

Directions for formatting an unbound report are given on page 152. Directions for footnotes are given in 83c, page 151. Refer to these pages if necessary.

stroke keys
with a flowing
rhythm

If necessary, refer to 57d, page 106, for spacing directions.

120d ● Formatting Problem: Report and Outline

Directions: Problem 1   Unbound Report
Key the one-page unbound report below. Place the footnote in the correct position at the bottom of the page.

THE LIBRARY AS A RESOURCE

The library has always been a special place to study, do research or just to read for fun. No other room in your school is quite like the library; it is more than just four walls with tables and chairs. It is a room where you can find the keys to unlock the doors to many new and old worlds. It is here that you can become acquainted with a wide variety of people and places.

Socrates will not mind if you decide to turn back the pages of history to get his views on philosophy--neither will Chopin mind if you want his advice in composing music. On the lighter side, if you feel like laughing, Bennett Cerf will be delighted to oblige with many of the funniest stories in print.

Libraries have changed greatly in the past twenty years. Not too long ago libraries were primarily a storehouse of books and magazines. Today's modern library has a wealth of audio and visual materials. A few examples are cassette tapes, films, VCR tapes, and computer software. Also available is the equipment necessary to use this media.[1]

In addition to using the holdings of the library, you will find the library and its staff well trained and loaded with information to help you enjoy the library.

[1]"The Library," The New Book Encyclopedia (1989), XI, p. 47.

Directions: Problem 2   Topic Outline
Key the topic outline below on a half sheet of paper, (long edge at top). Indent, space, capitalize, and punctuate the outline correctly. Place it in the exact vertical center of the page.

using an encyclopedia

```
   I   Introduction
        A   importance of encyclopedia as a reference
        B   rules for library use
  II   body
        A   how to locate information
             1   look first in the regular alphabetical
                  place
             2   always look for last names of persons
        B   miscellaneous hints
 III   conclusion
```

120e ● Extra-Credit Activities

Directions: Problem 1

Key a note of regret to a friend who has asked you to a play. Look at 117c, Problem 2, page 201 for ideas, but write the message in your own words.

Directions: Problem 2

Key a postal card announcement for a club in your school. If necessary, refer to 117c, Problem 1, page 201, for help in arranging the material.

120f ● Enrichment Activity

Directions: 1. If you are using a computer, edit the note you keyed in 120e, Problem 1. Send it to a relative expressing regret at being unable to attend a hockey game. Replace only those words necessary. Use right margin justification.

2. Print the revised note.

28c ● Continuity Practice: Numbers

Directions: Key the ¶ two times DS.

all letters and numbers used

	gwam 3′
Today, in the decade of the 1990s, folks from	3 | 24
8 years of age to 80 are quite concerned about the	6 | 28
need to spend more time exercising. In fact, 64	10 | 31
percent of all Americans claim to exercise every	13 | 34
week. According to the American Health Magazine	16 | 38
54 million walk, 23 million jog, and 17 million	19 | 41
hike to stay physically fit.	21 | 42

gwam 3′ | 1 | 2 | 3 | 4 |

28d ● Paragraph Guided Writings

Directions: 1. Take a 1′ writing on ¶ 1. Figure *gwam*. Add four words to your *gwam* for a new goal.
2. Take two 1′ writings on the same ¶ as you strive to reach your new goal.

3. Repeat steps 1 and 2 for ¶ 2.
4. Take a 3′ writing on both ¶s combined. Figure *gwam*. Compare your new rate to your 1′ writing.

all letters used

		gwam 3′
¶1 1.2 si	One of these days, the experts say, we may	3 | 39
	drive cars that know right where they want to go.	6 | 42
	They will be equipped with computer systems that	10 | 45
	keep them out of traffic jams, space them evenly	13 | 49
	on the roads, and find them places to park. Cars	16 | 52
	will almost think, it seems.	18 | 54
¶2 1.2 si	Most of us will have to admit that this sounds	21 | 57
	a bit crazy now, but it is fun to contemplate. If	25 | 60
	cars can really be made to do these things, we may	28 | 64
	not have to build any more new highways and use up	31 | 67
	precious land. We would not run into each other	35 | 71
	so often either.	36 | 72

gwam 3′ | 1 | 2 | 3 | 4 |

8 minutes **119e ● Learn to Make a Division Sign**

Directions: 1. To make the *division sign,* type the colon; backspace and strike the hyphen.

2. Key each sentence 3 times SS; DS between 3-line groups. Key the correct figures in place of the ? marks.

Solve these three problems: 144 ÷ 12 = ??.   96 ÷ 8 = ??.   72 ÷ 9 = ?.

Solve additional problems: 132 ÷ 12 = ??.   54 ÷ 9 = ?.   108 ÷ 9 = ??.

LESSON 120

70-space line

5 minutes **120a ● Keyboard Review**

Directions: Key each sentence three times SS. DS between 3-line groups.

alphabet John quickly scanned the horizon the next evening from Briarwood Peak.

figure The team reported (in 1989) that 143 of the 276 violations were fixed.

long reaches My secretary probably just needs a new electric machine before Monday.

easy He may want to go to the city to finish the problems on the new motor.

| 1 | 2 | 3 | 4 | 5 | 6 | 7 | 8 | 9 | 10 | 11 | 12 | 13 | 14 |

5 minutes **120b ● Language Arts Skills: Number Expression Guides**

Directions: The following are number expression guides and sentences that illustrate those guides. Study each guide. Key the sentences that illustrate the guides twice SS; DS between 2-line groups.

Use figures to key dates. If a day comes before a month, use a figure and follow it with *th, st,* or *d.*
Classes begin on September 8, 1990. The party was on the 1st of June.

Spell a number beginning a sentence even if figures are used later in the sentence.
Fifteen were invited; 11 were present. Seventy cars were in the race.

5 minutes **120c ● Speed Builder**

Directions: 1. Take a 1' writing on the ¶ below. The last word keyed will be your goal word.
2. Take a 3' writing with the return called after each minute. When the return is called, start the ¶ over again. Try to reach your goal each minute as the return is called.

1.4 si

sit erect; feet flat on the floor

             .   4   .   8   .   12

One of the biggest jobs of counting in the world occurs every ten

 .   16   .   20   .   24   .

years when this nation takes its census. While the practice goes back

28   .   32   .   36   .   40

thousands of years, this country was the first large one to carry out

 .   44   .   48   .   52   .

such a great count of its people. The census is usually conducted in

56   .   60

the first year of a decade.

LESSON 29

7 minutes

29a ● Keyboard Review

Directions: Key each line twice SS. DS between 2-line groups.

keep fingers curved; arms and wrists still

alphabet She entered the main office through the back door.
          Judy now plans to take her driving quiz next week.

2, 0 Peg misread 00 for 22. She can multiply 20 by 20.

it it its city permit unit profit write either little

easy The world fuel crisis is a problem for most of us.

| 1 | 2 | 3 | 4 | 5 | 6 | 7 | 8 | 9 | 10 |

7 minutes

29b ● Technique Builder

return carrier quickly

Directions: Key each line two times from dictation SS. DS between 2-line groups.

1 and it|and it is|and it is the|and she|and she did

2 if it is|if it is the|if the duty is|if they do go

3 to do the|to do the work|and it did|and it did the

4 and it|and it is|and it is the|and she|and she did

5 she is|she is there|he is|he is there|she is there

6 we are|we are the|they are|they are the|we are the

7 you can|you can have|you have|you did|you did have

8 I will|I will|I will save|I will sign|I will spend

10 minutes

29c ● Listening for the End-of-Line Signal

Directions: 1. Set an exact 50-space line (center – 25; center + 25).

2. Move the right margin stop 5 to 8 spaces farther to the right. Doing this will give your copy better horizontal balance.

3. Key the ¶ below, listening for the end-of-line signal. When you hear the signal, finish the word you are on and return to the next line. If the carrier

locks before you are finished, depress the margin release key and complete the word.

4. Set a 60-space line by moving your left and right margin stops out five spaces beyond your margin for a 50-space line. Key the ¶ as you did for a 50-space line.

Note: If you are using a microcomputer, let the automatic word wrap determine your line ending.

all letters used   1.2 si

words

Hanging out at the shopping malls is not just   9

for kids these days. The craze to frequent what   19

they see as a very exciting place to be has caught   29

on with most adults too.   34

| 1 | 2 | 3 | 4 | 5 | 6 | 7 | 8 | 9 | 10 |

119b ● Language Arts Skills: Apostrophe Guides

Directions: The following are apostrophe guides and sentences that illustrate those guides. Study each guide. Key the sentences that illustrate the guides twice SS; DS between 2-line groups.

The apostrophe denotes possession. Do not use it merely to form the plural of a noun.
Three girls were assigned to a locker. This is the new girl's locker.

Add 's to form the possessive of any singular noun.
The president-elect's campaign began. Bill's ball is in John's glove.

Add 's to form the possessive of a plural noun that does *not* end in *s.*
The women's skirts were put on sale; however, the men's suits were not.

Add only an apostrophe after the *s* if a plural noun does end in *s.*
Nine girls shared six girls' books; five boys shared four boys' books.

To show possession, add an apostrophe and *s* to a proper name of one syllable which ends in *s.*
The Sims's land is several miles down the road from the Jones's place.

To show possession, add only an apostrophe to a proper name of more than one syllable which ends in *s.*
The entire group enjoyed visiting the Williams' estate near the river.

---

10 minutes

119c ● Paragraph Guided Writings

Directions: 1. Set goals of 40, 50, and 60 words a minute. Take two 1' writings at each rate. Try to reach your goal word as time is called.

2. Your teacher may call the quarter or half minutes to guide you.

3. Key additional writings at the 50- and 60-word rate as time permits.

all letters used   1.4 si

keep a steady, even rhythm

Most people who place a telephone call wonder what the person who
answers looks like. The way you can tell is by just listening to that
person's voice. The way an individual's voice sounds fixes a mental
picture. That is why it is quite critical to sound pleasant and zesty
when you answer the phone.

---

10 minutes

119d ● Skill Comparison

Directions: Take two 1' writings on each sentence SS. DS between 2-line groups. Compare your rate on the lowest syllable intensity sentence to your rate on each of the other sentences.

1.0 si   Each one must learn that it is a key thing to know our work load well.

1.2 si   We can learn to work, as there are many ways open to the right person.

1.3 si   Everyone should learn to work well with others on many kinds of tasks.

1.4 si   Workers who enjoy their duties will more often do their job very well.

| 1 | 2 | 3 | 4 | 5 | 6 | 7 | 8 | 9 | 10 | 11 | 12 | 13 | 14 |

11 minutes   **29d ● Skill Comparison**

Directions: Key two 1′ writings on each sentence SS. DS between 2-line groups.

Compare *gwam* on the four sentences.

key without pauses   easy   When both girls won, they put the town on the map.

one-hand   After my best race I served cases of red pop free.

figures   Room 19 played at 6:30, but Room 28 plays at 7:45.

script   *A pound of pluck is worth more than a ton of luck.*

---

10 minutes   **29e ● Timed Writings**

Directions: Take two 3′ writings on the copy below. Circle all errors.

Figure *gwam*. Submit the better writing.

all letters used

		gwam 3′
¶ 1 1.2 si	You do not have to spend lots of money or buy	3 | 34
	a jet plane ticket to learn about life in far away	6 | 37
	time zones. You can gain some of the benefits of	10 | 40
	world travel without leaving home. You can find	13 | 44
	yourself a pen pal.	14 | 45
¶ 2 1.2 si	By writing to a boy or girl who lives in some	18 | 48
	other part of the globe, you will be able to expand	21 | 51
	your knowledge and form a real friendship at the	24 | 55
	same time. A pen pal will answer many questions	28 | 58
	about what life is like in a different land.	30 | 61

gwam 3′ | 1 | 2 | 3 | 4 |

LESSON 30

50-space line

7 minutes   **30a ● Keyboard Review**

Directions: Key each line twice SS. DS between 2-line groups.

keep wrists low and still

alphabet   Your taxi driver avoided the biggest traffic jams.
He knew which plaza would be quiet at that moment.

6, 3   Half of 66 is 33. Amy is 36 years old; Sam is 63.

he   he her here head help she when where neither other

easy   Eight chairs were left in this field by the girls.

| 1 | 2 | 3 | 4 | 5 | 6 | 7 | 8 | 9 | 10 |

118c ● Formatting Problems

Directions: Problem 1   Personal/Business Letter

Key the letter below on a full sheet, 50 space line. Use modified block style, mixed punctuation. Begin the return address on line 12. Address an envelope. Fold and insert letter in envelope.

Return Address: 127 Golfcrest Drive | Iron River, WI 54847-2416 | Today's date | Letter Address: Miss Carla Devon | Carla's Clothing Shop | 17 East River Road | Madison, WI 54146-2378 | Dear Miss Devon

Thank you very much for sending me the information I requested on your new line of women's winter wear.

The variety of clothing available for young women is a very pleasant surprise. Everything that I will need for cold weather is available.

Enclosed is my first order for merchandise from your shop. I look forward to receiving the new ski jacket and the matching gloves.

Sincerely yours | Miss Cynthia Everett | Enclosure

Directions: Problem 2   Keying a Poem

Key the poem in the exact vertical center on a half sheet of paper DS. DS after the heading. Center the copy horizontally by the third line of the second verse.

space quickly with down-and-in motion of thumb

Horse Sense

A horse can't pull while kicking.
This fact I merely mention.
And he can't kick while pulling,
Which is my chief contention.

Let's imitate the good old horse
And lead a life that's fitting;
Just pull an honest load, and then
There'll be no time for kicking.

Unknown

Directions: Problem 3   Personal/Business Letter

Using a full sheet, 50-space line, key the letter in Problem 1 again. Use block style, open punctuation.

LESSON 119

70-space line

5 minutes

119a ● Keyboard Review

Directions: Key each sentence three times SS. DS between 3-line groups.

alphabet We could give exact reasons for most of the crazy quips and bad jokes.

figure The market average during that day--June 9, 1988--rose over 31 points.

left hand Fred started a great new test beverage and a vast estate was a reward.

easy It is true that one who does not drive the auto right may not be left.

| 1 | 2 | 3 | 4 | 5 | 6 | 7 | 8 | 9 | 10 | 11 | 12 | 13 | 14 |

30b ● Timed Writings

Directions: Take two 3' writings on the ¶ below DS. Circle errors. Figure *gwam*.   Submit the better writing.

all letters used   1.2 si

	gwam 1'	3'
It has been said that the only sure and safe	9	3	29
way for people to double their money is to fold it.	20	7	33
While this remark was likely made in jest, there is	30	10	36
more than a little truth in it. Before you decide	40	13	40
where to invest the money you earned, give a good	50	17	43
deal of thought to the task. You may want to quiz	60	20	46
an expert in these matters. Money comes too hard	70	23	50
for you to squander it in the wrong place.	79	26	53

gwam 1' | 1 | 2 | 3 | 4 | 5 | 6 | 7 | 8 | 9 | 10 |
3' | 1 | 2 | 3 | 4 |

18 minutes

30c ● Tab Control

Directions: 1. Clear all tab stops.
2. Check to see that margin stops are set for a 50-space line.
3. Set the tab stop for the second column 21 spaces from the left margin.

Set the tab stop for the third column 21 spaces from the first tab stop. Return the carrier to the left margin.
4. Key each line DS; tab between words. Repeat if time permits.

margin   tab   tab
|◄——21 spaces——►| |◄——21 spaces——►|

buffer	memory	program
computer	modem	software
diskette	network	storage

10 minutes

30d ● Listening for the End-of-Line Signal

Directions: Key the ¶ below with a 50-space line, then with a 60-space line. Let the end-of-line signal guide you in returning the carrier. Use the margin-release key to allow you to key beyond your margin stop.

all letters used   1.2 si

Note: If you are using a microcomputer, let the automatic word wrap determine your line ending.

words

keep fingers deeply curved

If you do not have any one person you can talk — 9
to about your problems, you might want to keep a — 19
journal. It is a good place for you to express your — 30
thoughts on what happened during the day, such as a — 40
low grade on a quiz or an argument with a friend. — 50

Directions: Problem 3   Postal Card Announcement
Follow the directions given in Problem 1.   telephone number as the chairperson.
Use your own name, address, and

LESSON 118   70-space line

5 minutes   **118a ● Keyboard Review**

Directions: Key each sentence three times SS. DS between 3-line groups.

keep fingers
deeply curved

alphabet The full puzzling views will be quickly explained to most of the jury.

figure The longest anyone went without sleep was for 288 hours in June, 1974.

both hands Bob had the idea to go to the top before dark to meet the new friend.

easy It was less painful to lose just one battle than to lose more of them.

| 1 | 2 | 3 | 4 | 5 | 6 | 7 | 8 | 9 | 10 | 11 | 12 | 13 | 14 |

---

10 minutes   **118b ● Speed Builder**

Directions: Take two 1' writings on each ¶; try to increase speed on the second writing. Figure *gwam.*

Alternate Procedure: Work for speed as you take one 5' writing on all four ¶s combined. Figure *gwam.*

all letters used   1.4 si   gwam 1'   5'

	gwam 1'	5'
Television viewing has really changed in the last twenty years.	13	3	46
It is no longer just a matter of choosing a program to watch from a list	28	6	49
of three or four choices. We now have quite a long list of dozens of	42	8	51
choices from old and new comedy to the latest music videos.	53	11	54
What made this great change in TV viewing? A great deal of the	13	13	56
credit has to go to the marketing of cable TV. No longer is the viewer	27	16	59
tied to channels that can be picked up by an antenna; now anything being	42	19	62
sent by cable can be viewed.	47	20	63
As important as cable has been to more TV viewing choices, you can	13	23	66
not forget about the role of VCRs. The viewer who has a VCR can rent	27	26	69
tapes to be played on the TV set. Instead of reruns viewers can choose	42	28	71
first-run movies, instructional material, and just-for-fun videos.	55	31	74
What excitement can we expect next from television? We already	13	34	77
know about shopping from TV catalogs; however, we may soon be able to	27	36	79
place orders for goods that we want right on the TV set. Interactive	41	39	82
video is already a reality. On-screen newspapers and magazines do exist	55	42	85
and will become quite popular.	61	43	86

gwam 1' | 1 | 2 | 3 | 4 | 5 | 6 | 7 | 8 | 9 | 10 | 11 | 12 | 13 | 14 |
      5' | 1 | 2 | 3 |

Unit 5 ■ Learning the Basic Symbol Keys (Lessons 31–35)

Learning Goals:

1. To strike the symbol keys by touch, using correct fingering.

2. To space correctly after punctuation marks and symbols.

3. To improve basic skill by further refinement of stroking and operating techniques and by continued practice of skill-building drills and timed writings.

General Directions

Use a 60-space line for all lessons in this unit (center − 30; center + 30 + 5). SS sentences and drill lines. DS between repeated groups of lines. DS paragraph copy. Set machine for a 5-space paragraph indention.

LESSON 31

5 minutes **31a ● Keyboard Review**

Directions: Key each sentence twice SS. DS between 2-line groups.

alphabet Jenny loved to quote wild, crazy things from textbook pages.

figures More than 350 kids from 14 schools competed here on June 26.

easy I know that she told them to sit down in their usual chairs.

| 1 | 2 | 3 | 4 | 5 | 6 | 7 | 8 | 9 | 10 | 11 | 12 |

---

7 minutes **31b ● Location of $ (dollar), # (number or pounds), and / (diagonal)**

Reach to $ (dollar sign)

1. Shift, then reach up to $ with the f finger.

2. Touch $f lightly without moving other fingers from their home position.

Reach to # (number sign)

1. Shift, then reach up to # with the d finger.

2. Touch #d lightly without moving other fingers from their home position.

f4f f$f f4f f$f $f $f $4   Key twice on same line   d3d d#d d3d d#d #d #d #3

Reach to $

Reach to #

Reach to /

Reach to / (diagonal)

1. Reach down to / with the ; finger.

2. Touch /; lightly without moving other fingers from their home position.

;/; ;?; ;/; /; ;/

Lesson 31   **54**

LESSON 117

5 minutes **117a ● Keyboard Review**

Directions: Key each sentence three times SS. DS. between 3-line groups.

alphabet I have been lucky to exceed my first high quota and win a major prize.

figure The largest amusement park has 27,443 acres and cost $400 million new.

adjacent keys Right after their retirement, other writers returned to the territory.

easy To keep your mind quite sharp, you should use it as often as possible.

| 1 | 2 | 3 | 4 | 5 | 6 | 7 | 8 | 9 | 10 | 11 | 12 | 13 | 14 |

---

10 minutes **117b ● Concentration Practice**

Directions: Key the ¶ below as many times as possible in the time given SS. DS each time you begin the paragraph over.

words

  The college-age population has been shrinking, and fewer students 13

are choosing to major in science and engineering; yet demand for these 27

majors is growing at an annual rate of 7%, compared with a 2% rate for 42

the U.S. work force as a whole. A shortage of future scientists and 55

engineers will certainly exist. 61

| 1 | 2 | 3 | 4 | 5 | 6 | 7 | 8 | 9 | 10 | 11 | 12 | 13 | 14 |

117c ● Formatting Problems 30 minutes

Directions: Problem 1 Postal Card Announcement
1. Insert a postal card or paper cut to size (5½″ × 3¼″) into your machine.
2. Center the announcement at the right horizontally and vertically. (If necessary, refer to 40c, page 73, for finding the center of odd-size paper.)
3. Address the card to yourself on the opposite side (no return address needed).

Note: If you are using a computer, rule the outline of the card size on your printer paper.

EDUCATION-INDUSTRY PARTNERSHIP MEETINGS
VERNON HIGH SCHOOL AUDITORIUM

Please watch bulletins for dates and times

For additional information, call:

Miss Wilma Marshall, Chairperson
3219 Davidson Lane, 555-3467

Directions: Problem 2 Informal Regret
1. Key the informal regret note at the right on a half sheet of paper with the short side up as you did in 73c, page 133.
2. Use modified block style with open punctuation. Use your address as the return address and sign your name.

Current date/Dear Robert

Leonard and I thank you for your thoughtfulness in inviting us to attend the special events concert on Friday of next week. Unfortunately, we are having a committee meeting at our house on that date.

Thank you again, Robert, for thinking of us. I hope we can take a rain check for a future date./Sincerely

continued on next page

31c ● Location Drills $, #, and /   8 minutes

Directions: Key each line twice SS. DS between 2-line groups.

Note: Do not space between $, #, or / and a figure.

$ Their four lunches cost them $4.25, $4.55, $4.75, and $4.95.

\# She wrote 33 pounds as 33#.   Number 134 can be written #134.

/ Use the / to make fractions, as 1/3, 1/5, 1/8, 11/16, 15/16.

---

10 minutes

31d ● Comparison Sentence Skill Builder

Directions: Key two 1' writings on each sentence SS.

Compare rates on the three sentences.

easy   Six of the eight girls signed both forms with the right pen.

fig/sym   Our store priced Item #4685 at $37.50 beginning on 12/30/92.

shift   Winners are Rod Monroe, Lana Wolf, Her Mee, and Wei Yen Lee.

| 1 | 2 | 3 | 4 | 5 | 6 | 7 | 8 | 9 | 10 | 11 | 12 |

---

15 minutes

Your teacher may call half minute guides. You should be at or past the first . at 30" to finish the ¶ in 1'.

return
carrier
quickly

31e ● Speed Ladder Paragraphs

Directions: 1. Take a 1' writing on ¶ 1 DS. **2.** When you complete ¶ 1 in 1', continue on to ¶ 2. Repeat this procedure as you try to complete all five ¶s in the given time. **3.** Take three 1' writings on any ¶ you cannot finish in 1'.

all letters used   1.2 si   gwam 1' | 3'

One bit of advice you should heed is to keep your sense   11 | 4
of humor, even when things look their worst.   20 | 7

In fact, being able to laugh at oneself may well be the   11 | 11
secret to a good life and real success. That is no joke   23 | 14
either.   24 | 15

A good laugh can make living much easier. A joke cuts   11 | 19
problems down to size. It lowers tension if tempers start to   23 | 23
flare and things get out of hand.   30 | 25

Humor brings out the best in other folks too. It helps   11 | 29
them relax so they can enjoy being with you. They respond   23 | 33
in kind when facts are given to them in a clever, funny way.   35 | 37

The greatest thing about a sense of humor, however, is   11 | 41
that it is so good for your health. A quip can do as much   23 | 44
for how a person feels as jogging around the block. People   35 | 48
who laugh, they say, last.   40 | 50

gwam 1' | 1 | 2 | 3 | 4 | 5 | 6 | 7 | 8 | 9 | 10 | 11 | 12 |
     3' | 1 | 2 | 3 | 4 |

116d ● Speed Ladder Paragraphs

Directions: Take a 1' writing on ¶1 DS until you complete the ¶ in 1'. When you complete ¶1 in 1', continue on to ¶2. Repeat this procedure as you try to complete each of the ¶s in the given time.

Alternate Procedure: Take a 1' writing on ¶1 DS. Move to the second and succeeding ¶s only when you have completed each one within the error limit specified by your teacher.

all letters used   1.4 si

	gwam 5'

use quick
sharp strokes

Acid rain is the common term used for rain or other precipitation   3 | 55

with higher than normal acid content.   In the eastern and northern parts   6 | 58

of our nation, it has been blamed for the decline of the trees, fish,   8 | 60

and other wildlife.   9 | 61

The higher than normal acid content of rain can be traced mainly   12 | 64

to the burning of coal, oil, and gas by heavy industry and the utilities.   15 | 67

Burning these fuels releases sulphur and nitrogen oxides to the air   17 | 69

where they combine with water vapor.   19 | 71

The combination of water vapor and oxides produces large amounts   22 | 74

of sulfuric and nitric acid.   These acids in our air are carried downwind   24 | 76

sometimes for a great number of miles and deposited on the surface of   27 | 79

earth in the form of rain, snow, or other precipitation.   29 | 81

It is still hard to say just what the final net effects of acid   32 | 84

rain are.   There is a lot of hard evidence that claims this rain is   35 | 87

responsible for the death of fish in ponds and lakes, death of forest   37 | 89

trees, and changes in the soil.   It is also linked to human disease.   40 | 92

The question is what can be done to lessen the threat of acid rain.   43 | 95

The key to the puzzle is to reduce the amount of sulfur and nitrogen   46 | 98

from flue gases.   One way to do this may be increased use of hydro and   48 | 100

nuclear power to produce electricity and more use of fossil fuels that   51 | 103

are very low in sulfur.   52 | 104

gwam 5' | 1 | 2 | 3 |

LESSON 32

32a ● Keyboard Review

5 minutes

Directions: Key each sentence twice SS. DS between 2-line groups.

alphabet Karen just expected him to acquire a zest for living by now.

fig/sym Our order #439, for 2 7/8 lbs., is made out for just $15.60.

easy When she tried to go back to first base, she was thrown out.

| 1 | 2 | 3 | 4 | 5 | 6 | 7 | 8 | 9 | 10 | 11 | 12 |

7 minutes

32b ● Location of % (percent), & (ampersand), and - (hyphen) or -- (dash)

Reach to % (percent)
1. Shift, then reach up to % with the f finger.
2. Touch %f lightly without moving other fingers from their home position.

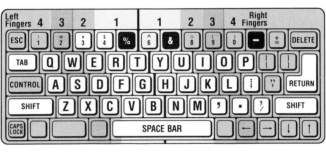

Reach to & (ampersand)
1. Shift, then reach up to & with the j finger.
2. Touch &j lightly without moving other fingers from their home position.

f5f f%f f5f f%f %f %f %5

Key twice on same line

j&j j&j j7j j&j &j &j

Reach to % (percent)

Do not space between a figure and %.

Reach to -
Do not space before or after - (hyphen) or -- (dash)

Reach to - (hyphen) or -- (dash)
1. Reach up to - with the ; finger.
2. Touch -; lightly without moving other fingers from their home position.

;-; ;-; -;- -;- -- -;

32c ● Location Drills %, & and -   8 minutes

Directions: Key each line twice SS. DS between 2-line groups.

% Interest rates at four banks were 9%, 8.5%, 8.75%, and 9.2%.

& Haller & Ling ordered 77 pairs of shoes from Sanchez & Sons.

- In mid-April we received a 4-star rating--the best possible.

Reach to & (ampersand)

Space before and after the &, which may be used in place of the word *and*.

all letters used 1.2 si

32d ● Script Skill Builder   10 minutes

Directions: Key the following ¶ twice DS. Take two 1' writings. Figure *gwam*.

gwam 1'

Noise is now such a vexing problem that at least one 11

town we know has hired two cops to cite those who get out of ... 23

line. To get their job done, they use a sound analyzer. So 35

far they have quieted a few saloons, a noisy parrot, and one ... 47

loudmouthed rooster. 51

Unit 14 ■ Improving Your Basic Skills—Measurement

(Lessons 116–120)

Learning Goals:

1. To continue to develop punctuation and number expression language arts skills.

2. To evaluate the skills and understanding acquired in keying a variety of personal applications by keying additional related applications with a minimum of direction.

General Directions

Use a 70-space line for all lessons in this unit (center – 35; center + 35 + 5) unless otherwise directed. SS sentences and drill lines; DS paragraphs.

This unit includes measurement of straight-copy and problem keying skills similar to problems covered in Cycle 3. You will be expected to format/key these problems with less directional material by applying what you have learned in previous lessons.

LESSON 116

5 minutes | **116a ● Keyboard Review**

Directions: Key each sentence three times SS. DS between 3-line groups.

alphabet | I believed that a jet trip from Arizona to Yonkers was quite exciting.

shift | Pete O'Brien and Lucy J. Wong work for Apple & Smith on Barrel Avenue.

figure | From mid-April to mid-November the number of players grew over 12,500.

easy | It is much fun to run near the ice and be close to the people fishing.

| 1 | 2 | 3 | 4 | 5 | 6 | 7 | 8 | 9 | 10 | 11 | 12 | 13 | 14 |

10 minutes | **116b ● Paragraph Guided Writings**

Directions: 1. Set goals of 40, 50, and 60 words a minute. Take two 1′ writings at each rate. Try to reach your goal word as time is called.

2. Your teacher may call the quarter or half minutes to guide you.

3. Key additional writings at the 50- and 60-word rate as time permits.

1.3 si

key without pauses between words

$$\overset{.}{} \quad \overset{4}{} \quad \overset{.}{} \quad \overset{8}{} \quad \overset{.}{} \quad \overset{12}{}$$

If you are to be successful in school and in the business world, you must also be successful in your reading skills. You can do this by working on procedures that will help you read better. These procedures indicate that when you read you must scan the material, think as you read, and make brief notes.

10 minutes | **116c ● Technique Builder: Stroking**

Directions: Take two 1′ writings on each sentence SS. DS between 2-line groups.

1st finger | First I did not buy my fur to fit, thus had to return it to the store.

2d finger | The kids did get a kick out of picking out the new kites from the den.

3d finger | All old notices I saw are too low on our list to allow for good sales.

4th finger | Pam is too zapped to puzzle whether to postpone a paper or pass it in.

| 1 | 2 | 3 | 4 | 5 | 6 | 7 | 8 | 9 | 10 | 11 | 12 | 13 | 14 |

32e ● Technique Builder

Directions: Key each line twice SS. DS between 2-line groups.

1 three happy jetty room bill week inn message sleep mood well

2 issue guess look good less rubber apply proof speed too free

3 buzz allow apply feel fall soon funny offer muzzle add bluff

---

10 minutes **32f ● Timed Writings**

Directions: Key two 3′ writings on the   Submit the better of the two writings.
¶ s below. Figure *gwam*.

	all letters used	*gwam* 1′ | 3′

¶1 1.2 si   Ever since the keyboard we now use was first designed,   11 \| 4

dozens of people have tried to improve on it. A problem they   23 \| 8

want to solve is that a few of our least frequently used keys   36 \| 12

can be stroked with ease, but all the common ones cannot.   47 \| 16

¶2 1.2 si   One expert has come up with a device that has but eight   11 \| 20

keys, each with three positions. The fingers do not have to   23 \| 24

jump around so much, and keys are moved back and forth rather   36 \| 28

than struck. Another new machine is split in the middle so   48 \| 32

that it looks like an open book face down.   56 \| 35

¶3 1.2 si   Still others are working on ways to lessen the load of   11 \| 38

those who have to spend a lot of time at the computer each   23 \| 42

day. An office products firm now sells a foam wedge that   34 \| 46

tips the keyboard toward the user. Its purpose is to relieve   47 \| 50

strain on the hands, neck, and eyes.   54 \| 53

```
gwam  1′ |  1  |  2  |  3  |  4  |  5  |  6  |  7  |  8  |  9  |  10  |  11  |  12  |
      3′ |        1        |        2        |        3        |        4        |
```

LESSON 33   60-space line

5 minutes **33a ● Keyboard Review**

Directions: Key each sentence two times SS. DS between 2-line groups.

alphabet Rick Wells put five dozen quarts of jam in the box for Gary.

fig/sym Only 60% can do the 25 push-ups required by the H & F tests.

easy Fix the handle so tight that he will not be able to turn it.

```
| 1 | 2 | 3 | 4 | 5 | 6 | 7 | 8 | 9 | 10 | 11 | 12 |
```

10 minutes   **115b** ● **Timed Writings**

Directions: 1. Take two 1' writings on
¶ 1, 101d, page 179. Figure *gwam* on
the better writing.

2. Take a 5' writing on all five ¶ s
combined. Circle errors and figure *gwam*.

---

30 minutes   **115c** ● **Formatting Problems**

Directions: Problem 1   Notice and Agenda of a Meeting

1. Key the notice and agenda in 97c,
Problem 1, page 172, as directed in the
problem.

2. Use the new center point and key the
page number.

Directions: Problem 2   Minutes of Meetings

1. Key the minutes in 98c, page 175,
following the directions in the problem.
2. Use the new center point and place
the page number in the correct position.

After you complete the minutes,
assemble your style guide in the correct
order. Staple the report at the left.

115d ● **Extra-Credit Activity**

Directions: 1. Key the unbound report
below on a full sheet of paper; 60-space
line DS.
2. Leave a 2″ top margin; center an

appropriate heading using the backspace
from center method.
3. Make corrections as indicated.

keep eyes and
mind on copy

	words
Turning waste into building ~~items~~ *blocks* is the newest proposal	12
for reducing⌃the increasing supply of ga⌒bⓇage. A new company	24
has developed a process that pulverizes solid waste, removes	36
the scrap metal, and then mixes the remains with ~~water~~ *liquid* wastes	49
and clay to produce a pellet. t̲he pellets are fired in a kiln	61
at 2,200 degrees.	65
The e̲nd product is a solid aggregate, which the company sug-	77
gests as an alternativⓔe to other clay⌃products used in the	88
~~building~~ *construction* industry. The fi⌒anl product weighs 30 per⌒cent less	100
than other aggregates commonly used in cement products. The	113
pro⌒cess appears to be a good way to use up ~~our~~ *solid* wastes.	125

115e ● **Enrichment Activity**

Directions: If you are using a computer,
1. Reformat the unbound report you
keyed in 115d above into a leftbound
report. Use 1½″ left and 1″ right
margins.

2. Replace all the words that were
inserted in the rough draft with the
original words they replaced.
3. Print the revised report.

33b ● Location of (and) (parentheses)

Reach to ((parenthesis)
1. Shift, then reach up to (with the I finger.
2. Touch (I lightly without moving other fingers from their home position.

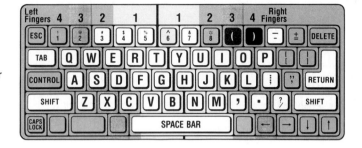

Reach to) (parenthesis)
1. Shift, then reach up to) with the ; finger.
2. Touch); lightly without moving other fingers from their home position.

191 1(1 191 1(1 (1 (1 (9   Key twice on same line   ;0; ;); ;0; ;);););)0

Reach to (

Reach to)

33c ● Location Drills: (and)   10 minutes

Directions: Key each line twice SS. DS between 2-line groups.

Note: Do not space between ( ) and the words they enclose.

(Strike the 9, then shift to key (. Key the 9, then key (99.

) Strike the 0, then shift to key). Key the 0, then key 00).

Send your letters (keep them short, please) to me at Box 90.

( ) Do not hang sweaters (or clothes that stretch). (They sag.)

Beth Martin (Grade 8) had the top speed (42 words a minute).

Almost 900 kids attended the concerts in Babylon (New York).

33d ● Continuity Practice

Directions: 1. Key the ¶ below one time DS. Circle all errors.
2. Try to key correctly three times the words in which you made an error.

3. Try to key the entire ¶ without errors as many times as you can in the time remaining.

all letters 1.2si

words

keep fingers deeply curved

The job of carrying papers is not for the lazy person. 11

You have to get up early each day, and you have to work in 23

all kinds of weather. Once in a while you have to call on 35

people who forget to pay their bill. Those are some of the 47

reasons that explain why many boys and girls quit after only 59

three to six months. 63

| 1 | 2 | 3 | 4 | 5 | 6 | 7 | 8 | 9 | 10 | 11 | 12 |

Directions: Problem 2   Leftbound Report

1. Key the report in 83d, pp. 151–152, in the form illustrated.

2. Use the new center point and place the page number in the correct position.

LESSON 114

70-space line

5 minutes

114a ● Keyboard Review

Directions: Key each sentence three times SS. DS between 3-line groups.

alphabet I know the job is expensive to organize and carefully equip the women.

fig/sym Your bonds that sold for $568.60 in 1969 had risen to $974.30 by 1989.

adjacent keys The captain is astonished to see several new sailors very fast asleep.

easy Both of the men had to ride the bus to work in the busy city each day.

| 1 | 2 | 3 | 4 | 5 | 6 | 7 | 8 | 9 | 10 | 11 | 12 | 13 | 14 |

---

10 minutes

114b ● Timed Writings

Directions: 1. Take two 1' writings on ¶ 1, 96d, page 171. Figure *gwam* on the better writing.

2. Take a 5' writing on all five ¶s combined. Circle errors and figure *gwam*.

---

30 minutes

114c ● Formatting Problems: Outlines

Directions: Problem 1   Sentence Outline

1. Key the outline in 57d, Problem 1, page 106, according to the directions given.

2. Use the new center point; key the page number.

Directions: Problem 2   Topic Outline

1. Key the outline in 87c, Problem 1, page 158, following the directions given.

2. Use the new center point and key the page number.

LESSON 115

70-space line

5 minutes

115a ● Keyboard Review

Directions: Key each sentence three times SS. DS between 3-line groups.

alphabet All good citizens have to quickly face toxic waste as a major problem.

fig/sym In June, 1986, about 18% of the 43 workers were making $1,200 a month.

long reaches My uncle announced that he has many great pictures of new fox hunters.

easy It is their wish to pay their bills in cash each time they become due.

| 1 | 2 | 3 | 4 | 5 | 6 | 7 | 8 | 9 | 10 | 11 | 12 | 13 | 14 |

33e ● Timed Writings

Directions: 1. Take one 3′ writing. Figure *gwam*.
2. Take two 1′ writings on each ¶.

3. Take one 3′ writing. Figure *gwam*. Compare this rate with your first 3′ writing.

all letters used

| | *gwam* 1′ | 3′ |

¶ 1 1.2 si
Studies show that most of us now have our car washed as   11 | 4 | 30
frequently as once a month. More often than not, we hire   23 | 8 | 34
someone else to do the job for us. At least that is what the   35 | 12 | 38
carwash people say.   39 | 13 | 40

¶ 2 1.2 si
Their research found out too, though, that a sizable   11 | 17 | 43
number of car owners expect to wash their cars right at home.   23 | 21 | 47
They still like to keep all the family wheels clean with a   35 | 25 | 51
hose, bucket, and sponge.   40 | 26 | 53

gwam 1′ | 1 | 2 | 3 | 4 | 5 | 6 | 7 | 8 | 9 | 10 | 11 | 12 |
3′ | 1 | 2 | 3 | 4 |

LESSON 34

60-space line

34a ● Keyboard Review

Directions: Key each sentence twice SS. DS between 2-line groups.

keep arms and
wrists quiet

alphabet Bob Jade was given extra maps quickly as he was in a frenzy.
fig/sym Exactly 465 runners (of all ages) competed on July 30, 1992.
easy He will throw the rocks out of sight at the end of the lane.

| 1 | 2 | 3 | 4 | 5 | 6 | 7 | 8 | 9 | 10 | 11 | 12 |

34b ● Numbers and Symbols   5 minutes

Directions: Key the ¶ below once DS.

all letters used

words

A recently published book paints a unique (and amazing)   11
picture of America.   Here are some interesting excerpts from   23
it: Americans eat 24,657,534 hot dogs every day and purchase   36
100 million M & Ms; the president of the U.S. earns $547.95   48
each day, while Michael Jackson makes $164,383.56; and women   60
spend 59 minutes (of each 24-hour period) cleaning house--   72
but men spend only 26.   76

| 1 | 2 | 3 | 4 | 5 | 6 | 7 | 8 | 9 | 10 | 11 | 12 |

112b ● Timed Writings

Directions: 1 Take two 1' writings on
¶ 1, 86d, page 157.

2. Take a 5' writing on all 5 ¶s
combined. Circle errors and figure *gwam*.

---

30 minutes

112c ● Formatting Problems/Keying Letters

Directons: Problem 1   Personal/Business Letter in Block Style

1. Key the letter in 78d, Problem 1,
page 142. Follow the directions given in
the problem.

2. Place the page number in the correct

position.

3. Remember that the center point
should be 3 spaces to the right of the
point normally used.

Directions: Problem 2   Personal Letter

1. Key the letter in 75c, page 136.
Follow the directions given for the
problem.

2. Place the page number in the correct

position.

3. Staple the letter on an 8½" × 11"
sheet of paper, placed so it appears
centered when bound at the left margin.

LESSON 113

70-space line

5 minutes

113a ● Keyboard Review

Directions: Key each line three times SS. DS between 3-line groups.

keep wrists
and arms quiet

alphabet	I was very delighted to have just the exact numbers for a quick prize.
figure	In 1987, a record 12,950 U.S. outlets changed the name of their firms.
combination	if it is to get, if it is to pull, if it is to join, if it is to trace
easy	Half of the team slept for more than eight hours each and every night.

| 1 | 2 | 3 | 4 | 5 | 6 | 7 | 8 | 9 | 10 | 11 | 12 | 13 | 14 |

---

10 minutes

113b ● Timed Writings

Directions: 1. Take two 1' writings on
¶ 1, 91c, page 164. Figure *gwam* on the
better writing.

2. Take a 5' writing on all five ¶s
combined. Circle errors and figure *gwam*.

---

30 minutes

113c ● Formatting Problems: Reports

Directions: Problem 1   One-Page Report

1. Key the report on page 100. Follow
the directions given in 53c, page 99.

2. Use the new center point and place
the page number in the correct position.

continued on next page

5 minutes   **34c ● Location of ' (apostrophe) and ! (exclamation point)**

Reach to ' (apostrophe)

1. The ' is to the right of the ; and is controlled by the ; finger.

2. Touch '; lightly without moving other fingers from their home position.

Reach to ! (exclamation)

1. Shift, then reach up to ! with the a finger.

2. Touch !a lightly without moving other fingers from their home position.

;'; ;'; ;'; ;'; '; ;' ';   Key twice on same line   a!a a!a a!a a!a !a a! !a

---

34d ● Location Drills: ' and !   8 minutes

Directions: Key each line twice SS. DS between 2-line groups.

> Space twice after ! at the end of a sentence, which may be a single exclamatory word.

Reach to '

Reach to !

' Mr. and Mrs. O'Grady can't pay the bill for Karen's tuition.

Jack O'Bannion says he won't ever eat at Mandy's Cafe again.

! Get ready! Begin! Run faster! Try harder! Hurry! Great!

He won first place! Priscilla was elected! I hate spinach!

'! Keep your eye on them! Don't give up! Get off Kelly's car!

Danger! Stop! I can't see the bridge to O'Donnell's house!

34e ● Continuity Practice   7 minutes

Directions: 1. Key the ¶ below one time DS. Circle all errors.

2. Try to key correctly three times the words in which you made an error.

3. Try to key the entire ¶ without errors as many times as you can in the time remaining.

all letters used   1.2 si

	words
If you go for things like bruised shins, flying straight	11
up high walls, and turning over once or twice in the ozone,	23
skateboarding is the sport for you. Of course you should be	36
sure to wear a helmet, wrist guards, and kneepads to ward	47
off the injuries. Get set to crash quite often, and do not	59
expect any net or pool of water to cushion your falls.	70

| 1 | 2 | 3 | 4 | 5 | 6 | 7 | 8 | 9 | 10 | 11 | 12 |

Directions: Problem 2 Table of Contents

1. Key the table of contents below for your style guide.

2. Set your margins for a 60-space line. (Remember that the center point should be 3 spaces to the right of the point normally used.)

3. Leave a 2″ top margin. QS between the title and the heading. DS between items.

4. Insert leaders as you did in 103c, page 182.

Note: Align periods with those in the first line, noting whether you start the periods on an odd or even number.

TABLE OF CONTENTS
QS

Personal Business Letter in Modified Block Style 1
DS
Personal Business Letter in Block Style 2

Personal Letter in Semibusiness Form 3

One-Page Report 4

First Page of Report with Footnotes 5

Sentence Outline 6

Topic Outline 7

Notice and Agenda of a Meeting 8

Minutes of a Meeting 9

Directions: Problem 3 Personal/Business Letter in Modified Block Style

1. Key the letter in 47e, Problem 1, page 87. Use the directions given for the problem.

2. Set margins for a 50-space line using the new center point.

3. Refer to the style guide general information given on page 194 for the placement of the page number.

LESSON 112

5 minutes

112a ● Keyboard Review

Directions: Key each line three times SS. DS between 3-line groups.

keep fingers
deeply curved

alphabet To organize and make plans for an exquisite display was the objective.

figure The Pacific Ocean is #1 in area, and its deepest point is 35,958 feet.

4th finger paws quiz zeal was quake say quack and upon polite zone pay saw police

easy I wish to pay by check for the video disk player they said is so good.

| 1 | 2 | 3 | 4 | 5 | 6 | 7 | 8 | 9 | 10 | 11 | 12 | 13 | 14 |

Your teacher may call half minute guides. You should be at or past the first . at 30″ to finish the ¶ in 1′.

34f ● Speed Ladder Paragraphs

Directions: **1.** Take a 1′ writing on ¶ 1 DS. **2.** When you complete ¶ 1 in 1′, continue on to ¶ 2. Repeat this procedure as you try to complete all five ¶s in the given time. **3.** Take three 1′ writings on any ¶ you cannot finish in 1′.

strike keys with quick, sharp strokes

all letters used   1.2 si   *gwam* 1′ | 3′

	1′	3′
Friends fill a vital role in life. They provide comfort	11	4
as they let you know you are not all alone.	20	7
With every new friend you explore a new path in life.	11	10
You will learn more and more the wider your circle of friends	23	15
becomes.	25	15
You might just hit it off with someone right away, or	11	19
it may take months before you do so. Recognize that each	22	23
new friendship moves at its own speed.	30	25
One of the very best times to meet new people is when	11	29
the school year begins. Then you have some good chances to	23	33
get acquainted with those outside your circle of old friends.	35	37
While we know how important our friends are to us, this	11	41
discussion will not be complete without some words of caution.	24	45
The advice may be trite, but it's true. To have a friend,	36	49
you must also be one.	40	51

gwam 1′ | 1 | 2 | 3 | 4 | 5 | 6 | 7 | 8 | 9 | 10 | 11 | 12 |
3′ | | 1 | | 2 | | 3 | | 4 |

LESSON 35   60-space line

35a ● Keyboard Review

Directions: Key each sentence twice SS. DS between 2-line groups.

alphabet   Bud Roper may take this quiz next week if Jack will give it.

fig/sym   It's unbelievable that Jan's team won 106 to 98 in overtime!

easy   Most of us show what we are by what we do with what we have.

| 1 | 2 | 3 | 4 | 5 | 6 | 7 | 8 | 9 | 10 | 11 | 12 |

Unit 13 ■ Preparing a Student-Writer's Style Guide (Lessons 111–115)

Learning Goals:

1. To organize and prepare a writer's style guide, including a title page, table of contents, and samples of business papers keyed in earlier units.

2. To review procedures used in formatting a wider left than right margin in order to bind the guide at the left and to center headings over a center point shifted three spaces to the right of the normal centering position.

General Directions

Use a 70-space line for all lessons in this unit (center – 35; center + 35 + 5) unless otherwise directed. SS sentences and drill lines; DS paragraphs.

LESSON 111

5 minutes

111a ● Keyboard Review

Directions: Key each line three times SS. DS between 3-line groups.

alphabet	Jack got zero on his final exam simply because we have hard questions.
fig/sym	Their new 3-year policies for $30,000 and $75,000 are #1896 and #2564.
direct reaches	wreck cedes mumble sum herb fun peck county bramble breeze unique bums
easy	The new sign may handle the problem if it is found and set up in time.

| 1 | 2 | 3 | 4 | 5 | 6 | 7 | 8 | 9 | 10 | 11 | 12 | 13 | 14 |

10 minutes

111b ● Timed Writings

Directions: 1. Take two 1' writings on ¶ 1, 81d, page 147. Figure *gwam* on the better writing.

2. Take one 5' writing on all five ¶s combined. Circle errors and figure *gwam*.

5 minutes

111c ● Formatting Problems: Student Writer's Style Guide

General Information:

1. In the problems in this unit, you will prepare a booklet entitled STUDENT WRITER'S STYLE GUIDE. Keep the pages you prepare until the entire booklet is finished. The booklet will contain 11 pages in all.

2. Correct all errors.

3. The booklet will be stapled at the left side. Refer to leftbound reports, 84b, page 153, for formatting procedures, if necessary.

4. Number the pages as indicated in the table of contents. Key page numbers on the fourth line space from the top, 1" from the right edge of the paper.

5. The center point for all pages in the booklet is 3 spaces to the right of the point normally used. Use this center point in centering titles and in setting margins when the directions call for setting a certain space line, such as a 50-space line.

25 minutes

Directions: Problem 1   Title Page of Style Guide

Prepare a title page similar to the one shown in 85c, page 155. Key the title, STUDENT WRITER'S STYLE GUIDE, your name, and the current date on the page.

continued on next page

7 minutes

35b ● Location of '' (quotation marks), * (asterisk), and __ (underline)

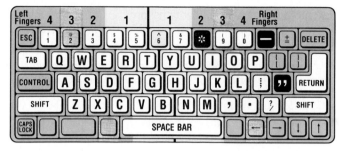

Reach to '' (quotation)

1. The '' is the shift of the ' and is controlled by the ; finger.

2. Touch ''; lightly without moving other fingers from their home position.

;'; ;''; ;'; ;''; ''; ;''

Key each drill twice

Reach to __ (underline)

1. Shift, then reach up to __ with the ; finger.

2. Touch __ lightly without moving other fingers from their home position.

;-; ;_; ;-; ;_; _; ;_ _;

Reach to * (asterisk)

1. Shift, then reach up to * with the k finger.

2. Touch *k lightly without moving other fingers from their home position.

k8k k*k k8k k*k *k k* *k

8 minutes

35c ● Location Drills: '', *, and __

Directions: Key each line twice SS. DS between 2-line groups.

Don't confuse "to" and "too" or "principal" and "principle."

Read three articles: "Show Time," "Smile," and "Vacations."

Use * for a footnote below.   My quote was from George Bush.*

— Indent <u>five</u> spaces. Use your <u>right</u> thumb. Please come <u>now</u>.

''— This report is called "At Risk." The book title was <u>Shogun</u>.

— They were assigned <u>The Covenant</u> and <u>All the President's Men</u>.

To *underline*. Key the material, then backspace to the first letter, shift and strike the underline. Use the shift lock if several words are to be underlined. The underline is not broken between words unless each word is to be underlined separately.

Note: If you are using a microcomputer, see the user's manual for instructions on underlining.

7 minutes

35d ● Technique Builder

Directions: Key each line three times SS. DS between 3-line groups.

Key with a steady rhythm

1 if they | they were | if they were | if she | she saves | if she saves

2 and he | and he | reads | reads | and he reads | and she | and she reads

3 they did | they did | they did only | she may | she may | she may only

4 to the | to the | race | race | to the race | for their | for their race

110b ● Timed Writings

Directions: 1. Take two 5' writings on 106c, page 187. Work for best possible speed with a minimum of errors.

2. Figure *gwam;* submit the better of the two writings to your teacher.

---

25 minutes

110c ● Formatting Problems: Justifying the Right Margin

School newspapers are sometimes keyed so that all the lines, except the last line in a paragraph, are even at the right margin. The copy then has the appearance of a printed page.

Note: If you are using a machine that automatically justifies the right margin, *do not* use the automatic function. Learn to justify the right margin in the typewriter mode.

Directions for justifying right margin:

1. Key a line of diagonals to indicate maximum line length (pica 30; elite, 36).

2. Key the article. Add diagonals to the short lines to make them even with the line of diagonals at the top.

3. Rekey the article. Add one extra space between words for each diagonal in the line. Avoid putting extra spaces in one line under extra spaces in the line above.

Directions: Problem 1   Article with Justified Right Margin

1. Prepare the article below on 4¼" × 11" paper. Key the first draft with diagonals for short lines; then key the final draft with justified lines.

2. Use directions in 108c, page 190, for preparing newspaper copy, but justify right margin. Use the title for this article: COMPUTER FUTURE.

```
///////////////////////////////
    You can be sure that in the
future each home and business/
will have a computer.  All of/
us need to be well trained in/
how they will be used and in//
their operation.  Take every//
opportunity you can obtain to/
''know'' all computers soon.////
The future is tomorrow!
```

```
    You can be sure that in the
future each home   and business
will have a computer.  All of
us need to be well   trained in
how they will be used   and in
their operation.  Take every
opportunity you can obtain to
''know''  all computers soon.
The future is tomorrow!
```

Directions: Problem 2   Article with Justified Right Margin
Prepare 94c, page 168, in a form suitable for a school newspaper. Justify the right margin; use as the title DOING YOUR BEST.

110d ● Enrichment Activity

Directions: Prepare the two topics you did not use in Problem 2 of 109c, page 192, as feature stories for your newspaper. Use proper newspaper format.

Note: If you are using a machine that automatically justifies the right margin, use this feature in completing this activity.

10 minutes **35e ● Timed Writings**

Directions: Key two 3′ writings on the ¶s below. Figure *gwam*. Submit the better writing.

all letters used   *gwam* 1′ | 3′

			gwam 1′	3′

¶1 1.2 si   Now that scientists have found out how to launch the   11 | 4 | 56

parts of satellites and then assemble them in space, one of   23 | 8 | 60

their major dreams will at last come true.   This technique   34 | 11 | 64

makes it possible for them to build a new home in the sky.   46 | 15 | 68

¶2 1.2 si   These space stations, as they float way high above the   11 | 19 | 71

clouds, will get the energy they need from sunlight that is   23 | 23 | 75

collected on large panels.   The men and women who live and   35 | 27 | 79

work in this new space home will be taxied back and forth   46 | 31 | 83

from the earth in a shuttle.   52 | 33 | 85

¶3 1.2 si   The thought of space stations is not new.   They have   11 | 36 | 89

been seen both in print and in the movies for a long time.   23 | 40 | 93

In fact, the first story of a manned space station appeared   35 | 44 | 97

in a magazine well over a hundred years ago.   It was a hollow   47 | 49 | 101

brick sphere that could be shot into space by a cannon.   58 | 52 | 105

gwam 1′ | 1 | 2 | 3 | 4 | 5 | 6 | 7 | 8 | 9 | 10 | 11 | 12 |
      3′ | 1 | 2 | 3 | 4 |

Punctuation Guide

1. Space twice after end-of-sentence punctuation.

2. Do not space after a period within an abbreviation. Space once after an abbreviation; twice if that period ends a sentence.

3. Space once after a comma.

4. Space twice after a colon. Do *not* space before or after a colon when stating time.

5. Key the dash with two hyphens; do not space before or after.

6. Do not space before or after the hyphen in a hyphenated word.

35f ● Spacing After Punctuation Marks: Review   8 minutes

Directions: Key each line one time SS.

1 Sit in the bleachers. The game starts soon. I hope we win.

2 Where is it? Will he go? Can they see? Who ate the fries?

3 Don't run! Be quiet! Turn down the volume! We'll be late!

4 Mr. and Mrs. White left at 10 a.m. We met the 1 p.m. plane.

5 Heather, Kaitlin, and Amy spent the summer in Paris, France.

6 Jot down these numbers: 35, 42, and 50. I arrived at 4:10.

7 Drop us a line--about 100 words or less--before September 5.

8 Our teacher said Mandy Jones-Carr turned in a 15-page paper.

   | 1 | 2 | 3 | 4 | 5 | 6 | 7 | 8 | 9 | 10 | 11 | 12 |

Lesson 35   63

109b ● Skill Builder from Rough Draft Copy

Directions: Take two 1' writings on each sentence.

words

1. Buy cloths that (good\look) on you, not just because they are instyle. 14
2. A ward⁀robe must meet your age level and also your type of personalitty. 14
3. [   ]All your clothing needs to be kept clean, pressed, and in good repair. 14
4. You can't look your best on any occasion if your clothes are not ~~ironed~~ neat. 14

109c ● Problem Formatting: Preparing Newspaper Copy

Directions: Problem 1   Items of Special Interest

1. Key an article entitled (*Use Your Name*) SAYS--. Make the article consist of the items listed below.

2. Follow the directions for preparing newpaper copy given in 108c, page 190. Compose an appropriate side heading for each item.

86c	Skill Builder from Script	page 156
87b	Skill Builder	page 158
102c	Skill Builder from Script	page 181

Directions: Problem 2   Feature Story

1. Compose on a full sheet in rough-draft form a feature story on one of the following topics. The reference following each topic is to a similar article in the textbook. You may get ideas from these articles, but do not copy them; compose your own story.

2. Make a final copy of your feature article on 4¼" × 11" paper in the same form you used for keying the other items for the school newpaper.

3. Use your name as the author; give your story an appropriate title.

Writing For A School Newspaper (73b Speed Builder page 132)

Travel Changes (88b Speed Builder 159)

Successful Selling (98b Speed Builder page 174)

LESSON 110

70-space line

110a ● Keyboard Review

Directions: Key each sentence three times SS. DS between 3-line groups.

alphabet Both just received six dozen packages of winter quilts from a factory.

fig/sym As of September 1, 1988, the nation was importing only 25% of its oil.

adjacent keys People acquire more rewards from walking short treks to Worth Station.

easy Time can be like money; the less you have the longer you make it last.

| 1 | 2 | 3 | 4 | 5 | 6 | 7 | 8 | 9 | 10 | 11 | 12 | 13 | 14 |

Cycle 2   *Basic Personal Applications*

Directions: Problem 1 Feature Article

1. Prepare a copy of 101d, page 179, as a feature story for your school newspaper. Use the following heading: STRESS IN THE WORKPLACE.

2. When preparing your copy, follow the general directions given on page 190. Your copy should look like the copy in the partial illustration at the right.

```
         STRESS IN THE WORKPLACE

    Today's health experts cite
as their current concern the
amount of stress that a worker
must face on the job each day.
They say stress can be a real
threat to a person's physical
and mental condition.  Research
agrees with this.

    If you had to identify which
jobs place people under the
greatest stress, you might
```

Directions: Problem 2 Special Items

1. The second sentence in some Keyboard Reviews in Cycle 3 is a factual statement of general interest. Select six or more of these sentences for an article. Use the following heading: FACTS OF LIFE. Use your name as the author.

2. Your copy should look like the copy in the partial illustration at the right.

```
            FACTS OF LIFE
            Use Your Name

    A crowd of 49,936 witnessed
the 1966 All-Star game in 100-
degree heat.

    In our country, more than
40.65 million homes, or 23%, own
a computer.
```

To review centering lines on odd size paper, refer to page 73.

Directions: Problem 3 Short Item

Prepare the paragraph in 77b, page 139, as an item for your newspaper. Give the item a suitable title; use your name as the author.

LESSON 109

5 minutes

109a ● Keyboard Review

Directions: Key each sentence three times SS. DS between 3-line groups.

alphabet My exploits as a jockey amazed quite a few after they began to arrive.

fig/sym Arabic numbers like 5, 6, and 7 are sometimes keyed (5), (6), and (7).

left hand We read that a brave crew saved a craft as great west breezes started.

easy It is easy to get moving if you begin very early and go right to work.

| 1 | 2 | 3 | 4 | 5 | 6 | 7 | 8 | 9 | 10 | 11 | 12 | 13 | 14 |

You are now ready to build upon and apply the basic skills you learned in Cycle 1. The following is a preview of some of the problems you will be working on in Cycle 2.

Notices, Personal Notes, and Letters

You will learn procedures for keying announcements, personal notes, and personal business letters in acceptable form.

Themes, Outlines, and Tables

These papers are an important part of school work. The guides that you will be given are those most commonly used in keying themes, outlines, and tables.

Language Arts Development

One of your goals in this course is to be able to compose school and personal papers at the keyboard. The drills, spelling aids, and capitalization guides included in this cycle will help you achieve this goal.

Extra-Credit Assignments

Problems are given at the end of some lessons for students who finish assignments ahead of schedule. Key these problems as time permits.

Building Basic Skills

The more you improve your keying skills, the easier it will be for you to concentrate on the papers you are preparing.

Help Yourself to Improve

Much of what you get out of the lessons in Cycle 2 will depend upon you. Here are some points to keep in mind as you prepare your lessons:

1. Have the desire to improve. You learn best when you really want to learn.

2. Have a clear goal in mind for each exercise. You cannot learn if you do not know what you should be learning. Keep your goals in mind as you key the drills and problems.

3. Learn to plan your work. Part of this job requires you to read and hear directions correctly. In order to accomplish your goals, you must learn to follow directions carefully.

Unit 6 ■ Centering Notices and Announcements (Lessons 36–40)

Learning Goals:

1. To format/key copy that is centered vertically and horizontally on full sheets, half sheets, and odd-size paper or cards.
2. To format/key reports with centered headings.
3. To answer questions as an aid to composing at the keyboard.
4. To key correctly words that are commonly misspelled.
5. To format/key rough draft reports containing common proofreader's marks.
6. To use basic correction procedures in correcting keying errors.
7. To increase keying skills by further refining basic techniques.

General Directions

Use a 60-space line for all lessons in this unit (center − 30; center + 30 + 5). SS sentences and drill lines. DS between repeated groups of lines. DS paragraph copy.

Instructions for making corrections are given in Lesson 39 of this unit. Your instructor will tell you whether or not you are to correct errors on problems in Lessons 39 and 40.

LESSON 36

5 minutes   36a ● **Keyboard Review**

Directions: Key each sentence three times SS. DS between 3-line groups.

use quick
sharp strokes

alphabet   Juan Vasquez knows of body building exercise plans for them.

fig/symbol   He read 24 books in 1992--including The Russians and Poland.

easy   Those who were in good shape ran down the field at halftime.

| 1 | 2 | 3 | 4 | 5 | 6 | 7 | 8 | 9 | 10 | 11 | 12 |

108b ● Speed Builder

Directions: Take two 1' writings on each ¶; try to increase speed on the second writing. Figure *gwam.*

Alternate Procedure: Work for speed as you take one 5' writing on all three ¶s combined. Figure *gwam.*

all letters used   1.3

	gwam	1'	5'
Entrance requirements for college have become much more demanding	13	3	36
in recent years. More and more people want to go to college and are now	28	6	39
expecting to stay longer. As a result, it is very important that stu-	42	8	41
dents quickly realize they must be very well prepared in their early	56	11	44
school years.	59	12	45
Besides being prepared by taking the right courses and doing well,	13	14	47
would-be college students must be very careful to make plans as to what	28	17	50
school they want to attend. To pick the school, a choice must be made	42	20	53
as to which college major should be pursued.	51	22	55
In making a choice of school major, a person must have a career	13	24	57
plan in mind. In order to make this plan, it is important to read a	27	27	60
great deal and to talk to those who are in the field of work interest.	41	30	63
Once armed with the right education and a plan, the rest will be easy.	55	33	66

gwam 1'	1	2	3	4	5	6	7	8	9	10	11	12	13	14
5'		1			2			3						

108c ● Formatting Problems: Preparing Newspaper Copy

Many schools, clubs, and other organizations prepare and issue newspapers and newsletters of the type you will prepare in the next 3 lessons. Items of interest are composed and prepared in accordance with set rules and are submitted to an editor. The editor checks the items and arranges the copy on plan sheets. When all copy is arranged, the paper is duplicated or printed, assembled, and distributed.

In the next three lessons, you will prepare copy for an editor. The copy will be part of a newspaper duplicated on 8½" × 11" paper.

Directions for Preparing Newspaper Copy:
1. Cut several sheets of paper in half lengthwise (4¼" × 11").
2. Make a rough-draft copy of your item on a separate sheet of paper. Proofread; mark errors.
3. Prepare your final copy on 4¼" × 11" paper. Set margins for a 3" line (pica, 30 spaces; elite, 36 spaces). If the right margin is to be justified (see page 193), the maximum line length is 30 or 36 spaces.
4. Center and key main headings in all capitals. If a side heading is used, capitalize the initial letter of each main word in the heading. Double space before and after a side heading. Single space paragraph copy; double space between paragraphs. Indent paragraphs 3 spaces. Leave a 1" top margin on each sheet.

(continued on next page)

5 minutes

keep fingers
deeply curved

36b ● Technique Builder: Stroking

Directions: Key each sentence three times SS. DS between 3-line groups.

top row   Robert Piret tried to key your pottery reports very quietly.

direct reaches   I myself doubt that any cellists will bring any cello music.

bottom row   Can anyone, man or woman, explain the exact name of my band?

| 1 | 2 | 3 | 4 | 5 | 6 | 7 | 8 | 9 | 10 | 11 | 12 |

---

8 minutes

key without pauses
between words

36c ● Language Arts Skills: Spelling and Proofreading Aid

Directions: **1.** Key each line three times SS. DS between each 3-line group.
2. Note the spelling of each word as you key this drill.

3. Proofread carefully. Check any word about which you are uncertain against the original copy. Circle all errors.

1   attempt coming fourth library prior finally until using paid

2   quantity excellent privilege particular substantial mortgage

3   efficient continuing guarantee superintendent accommodations

---

17 minutes

keep wrists
and arms quiet

36d ● Paragraph Guided Writings

Directions: **1:** Take a 1' writing on ¶ 1. Figure *gwam*. Add four words to your *gwam* for a new goal.
2. Take two 1' writings on the same ¶. Try to reach your goal on each writing.

3. Take a 1' writing on the same ¶. Drop back two to four *gwam*. Your goal is to key without errors.
4. Repeat Steps 1, 2, and 3 for the second and third ¶s.

all letters used   1.2 si

gwam 3'

Labor experts say very few workers had planned to hold	4	39
the kinds of jobs they presently have. This does not mean	8	43
they are lazy; most are doing what they do just because of	12	46
chance or a lack of choice.	13	48
As a result many of them are trapped in some type of	17	52
work that is less than what they could do. Quite a number	21	56
look at their jobs as necessary evils.	24	59
The need for higher skills is vital if you want to be	27	62
employed at work you truly like. Find out now what your	31	66
career options are and then take steps to prepare for them.	35	70

gwam 3' | 1 | 2 | 3 | 4 |

107c ● Formatting Problems: Bulletin Board Notices   30 minutes

To review spread headings, refer to page 146.

Directions: Problem 1

On a half sheet, long edge at top prepare the bulletin board notice shown below. Center the notice vertically and horizontally; set margins at each side of the main heading; align third line of notice at each margin.

```
                           *
           *          *                                    DS
M E T R O P O L I T A N   K E Y B O A R D I N G   C O N T E S T
           *          *                                    SS
                      *
                     QS
```

Notice to All Contestants
                          DS
SCHOOL BUS LEAVES FOR NOLAN MIDDLE SCHOOL
                                        DS
School Parking Lot   Friday, June 6
                                                          DS
                     2:00 p.m.

Directions: Problem 2

On a half sheet, prepare the notice shown below. Center the notice vertically; set a 70-space line and begin the first entry at left margin; center second entry; make third entry end at right margin. Space copy vertically as you did in Problem 1.

To review centering items under headings, refer to page 123.

OUR LEADERS IN BASEBALL

Best Slugging Average	Best Pitching Average	Best Fielding Average
Thomas Wingfoot	Aurelio Lopez	Russell Haver

OUR LEADERS IN BASEBALL

LESSON 108   70-space line

5 minutes   **108a ● Keyboard Review**

Directions: Key each sentence 3 times SS. DS between 3-line groups.

strike keys with quick, crisp, short strokes

alphabet They were required to save the jigsaw puzzles in the black box for me.

figure Going 90 miles per hour, a skier jumped 282 feet on February 26, 1933.

direct reach My cousin Brad brought my brother and aunt to Briton for the symphony.

easy They were told to key their last names below the title of the article.

| 1 | 2 | 3 | 4 | 5 | 6 | 7 | 8 | 9 | 10 | 11 | 12 | 13 | 14 |

10 minutes

36e ● Language Arts Skills: Composing at the Keyboard

Directions: 1. Key an answer to each question. Use complete sentences as shown in the sample answer.

2. If time permits, key any sentences in which you made errors.

Questions

1. What is your favorite subject?
2. What is your favorite sport?
3. What is the name of your school?
4. What is your keyboarding teacher's name?
5. Name the state in which you live.
6. Name the city in which you were born.

Sample Answer: My favorite subject is history.

LESSON 37

60-space line

5 minutes

37a ● Keyboard Review

Directions: Key each sentence three times SS. DS between 3-line groups.

keep arms and
wrists quiet

alphabet Marvel Jackson was requested to pay a tax for the big prize.

fig/sym Thirty of the 120 students (25%) missed questions #79 & #80.

easy They paid for their eight chairs with the profits they made.

| 1 | 2 | 3 | 4 | 5 | 6 | 7 | 8 | 9 | 10 | 11 | 12 |

---

5 minutes

37b ● Language Arts Skills: Keying from Dictation and Spelling Checkup

Directions: Your teacher will dictate the words in 36c, page 66. Key the words from dictation. Check your work for correct spelling. Rekey any words in which you made an error.

---

10 minutes

37c ● Timed Writings

Directions: Take two 3' writings on 36d, page 66. Figure *gwam*.

Submit the better of the two writings.

---

25 minutes

37d ● Learn to Center Vertically

Centering material so that it will have uniform top and bottom margins is called vertical centering.

Step 1 Count the lines in the copy to be centered. If your copy is to be double-spaced, remember to count the spaces between the lines. There is only 1 line space following each line of copy when material is double-spaced.

Step 2 Subtract the total lines to be used from the lines available on the paper you are using. (There are 33 lines on a half sheet, 66 on a full sheet).

Step 3 Divide the number of lines that remain by 2. The answer gives you the number of lines in the top and bottom margins. If the result contains a fraction, disregard it.

Step 4 Space down from the top of your paper or screen the number of line spaces obtained in Step 3. Start keying 1 line space below the number you calculated for your top margin.

(continued on next page)

10 minutes **106d ● Composing at Your Machine**

Directions: Compose a paragraph, telling in your own words what the following quotation means to you.

"The best place to find a helping hand," Banks said, "is at the end of your arm."

LESSON 107

70-space line

5 minutes **107a ● Keyboard Review**

Directions: Key each sentence three times SS. DS between 3-line groups.

do not pause
between words

alphabet We have just realized Gil's black picture frame is not exactly square.

figure One 900 A.D. Viking ship was 23.3 meters long and 5.3 meters in width.

adjacent keys It was very sad for her to hear the reporter's opinions on this topic.

easy The house was shaken by the gale winds and by very strong rain storms.

| 1 | 2 | 3 | 4 | 5 | 6 | 7 | 8 | 9 | 10 | 11 | 12 | 13 | 14 |

---

10 minutes **107b ● Language Arts Skills: Punctuation Guides (Quotation Marks)**

Directions: The following are guides for the use of quotation marks and sentences that illustrate the use of those guides. Study each guide; then key the sentence that illustrates the guide. Key each sentence twice SS; DS between groups.

reach to the
shift key
quickly and
firmly

Place quotation marks around the exact words of a speaker.
"Not a bad profit," my partner said, "for a firm that has just begun."

When the quotation is broken to identify the speaker, put quotation marks around each part.
"The deepest mine in the world," they continued, "is 9,811 feet deep."

If the second part of the quotation is a new sentence, use a capital letter.
"We are going to Alaska," she said quietly. "Where are your tickets?"

Use no quotation marks with an indirect quotation.
The advertising director announced that the new sale would begin soon.

Use quotation marks around the titles of articles, songs, poems, themes, short stories, and the like.
Lois Adams wrote the new best-selling single title, "Where I Started."

Always place the period or comma inside the closing quotation mark.
Mr. Nelson stated, "I would like to read your article in the journal."

37d, continued **Vertical Centering**

Directions: Problem 1
1. Center the ¶ below vertically on a half sheet of paper (long side up).
2. Key the ¶ line-for-line. Use a 60-space line DS.

Directions: Problem 2
1. Center the ¶ below vertically on a full sheet of paper.
2. Key the ¶ line-for-line. Use a 60-space line DS.

---

		words
1		
2		
3		
4		
5		
6		
7		
8	Start on	
9	Line 9	Vertical centering means you arrange your copy so that — 11
10		
11		it has equal top and bottom margins. Material formatted this — 23
12		
13		way looks neat and is pleasing to the eye. — 32
14		
15		To center copy vertically, count the lines you are going — 45
16		
17		to key; also count the blank lines you plan to leave between — 56
18		
19		the keyed ones. Subtract this total from 33 for a half sheet — 68
20		
21		of paper or from 66 for a full sheet. Divide the difference — 81
22		
23		by 2 to determine how far down to come before keying your — 93
24		
25		first line. If the result contains a fraction, disregard it. — 105

Lines on half sheet 33
Lines and line spaces in copy 17
Line spaces in top and bottom margins 16
Divide by 2. Top margin 8*
Bottom margin 8

* Start keying on the 9th line space from the top of paper or screen.

LESSON 38

60-space line

5 minutes **38a ● Keyboard Review**

Directions: Key each sentence three times SS. DS between 3-line groups.

keep feet flat on floor

alphabet Pamela gave Nick exquisite old jewelry for the bazaar today.

symbol A record 127 people cast votes for Ramona as vice-president!

easy He tried to learn to keep his eyes on the ball at all times.

| 1 | 2 | 3 | 4 | 5 | 6 | 7 | 8 | 9 | 10 | 11 | 12 |

Lessons 37 & 38   **68**

20 minutes **106c ● Speed Ladder Paragraphs**

Directions: Take 1' writings on each ¶ as you did in 96d, page 171.

all letters used   1.3 si

gwam 5'

Among the most feared warrior groups of all times were the Vikings.	3	55
Living on or near the sea, they depended on warlike efforts to live.	6	58
They roamed thousands of miles, exploring for any items of value they	8	60
could find.	9	61
The boats they used, though very tiny, were their pride and joy.	11	63
Often described in Viking writings, these trim ships were the key to the	14	66
success of their warriors. In fact, it was not unusual for a chief to	17	69
have his boat buried with him.	18	70
The ships drew very little water and were well suited for battle in	21	73
rivers and inland waters. They were light and quick and built to be	24	76
strong in surprise attacks. Though their low sides were a disadvantage	27	79
in rough seas, the Vikings' sailing skills won out.	29	81
Viking ships were sized by the number of oars they had on board.	31	83
Thirteen pairs was the very least that a warship would have. Besides	34	86
being propelled by oars, the ships also had sails for power in windy	37	89
weather. A single square sail made of coarse cloth was the typical	40	92
choice.	40	92
The ships were constructed of fir wood planking fastened to curved	43	95
wooden ribs. The keels were fashioned of oak. The hulls were tarred,	46	98
and cow hair or thread used for caulking. A carved dragon's head adorned	49	101
the prow of their vessel. The stern might repeat the design or display	51	103
a dragon's tail.	52	104

gwam 5' | 1 | 2 | 3 |

38b ● Paragraph Guided Writings

Directions: 1. Take a 1' writing on ¶ 1. Figure *gwam*. Add four words to your *gwam* for a new goal.

2. Take two 1' writings on the same ¶. Try to reach your goal on each writing.

3. Take a 1' writing on the same ¶. Drop back two to four *gwam*. Your goal is to key without errors.

4. Repeat Steps 1, 2, and 3 for the second and third ¶ s.

all letters used   1.2 si

	gwam 3'
Most of us are so pressed for time these days that those	4 | 40
who market goods and services have a hard time keeping up.	8 | 44
In the era of fax machines and microwaves, what once seemed	12 | 48
fast is not quite fast enough anymore.	14 | 51
We think pizza should be delivered to the house in half	18 | 55
an hour or less. We get upset if someone makes us wait more	22 | 59
than a minute or so for a burger and fries.	25 | 62
If we do save bits of time here and there, perhaps the	29 | 66
real challenge is to learn what to do with them. Extra time	33 | 70
is worth something when it is enjoyed and used wisely.	36 | 73

gwam 3' | 1 | 2 | 3 | 4 |

38c ● Learn to Center Horizontally

Centering material so there will be equal left and right margins is called horizontal centering.

Step 1 Check the placement of the paper guide. Turn to page xi, and read the directions for adjusting the paper guide.

Step 2 Clear tab stops. Set tab at center point of paper (elite 51; pica 42) for paper 8½ inches wide.

Step 3 Backspace from center point once for every 2 characters or spaces in the line to be centered. If there is one character left, do not backspace for it. Begin to key at the point where you complete the backspacing.

Note: Microcomputers and some typewriters are equipped with automatic centering. To center horizontally on your particular machine, consult the user's manual.

Directions: Problem 1

1. Key the announcement below on a half sheet of paper following the directions above.

2. DS below the heading and between all other lines.

3. Begin on Line 14. When you complete the line, return to center point and repeat the steps for each line.

ATTENTION ESL CLUB MEMBERS
DS
Important Meeting
DS
Thursday, April 10
DS
Room 243, West Wing, 12:30 p.m.

(continued on next page)

105c ● Formatting Problem: Dinner Program and Menu

Directions: Key the Dinner Program and Menu shown below. Follow the directions given in 104d, page 184.

Space and arrange the copy attractively on both pages of the fold-over sheet.

Cover Page

D I N N E R   M E E T I N G

STUDENT GOVERNMENT ASSOCIATION

```
        XX
      X    X
     X      X
    X  GA  X
     X    X
      X  X
       XX
```

Lincoln Dining Room

Lansing Hotel

November 18, 19--

Inside Page

P R O G R A M

Presiding	Wilma McDonald, President
Introductions	Mark Allen, Student Lansing Middle School
Keynote Address	"Winning or Losing" Agnes Dombrowski, Chairperson National Advisory Council
Award Presentations	Heinz Schader, Editor Lansing Journal

D I N N E R   M E N U

Mixed Salad	Carrot Casserole
Chicken Kiev	Biscuits and Butter
French Fried Potatoes	Chocolate Torte Cake

Coffee, Tea, Milk

LESSON 106

70-space line

5 minutes **106a ● Keyboard Review**

Directions: Key each sentence three times SS. DS between 3-line groups.

alphabet Liz knew that expensive habits can put making full quotas in jeopardy.

figure Lou bought a Model 10 744 electronic piano for $162 less than in 1978.

balanced/one-hand We saw them work and rest. Read my themes at noon. We saw your cars.

easy Keep your eyes fixed on the copy as you key any drill or new problems.

| 1 | 2 | 3 | 4 | 5 | 6 | 7 | 8 | 9 | 10 | 11 | 12 | 13 | 14 |

---

10 minutes **106b ● Skill Comparison**

Directions: Take two 1' writings on each sentence. Compare *gwam*. Try to match your "easy" sentence speed on the other sentences.

easy Do not rest your fingers on the keys if you wish to reach a high rate.

fig/sym The cost of 1994 computers (according to a 1990 study) could drop 17%.

rough draft the best way to cheer your self up is attempt to cheer up some body else.

shift Bill went with Jan to meet Mr. Rodgers at Zeeland Book Fair in August.

38c, continued

Learn to Center Horizontally

Directions: Problem 2

1. Center the announcement below vertically on a half sheet of paper (long side up).
2. Center each line horizontally.
3. DS below the heading and between all other lines.

Directions: Problem 3

1. Center the announcement below vertically on a half sheet of paper (long side up).
2. Center each line horizontally.
3. DS below the heading and between all other lines.

```
        SPECIAL ANNOUNCEMENT
                    DS
           Free Movie
                DS
          "Home Alone"
                DS
           Auditorium
                DS
     November 16, 7:30 p.m.
```

```
          ALL SOFTBALL FANS
                    DS
          Valley Finals
                  DS
      Cheer our Team to Victory!
                       DS
      Anderson Field, 3:30 p.m.
                    DS
              BE THERE
```

LESSON 39

5 minutes

39a ● Keyboard Review

Directions: Key each sentence three times SS. DS between 3-line groups.

alphabet Major taxes have clearly penalized quite a few bigger banks.

fig/sym Lot prices varied more than $765 during the years 1991-1992.

easy The profit you can make depends on both labor and materials.

| 1 | 2 | 3 | 4 | 5 | 6 | 7 | 8 | 9 | 10 | 11 | 12 |

8 minutes

39b ● Speed Ladder Sentences

Directions: **1.** Take 1' writings on each sentence. Try to key each sentence four times within the minute.
2. Your instructor will call the return each 15 seconds to guide you.
3. The rate increases 4 words a minute with each succeeding sentence.

		gwam 15"	words
keep your eyes on the copy	1 Sit up as you key these words.	24	6
	2 Your goal is to complete this line.	28	7
	3 Keep your eyes on the copy in your book.	32	8
	4 See if you can add some more words each time.	36	9
	5 Tap the return key quickly as the guide is called.	40	10

| 1 | 2 | 3 | 4 | 5 | 6 | 7 | 8 | 9 | 10 |

104d, continued

To center lines on paper of odd size, refer to directions on page 73 if necessary.

To key spread headings, refer to directions on page 146 if necesary.

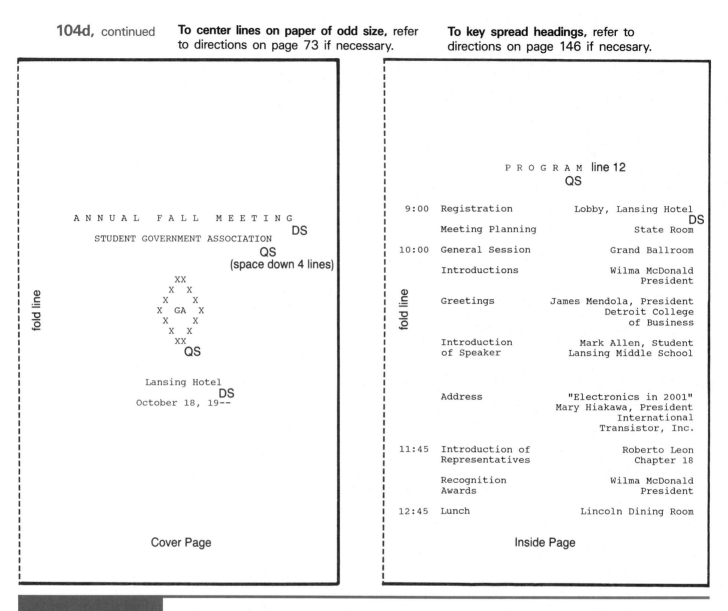

A N N U A L   F A L L   M E E T I N G
DS
STUDENT GOVERNMENT ASSOCIATION
QS
(space down 4 lines)

```
            XX
          X    X
         X      X
         X  GA  X
          X    X
           X  X
            XX
```
QS

Lansing Hotel
DS
October 18, 19--

Cover Page

P R O G R A M line 12
QS

9:00	Registration	Lobby, Lansing Hotel
	Meeting Planning	State Room
10:00	General Session	Grand Ballroom
	Introductions	Wilma McDonald President
	Greetings	James Mendola, President Detroit College of Business
	Introduction of Speaker	Mark Allen, Student Lansing Middle School
	Address	"Electronics in 2001" Mary Hiakawa, President International Transistor, Inc.
11:45	Introduction of Representatives	Roberto Leon Chapter 18
	Recognition Awards	Wilma McDonald President
12:45	Lunch	Lincoln Dining Room

DS (after Registration line)

Inside Page

fold line

LESSON 105

70-space line

5 minutes

105a ● Keyboard Review

Directions: Key each line three times SS. DS between 3-line groups.

sit erect as you key the copy

alphabet The judge will require several dozen back copies of my deluxe edition.

figure Nearly 68% of all adults that have reached age 35 jog or run daily.

long reach hunt curve twice doubt cent box my numb ace zebra zany brown nurse sum

easy The chief thought it was our place to visit with all the past players.

| 1 | 2 | 3 | 4 | 5 | 6 | 7 | 8 | 9 | 10 | 11 | 12 | 13 | 14 |

15 minutes

105b ● Timed Writings

Directions: 1. Take two 5' writings on 101d, page 179. Work for best possible speed with a minimum of errors.

2. Figure *gwam;* submit the better of the two writings to your teacher.

39c ● **Continuity Practice from Script**

Directions: Key the ¶ below at least two times on a 60-space line DS. Repeat if time permits.

all letters used   1.2 si

	words
There is an old saying that one should not judge a book	11
by its cover. Let us see how this maxim might apply to us	23
at the grocery store. If certain colors can really make a	35
person hungry, as some think they can, that orange bag of	47
pretzels may catch your eye. Don't be too quick to buy it	58
unless you are sure you want what is inside.	67

13 minutes

39d ● **Formatting Problem: Centering Paragraphs**   60-space line

Directions: 1. Center the report below vertically on a full sheet of paper DS.   2. Center the heading horizontally in all caps; QS below the heading.

Correcting Errors

Learn to use the basic methods for correcting keying errors. Several of these methods are explained in the ¶s at the right.

words

CORRECTING ERRORS   4

QS

Several different methods for correcting errors on written   16
documents are available today.   22

Many typewriters are equipped with a correction tape.   33
When you depress a special correction key, this tape lifts off   45
the undesired character from your paper.   53

If your machine does not have this special feature, you   65
have three basic methods from which to choose. To correct an   77
error with correction fluid, just paint over the incorrect   89
letter; make sure the fluid is dry before rekeying. In using   101
correction paper, place the paper between the ribbon and your   114
error; rekey your error, allowing powder from the tape to   125
cover the incorrect letter. When using an eraser, roll your   137
paper up two or three lines and hold the paper firmly against   150
the platen as you erase.   155

On microcomputers, incorrect characters are removed from   166
the screen by use of the backspace or delete keys.   176

LESSON 104

5 minutes

104a ● Keyboard Review

Directions: Key each sentence three times SS. DS between 3-line groups.

keep fingers
deeply curved

alphabet The project was quickly moved by anxious citizens to avoid any fights.

figure Laura ordered 17 3/4 yards of #506 silk at a cost of $8.90 for a yard.

home row All final cash sales of the flashy jade glass rings are finally added.

easy We are asking them to sign a blue form as soon as it is given to them.

| 1 | 2 | 3 | 4 | 5 | 6 | 7 | 8 | 9 | 10 | 11 | 12 | 13 | 14 |

---

5 minutes

104b ● Language Arts Skills: Punctuation Guides (Dash and Parentheses)

Directions: The following are guides for the use of the dash and parentheses and sentences that illustrate the use of the guides. Study each guide; then key the sentence that illustrates the guide. Key each sentence twice SS; DS between 2-line groups.

Use a dash to show a sudden break in thought.
We are returning your manuscript--even though it might have potential.

Use a dash before the name of an author when it follows a direct quotation.
"We have nothing to fear but fear itself."--Franklin Delano Roosevelt.

Use parentheses to enclose an explanation.
Most of the workers received their usual raise (about 6%) last August.

---

5 minutes

104c ● Skill Builder from Rough Draft

Directions: Take four 1' writings on the ¶; try to increase speed with each writing.

gwam 1'

Many of us are able to ~~type~~ key copy for one minute, however, 11

being able to do well on a longer writings is often much more 21

dif_ficult. In orders to have good ~~study~~ skill and accuracy in 32

keying copy, you must practice as much as possible. ~~In~~ there 41

is no beter way to build skill than to practice, practice, 52

and ~~they~~ then practice more. 54

Note: Some computer software will automatically align items at the right margin.

To align items at the right margin, set a tab stop at the right margin. After keying copy in the line beginning at the left margin, tab to the right margin; backspace for each letter or space in the item; begin keying where backspacing ends.

104d ● Formatting Problem: Program of a Meeting   30 minutes

Directions: 1. Fold an 8½" × 11" sheet of paper in half to 5½" × 8½".
2. Insert the folded sheet with the fold at the left (against the paper guide).
3. Arrange the copy for the cover page shown on page 185. Center all copy vertically; center each line horizontally; use spacing guides on the model.

4. After you finish the cover, remove the paper, reverse the fold, and reinsert the paper with the fold at the left.
5. Arrange the copy for the inside page as illustrated on page 185. Center all copy vertically; use ½" side margins. Items at the right of the page are aligned at the right margin.

(continued on next page)

12 minutes

39e ● Learn to Correct Rough Draft

Copy that has been keyed or printed may be corrected by the use of proofreader's marks. Study the proofreader's marks explained here; then follow the directions below for keying the announcement.

Common Proofreader's Marks

^	insert	ℓ	delete	/ or lc	lowercase
^,	insert comma	⊐	move right	tr or ∽	transpose
^.	insert period	⊏	move left	#	add space
⌣	close up	Cap or ≡	capitalize	¶	paragraph

Directions: **1.** Center the announcement vertically on a half sheet of paper (long side up).
2. Center each line horizontally. Backspace once for 2 characters or spaces as they will appear in the corrected copy.
3. DS below the heading and between all other lines.
4. Make the corrections as you key the announcement.

```
YOU ARE INVITED
by/the   [# add space]
Junior Pep Varsity club   [tr: Pep Varsity; ≡ under c: capitalize]
to attend the   [attend deleted]
Annual SwimFest   [/F lc]
Madisonville YMCA
Saturday^, December 12, 7:30 p. m.   [insert comma; close up]
```

LESSON 40

60-space line

5 minutes

40a ● Keyboard Review

Directions: Key each sentence three times SS. DS between 3-line groups.

use quick, sharp strokes

alphabet Have Fred explain why he objects to making up the last quiz.

fig/sym "Mike's address is 2874 North Alamar Avenue," replied Cindy.

easy Most of the tires on the bus are worn down and out of shape.

| 1 | 2 | 3 | 4 | 5 | 6 | 7 | 8 | 9 | 10 | 11 | 12 |

Leaders: Key the first line of the first column; space once and note whether the printing point indicator is on an odd or even number. Key a period, space, period in turns across the line; stop 2 or 3 spaces before the second column. On lines that follow, align the periods with those in the first line, keying on odd or even numbers.

Dollar Signs: Place a dollar sign before the first amount in a column and before the total. Align the dollar sign 1 space to the left of the longest amount in the column. Key an underline under the last item in the column to include the $ and extend to the end of the column. Then DS and key the total line. Indent the word "Total" 5 spaces from the left margin.

STUDENT ACTIVITIES OFFICE BUDGET
DS

19-- to 19--
DS

<u>Anticipated Income</u>
DS

National Bank, Interest Income . . . . $ 25.00
DS

Student Council Dance 1,200.00
DS

Booster Club Ticket Sales . . . .   <u>320.00</u>

    Total $1,545.00
DS

<u>Anticipated Expenditures</u>
DS

Dance Band Fees . . . . $ 380.00
DS

Printing 90.00
DS

Decorations 68.00

Booster Club Raffle Prizes 230.00

Awards 190.00

Donation to Athletic Fund . . . . . .   <u>300.00</u>

      Total $1,258.00
DS

Total Budgeted Income $1,545.00
DS

Total Budget Expenditures . . . .   <u>1,258.00</u>
DS

Total Budgeted Balance . . . . $ 287.00

Note: Some computer software will automatically align leaders using special tab features.

40b ● Timed Writings

Directions: Key two 3' writings on 38b, page 69. Figure *gwam*.   Submit the better of the two writings.

40c ● Finding Horizontal Center Point

In order to center headings on paper or cards of different sizes, you must learn how to find the center point.

Step 1 Insert the paper you will use to key 40d into your machine.

Step 2 Add the numbers on the line-of-writing scale at the right and left edges of the paper.

Step 3 Divide the sum by 2. The resulting figure is the horizontal center point of the paper.

40d ● Keying on Odd-Size Paper or Cards

Directions: Problem 1

1. Insert a half sheet of paper (5½ × 8½") with the short side up.
2. From the top edge of the paper, space down to the 20th line for the heading.
3. Find the horizontal center of the half sheet following directions in 40c. Set a tab stop at this point.
4. Key the announcement below, centering each line horizontally. DS below the heading and between all other lines.

Note: To do this assignment on a microcomputer or an electronic typewriter with automatic centering, you will need to reset your margins for a 5½" line. Check your user's manual for assistance.

There are six vertical line spaces to an inch. An 8½ inch sheet contains 51 vertical line spaces:
8½ × 6 = 51.

Lines available	51
Lines required	13
Lines remaining	38
Top margin	19
Begin on line	20

COMPTON COMPUTER CLUB

Announces

a Special Demonstration/Workshop

"Presentation Graphics Software"

Dr. Arlene Motz

Wednesday, February 8, 2:30 p.m.

Lab 13

Directions: Problem 2

1. Insert a half sheet of paper with the short side up.
2. Center the announcement at the top of page 74 vertically; center each line horizontally. DS below the heading and between all other lines.

(continued on next page)

10 minutes   **103b** ● **Speed Builder**

Directions: Take two 1' writings on each ¶; try to increase speed on the second writing. Figure *gwam*.

Alternate Procedure: Work for speed as you take one 5' writing on all three ¶s combined. Figure *gwam*.

all letters used   1.3 si

	gwam	1'	5'
The ads we see every day direct us to do a variety of things. A	13	3	37
few may tell us we need a new type of food product. This food item we	27	5	39
are told will make us healthy, attractive, popular, and a whole number	41	8	42
of things. We just know it can't keep all of these promises.	54	11	45
If we know a product cannot possibly do all the things which are	13	13	47
advertised, then why do so many people, including us, still go out and	27	16	50
buy the product? Why do the makers of these products spend so much of	41	19	53
their funds on ads for the public to see?	50	21	55
Producers spend a great deal of money on ads for they know that an	13	23	57
item will not sell unless people know about it. They want to maximize	28	26	60
their sales. Consumers quickly want to have all those very special	41	29	63
benefits that appear in the ad. So, even though their sense tells them	56	32	66
that it can't be that good, they still buy the product.	67	34	68

gwam 1' | 1 | 2 | 3 | 4 | 5 | 6 | 7 | 8 | 9 | 10 | 11 | 12 | 13 | 14 |
5' | 1 | 2 | 3 |

---

30 minutes   **103c** ● **Formatting Problem: School Organization Budget**

Directions: On a full sheet, key the school organization budget shown on the next page. Leave a 2" top margin; center copy vertically as directed on the model.

Center each heading horizontally; center the body copy using the longest item in each column; leave 10 spaces between columns. Use leaders to separate the two columns.

Lesson 103   **182**

RED WAVE BAKE SALE

at Cafeteria Entrance
Thursday, November 8
Donuts, Cookies, Cakes, Pies
High Quality and Low Prices
Send the Red Wave to the District Tournament

Directions: Problem 3

1. Insert a half sheet of paper with the short side up. DS below the heading and between all other lines.

2. Center the problem vertically; center each line horizontally.

Do not key lines within the copy. They indicate return points.

TIOGA JUNIOR HIGH SCHOOL | Pep and Cheer Try-outs | (Begin After Spring Break) | Information Meeting | Wednesday, April 18, 4:15 p.m., North Gym | ALL CANDIDATES MUST ATTEND

40e ● Extra Credit: Key from Rough Draft

When rough draft copy must be centered vertically, you may wish to key the corrected copy on practice paper first.
Directions: 1. Center the exercise vertically on a full sheet of paper, using a 60-space line.

You can then count the number of lines required and follow the usual procedure for vertical centering.
2. Provide an appropriate heading. QS below the heading and DS between all other lines.

(Provide appropriate heading)

Some of the most famous places on earth, odd as this may

seem, are not majestic mountains or fabulous buildings. They are

amusement parks--like Disney land and Walt Disney World,

to name a couple of the best known.

The oldest of these so called theme parks is Knott's

Berry Farm. beginning as a road side stand where Walter and

Cordelia Knott sold berries, it has expanded with the times and today

draws 5 million people a year to enjoy its many attractions.

102b, continued

Directions: Problem 2

1. On a half sheet, long edge at top, center the graph shown below.
2. Center both lines of the main heading

SS; QS between 2-line main heading and body of graph. Space body of graph as you did in Problem 1.

```
           KEYBOARDING SPEED DEVELOPMENT
                 FOR NIKKI TALBOT


        September    xxx
        October      xxxxxx
        November     xxxxxxxxxxxxx
        December     xxxxxxxxxxxxxxxxxxxxx
        January      xxxxxxxxxxxxxxxxxxxxxxxxxx
                     !           !           !
          GWAM       10         20          30
```

---

5 minutes

102c ● Skill Builder from Script

Directions: Take four 1′ writings on the ¶. Try to increase speed with each writing.

gwam 1′

Swimming is one of the best and safest ways to 10
improve overall physical fitness. It has been proven 22
that some exercises, while good for muscle building, 33
can result in damage to other parts of the body. For 49
example, jogging can often be very hard on the knees. 55

---

5 minutes

102d ● Building Skill on Figures and Symbols

Directions: Key each sentence three times SS. DS between 3-line groups.

keep locations of symbol keys fixed in your mind

1 Our new boat (purchased at Beth's Marina) goes over 50 miles per hour.

2 The story entitled "Winners and Losers" appeared on May 2 in Newsweek.

3 The new 6-month savings certificates are paying 8.25% annual interest.

LESSON 103

70-space line

5 minutes

103a ● Keyboard Review

Directions: Key each line three times SS. DS between 3-line groups.

alphabet The lost junk was moved by poor citizens quite anxious to stop fights.

figure The 4 planes flew a total distance of 27.89 million miles in 343 days.

4th finger polo zip lamp quiz pail soap pupil zap lap quit zipper palm quiz group

easy The right quick bids may take many items for the people who make them.

| 1 | 2 | 3 | 4 | 5 | 6 | 7 | 8 | 9 | 10 | 11 | 12 | 13 | 14 |

Unit 7 ▪ Keying Personal Notes and Letters (Lessons 41–50)

Learning Goals:
1. To key personal notes in block and modified block style.
2. To key messages on postal cards.
3. To key personal/business letters in block and modified block style.
4. To use open and mixed punctuation in letters and notes.
5. To address small and large envelopes.
6. To answer questions as an aid to composing at the machine.
7. To key correctly words that are commonly misspelled.
8. To apply capitalization guides in keying sentences.
9. To key from rough draft containing common proofreader's marks.
10. To increase keying skill by further refining basic techniques.

General Directions

Use a 60-space line for all lessons in this unit unless otherwise directed. SS sentences and drill lines. DS between repeated groups of lines. DS paragraph copy. Set machine for a 5-space paragraph indention. Your teacher will tell you whether or not to correct errors when keying problems.

LESSON 41

5 minutes   **41a ● Keyboard Review**

Directions: Key each sentence 3 times SS. DS between 3-line groups.

keep feet
on the floor

alphabet That back cover of my tax journal puzzled quite a few girls.
fig/sym Of their 96 new bikes, 72 are 10-speeds and 24 are 3-speeds.
easy Their big bus made a right turn at the signal light in town.

| 1 | 2 | 3 | 4 | 5 | 6 | 7 | 8 | 9 | 10 | 11 | 12 |

10 minutes   **41b ● Technique Builder: Flowing Rhythm**

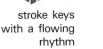

stroke keys
with a flowing
rhythm

Directions: Key each line 3 times SS from dictation. DS between 3-line groups.

1 if the | if the cases | if the cases | for the | for the | for the car
2 and the | and the date | and the date | and the seat | and the seats
3 she saw | she saw only | he did | he did care | they face | they faced
4 if you | if you ever | if you trade | and you | and you | and you were

10 minutes   **41c ● Sentence Skill Builder from Script**

Directions: Take two 1′ writings on each sentence. Figure *gwam*.

words

Your room is not the only place that is in a big mess today.   12

The planet that we live on now has some problems of its own.   12

We will need people like you who can learn to clean them up.   12

Lesson 41

75

5 minutes   **101e ● Continuity Practice**

Directions: Key the last ¶ of 101d as many times as you can in 5'. Work   for even, continuous stroking.

LESSON 102   70-space line

5 minutes   **102a ● Keyboard review**

Directions: Key each sentence three times SS. DS between 3-line groups.

return quickly   alphabet   With zip I could equal the very next track effort by jumping the best.

fig/sym   Invoice #373 (dated May 25) for $450.75 was sent to August & Co., Inc.

double letter   The office will tell the committee to offer the messages to the staff.

easy   The boss paid all the boys their total pay on time this fiscal period.

| 1 | 2 | 3 | 4 | 5 | 6 | 7 | 8 | 9 | 10 | 11 | 12 | 13 | 14 |

30 minutes   **102b ● Formatting Problems: Horizontal Bar Graphs**

Directions: Problem 1

1. On a half sheet, long edge at top, center the graph shown below. Use the directions on the model as a guide for spacing.

2. To determine the left margin, backspace once from the center for each 2 letters in the longest name, in the longest bar, and for spaces between names and bars. Set left margin. Space forward once for each letter in the longest name and for spaces between the names and bars. Set a tab here to begin the bars.

3. Each *x* represents one word a minute, beginning with 30 *gwam*. Place an exclamation point under the first *x* in each group of ten as shown. Center the figures under the exclamation points by depressing the backspace key or incremental spacer key if your machine has one.

```
              HIGHEST KEYBOARDING RATES IN 9:00 CLASS
                                                    DS
                         March 24, 19--
                  6 spaces               QS


        Brazell, James  |  xxxxxxxxxxxxxxxxxxxxxxxxx
                        |                            DS
        Ortiz, Ophfelia ↓  xxxxxxxxxxxxxxxxx
        Rohm, Dexter       xxxxxxxxxxxxxxxxxxxxxxxxxxxxx
        Repp, Roxanne      xxxxxxxxxxxxxxxxxxxxxxxxxxxxxxxxxxx
               GWAM        !        !        !        !
                          30       40       50       60
```

5 minutes

key each word
letter by letter

41d ● Language Arts Skills: Spelling and Proofreading Aid

Directions: Key each line 3 times SS. DS between 3-line groups.

1 toward similar practice valuable salary acknowledge hesitate

2 dollar financial procedure situation separate volume session

3 convenient responsibility circular calendar specific license

---

15 minutes

41e ● Paragraph Guided Writings

Directions: 1. Take a 1' writing on ¶ 1. Figure *gwam.* Add four words to your *gwam* for a new goal.
2. Take two 1' writings. Try to reach your goal on each writing.

3. Take a 1' writing on the same ¶. Drop back two to four *gwam.* Your goal is to key the ¶ without errors.
4. Repeat Steps 1, 2, and 3 for the second and third ¶ s.

keep wrists low
and arms quiet

all letters used   1.2 si

	gwam 3'
Before you start to look for your first job, you will be	4 | 42
wise to consider some techniques of job seeking that have been	8 | 47
helpful to others. They can also pay off for you.	11 | 50
For example, show that you are not lazy by listing the	15 | 54
kinds of work you have done. You might have delivered papers	19 | 58
or taken care of children. Be sure to include work for which	23 | 62
you did not get paid.	25 | 63
The strong points of your school record should be noted,	29 | 67
of course. It will help if you can say you missed only two	32 | 71
days of school in three years or that your keyboarding rate	36 | 75
was one of the best in the class.	39 | 77

gwam 3' | 1 | 2 | 3 | 4 |

LESSON 42

60-space line

5 minutes

sit erect;
keep feet
flat on
floor

42a ● Keyboard Review

Directions: Key each sentence 3 times SS. DS between 3-line groups.

alphabet Quint saw five black taxis jump the curbs and go zooming by.

fig/sym The Women's Club can meet at Olson's on April 30 and May 24.

easy Make sure he laid both world maps on the chair in row eight.

| 1 | 2 | 3 | 4 | 5 | 6 | 7 | 8 | 9 | 10 | 11 | 12 |

101d ● Speed Ladder Paragraphs

Directions: Take 1' writings on each ¶ as you did in 96d, page 171.

all letters used 1.3 si

	gwam 5'

Today's health experts cite as their current concern the amount of — 3 | 56

stress that a worker must face on the job each day. They say stress can — 6 | 59

be a real threat to a person's physical and mental condition. Research — 8 | 61

agrees with this. — 9 | 62

If you had to identify which jobs place people under the greatest — 12 | 65

stress, you might choose those where the most danger is involved. One — 15 | 68

job that may come to mind is that of working on a police force or being — 18 | 71

a window washer on a tall building. — 19 | 72

You might judge that those who have to make hard decisions each — 21 | 74

day lead the most stressful lives, but this is not the case. Most of — 24 | 77

the current studies suggest that stress at the top levels is quite often — 27 | 80

offset by much higher status and better level of pay. — 29 | 82

Factors other than decision making or danger seem to turn most any — 32 | 85

job into a stressful one for the person in it. Working with a boss who — 34 | 87

looks over your shoulder all day long is one of them. Another is working — 38 | 91

at tasks that are dull and boring. Liking our job usually means less — 41 | 94

stress. — 41 | 94

Computerized equipment is blamed by some as the chief reason for — 44 | 97

increased stress on the job site. They say that we are moving so much — 46 | 99

faster today that workers do not have time to relax. If this is true, — 49 | 102

then we should be ready to deal with much more hidden stress, because — 52 | 105

the computer is here to stay. — 53 | 106

gwam 5' | 1 | 2 | 3 |

42b ● Language Arts Skills: Keying from Dictation and Spelling Checkup

Directions: 1. Your teacher will dictate words in 41d, page 76. Key the words from dictation.

2. Check your work for correct spelling. Rekey any words in which you made an error.

42c ● Timed Writings

Directions: 1. Take two 3′ writings on 41e, page 76. Proofread; circle errors.

2. Figure *gwam;* submit the better writing.

42d ● Formatting Problems: Personal Notes in Block Style, Open Punctuation

Directions: Problem 1
1. Set margins for a 50-space line.
2. On a half sheet of paper, key the personal note below.

Begin the date on the 7th line from the top. Begin the salutation on the 4th line below the date.

---

begin 7 lines from
top

words

Date   May 8, 19--   2

4th line (return 4 times)
below date

Salutation   Dear Michelle   5
DS

Body   Congratulations on being elected as our new Student   15
Body President. I know from experience that you   25
will be the busiest person on campus next year.   35
DS

Will you please ask each of your officers to be   45
present at the special meeting of the old and new   55
student councils on Thursday afternoon. The meeting   65
will begin promptly at 3:45 in the cafeteria.   75
DS

I'm looking forward to seeing everyone there.   84
DS

Complimentary Close   Sincerely   85

In the block style, the date, salutation, and complimentary
close are keyed at the left margin. The lines of the paragraphs are blocked. Open punctuation is used in this note
(no marks of punctuation follow the salutation or complimentary close).

100c, continued

Directions: Problem 2 Composing a Postal Card

1. Assume the message in Problem 1 has been mailed to you. Compose an answer and prepare it in proper form on a postal card.

2. Explain that you can assist in the telephone campaign; however, you would need to use a school telephone.

LESSON 101

5 minutes **101a ● Keyboard Review**

Directions: Key each sentence three times SS. DS between 3-line groups.

keep key locations fixed in your mind

alphabet My fine puzzle was cut with a jigsaw and put in very equal knit boxes.

figure In our country, more than 40.65 million homes, or 23%, own a computer.

e,i Their eight friends were not believed, since neither box was received.

easy Be sure to place the newer books on the floor where they will be seen.

| 1 | 2 | 3 | 4 | 5 | 6 | 7 | 8 | 9 | 10 | 11 | 12 | 13 | 14 |

---

5 minutes **101b ● Language Arts Skills: Punctuation Guides (Colon)**

Directions: The following are guides for the use of the colon and sentences that illustrate the use of those guides. Study each guide; then key the sentence that illustrates the guide. Key each sentence twice SS; DS between 2-line groups.

keep feet flat on the floor

Use a colon to introduce a list of items or expressions.
The orders requested the following: ribbons, disks, paper, and forms.

Use a colon to separate hours and minutes when expressed in figures.
Louise left the airport at 8:15; she arrived at their offices at 9:33.

Use a colon to introduce a question or long quotation.
Colons tell a reader: "Here is something I must read very carefully."

---

10 minutes **101c ● Sentence Control Builder**

Directions: Take two 1' writings on each sentence. Try to complete each writing without error.

space quickly with a down-and-in motion

1 You cannot lead anyone any farther than you have dared to go yourself.

2 If you could get half your wishes, you would likely double your cares.

3 You have the right to risk those things if no one else will be harmed.

4 Those who think too much of themselves usually aren't thinking enough.

| 1 | 2 | 3 | 4 | 5 | 6 | 7 | 8 | 9 | 10 | 11 | 12 | 13 | 14 |

42d, continued

Directions: Problem 2
1. Set margins for a 60-space line.
2. On a half sheet of paper, key the personal note below.

As you did in Problem 1, begin the date on the 7th line from the top and the salutation on the 4th line below the date.

words

Today's date   3

4 line spaces (return 4 times
between date and salutation)

Dear Abby   5
DS

You probably remember writing the long report that Ms. Berg   17
always assigns her English 8 students during spring semester.   30
This year I'm the one who has the big job to do.   40
DS

I have decided to write my report on Yellowstone National   51
Park. Did you save any of the brochures we picked up when   63
we were there? If so, I'd really appreciate it if you would   75
send them to me right away.   81
DS

Sincerely   83

LESSON 43

60-space line

5 minutes

43a ● Keyboard Review

Directions: Key each sentence 3 times SS. DS between 3-line groups.

strike each key
with quick,
sharp strokes.

alphabet   They flew D. G. Chavez home quickly by jet at their expense.

fig/sym   Total fees amounted to $7,435--an 80% increase in 12 months!

easy   At least eight of their members work there in the same firm.

| 1 | 2 | 3 | 4 | 5 | 6 | 7 | 8 | 9 | 10 | 11 | 12 |

---

10 minutes

43b ● Sentence Skill Builder from Script

Directions: Take two 1' writings on each sentence. On the first writing, push for speed. On the second writing, drop back in speed and work for control.

words

If you do not know which career you want, you are not alone.   12

Even most college students are unsure of their career goals.   12

To find a career you like, you need to look inside yourself.   12

You should try to find out what activities satisfy you most.   12

LESSON 100

5 minutes

100a ● Keyboard Review

Directions: Key each sentence three times SS. DS between 3-line groups.

think each word
as you key

alphabet I was quite upset by hearing crazy music from her very old jukeboxes.

figure As of June 17, all Model 243 computers will be changed to Model 5690.

long reach Myron goes to a ceremony annually to celebrate a number of successes.

easy When all the work is finished, have them hand it to the team captain.

| 1 | 2 | 3 | 4 | 5 | 6 | 7 | 8 | 9 | 10 | 11 | 12 | 13 | 14 |

15 minutes

100b ● Timed Writings

Directions: 1. Take two 5' writings on 96d, page 171. Work for best possible speed with a minimum of errors.

2. Figure *gwam;* submit the better of the two writings to your teacher.

25 minutes

100c ● Formatting Problems: Postal Cards

Directions: Problem 1   Postal Card from Script Copy

1. Key the following message on a postal card or on paper cut to size (5½" × 3¼").

2. Insert the card into your machine with short side at left. Determine horizontal center; set margins 4 spaces in from each side of card.

3. Address the card to MS JANICE EVERS, 453 LOCUST DRIVE, RESTON VA 22019-5609.

4. Key the following return address in the upper left corner of the address side of the postal card: John Douglas, 18 Edgar Street, Reston, VA 22019-5209.

 Note: If you are using a computer, key the message so that the printed copy will fit on a postal card.

August 7, 19--

Dear Booster Club Member

Although the next school year is still almost a month away, your club officers are making plans for a successful fall.

We need your help during the next three weeks to get the word out about our fall activities. Please let me know if you can assist in a telephone campaign.

John Douglas, Secretary

(continued on next page)

43c ● Language Arts Skills: Composing at the Keyboard

Directions: Compose answers to as many of the questions below as time permits. Use complete sentences as you key your answers.

1. How many vertical line spaces are there on a full sheet of paper?

2. How many vertical line spaces are there on a half sheet of paper?

3. How many horizontal spaces (elite type) are there on a full sheet (8½"x11") of paper?

4. How many horizontal spaces (pica type) are there on a full sheet of paper?

43d ● Formatting Problems: Personal Notes in Modified Block Style, Open Punctuation

Directions: Problem 1

1. Key the note below; use half sheet and a 60-space line.

2. Begin dateline and complimentary close at the horizontal center point of the paper. Begin the salutation on the 4th line below the date at the left margin.

begin 7 lines from top

words

↓May 10, 19--   3
└─ center point

4th line (return 4 times) below date

Dear Paul↓   5
   DS

You are very thoughtful to write me a note of congratulations   17
for winning the election. After watching you this year, I   29
realize that I have some big shoes to fill.   38
   DS

Your plan to have the old and new officers meet right away is   50
a good one. All of our group will be there except Sharon, who   63
is competing in the track meet this afternoon. I'll take good   75
notes for her.   78
   DS

center point → Sincerely   80

In the modified block style, the date and the complimentary close are started at the center point of the paper. The paragraphs may be blocked or indented.

Directions: Problem 2

1. Key note at top of page 80 in modified block style, open punctuation, with indented paragraphs; use half sheet and a 60-space line.

2. Space down for date and salutation the same as Problem 1.

(continued on next page)

LESSON 99

5 minutes

99a ● Keyboard Review

Directions: Key each sentence three times SS. DS between 3-line groups.

alphabet Jan quickly realized how to beat the full bumps by driving extra slow.

figure A 1991 TV set cost less than a 1950 model did by more than 60 percent.

u,i We will build a new building which will be suitable for a public unit.

easy If they handle their work right, the firm may make a profit each time.

| 1 | 2 | 3 | 4 | 5 | 6 | 7 | 8 | 9 | 10 | 11 | 12 | 13 | 14 |

---

10 minutes

99b ● Control Builder

Directions: Key the ¶ twice at the control level. Repeat if time permits.

Goals: 2 or fewer errors per writing.

think the letters
and figures as
you key them

words

On June 9, 1991, that famous quacking fowl, Donald Duck, celebrated 14

his 57th birthday. This star is younger than his friend, Mickey Mouse, 28

who was 62 in November, 1990. Donald Duck's studio earned $100 million 42

from 130 cartoons, 4 feature films, and many books and products. During 57

World War II, over 400 military patches had this duck as their symbol. 71

| 1 | 2 | 3 | 4 | 5 | 6 | 7 | 8 | 9 | 10 | 11 | 12 | 13 | 14 |

99c ● Formatting Problems: Preparing Copy on 5″ × 3″ cards   30 minutes

Directions: Problem 1   Admission Tickets

1. Prepare 3 tickets of the kind illustrated below. Use 5″ × 3″ cards or paper cut to size. DS the copy and arrange it neatly as directed on the illustration below.

2. Note that some of the lines are centered and some are flush with the left and right margins. (See page 73 to review finding center point on odd-size paper).

3 Number your three cards in sequence beginning with No. 150.

Directions: Problem 2   Membership Cards

1. Prepare three membership cards of the kind illustrated below. Use 5″ × 3″ cards or paper cut to size. Arrange the copy neatly as directed on the illustration below.

2. After you finish the last line of centered copy, return 4 times and key 1½″ underlines flush with each margin for the signature lines. Center the titles under the underlines.

3. Number your three cards in sequence beginning with No. 86. Membership will last to June 1 of next year. Use the correct year on your cards.

Note: If you are using a computer, rule the outline of the card size on your printer paper.

	begin 3rd line from top edge of card No. 150	
½″ mar- gin	Admit One COURTNEY SCHOOL SPRING CONCERT Musical Review The Courtney Players Courtney School Auditorium Wednesday April 17, 19-- 7:00 p.m. Admission $1.50	½″ mar- gin

	begin on 3rd line from top edge of card No. 86	
½″ mar- gin	Official Membership Card BARBOUR ATHLETIC CLUB "Sportsmanship and Excellence" Barbour Middle School Year Ending June 1, 19-- *Tom Wickel* President *Barb Palmer* Secretary	½″ mar- gin

June 15, 19-- 3

Dear Stacy 5

 Next Friday is the big day! My flight is supposed to 16
arrive at 3:45 p.m. I can't wait to see all of the gang. 28

 Marty said he thought the picnic would be on Monday after- 38
noon, right after the game. I'm hoping you can find a spare 50
bike for me to ride. 56

 If there is anything I should do here before I leave, 66
please call me. Thanks a million for the invitation. 77

Sincerely 79

Note: To indent the first line of a ¶, space in 5 spaces from the left margin and set a tab stop.

Directions: Problem 3

1. Use a half sheet of paper inserted lengthwise into your machine (short side up). Set a 40-space line.

Note: If you are using a microcomputer, format the note as it appears in the illustration.

2. Key the note shown at the right. Begin the name and address of the writer (the return address) one-half inch from the top. Center each line of the return address.

3. Set off the return address by keying a line of hyphens from the left to the right edge of the paper, a line space or two below the return address.

4. Begin the date at the center point of the paper on the 3d line space below the hyphens under the return address. To find center point, refer to page 73; or fold your paper to bring the left and right edges together. Crease the paper lightly at the top.

5. Begin the salutation on the 4th line space below the date.

6. Begin the complimentary close at the center point of the paper a DS below the last ¶.

```
              RAMONA TREJO
          1427 Livermore Road
          Salinas
- - - - - - - - - - - - - - - - - - - - - - - - - - - -

                    June 15, 19--


Dear Stacy

     Next Friday is the big day!  My flight
  is supposed to arrive at 3:45 p.m.  I can't
  wait to see all of the gang.

     Marty said he thought the picnic would
  be on Monday afternoon, right after the
  game.  I'm hoping you can find a spare bike
  for me to ride.

     If there is anything I should do here
  before I leave, please call me.  Thanks a
  million for the invitation.

                    Sincerely
```

98c ● Formatting Problem: Minutes of Meetings   30 minutes

Directions: 1. On a full sheet, prepare the minutes of a meeting from the copy below.

2. Leave a 2″ top margin; use the directions on the model as a guide for spacing copy. Set a 1½″ left margin and a 1″ right margin because the minutes will be kept in a binder.

Minutes of Meetings
The minutes of a meeting are an exact record of what happened at a meeting. There is no set form which is used by all clubs and organizations for recording minutes. The form recommended in this lesson is acceptable and widely used.

Note: When reports will be bound on the left side, the center point is 3 spaces to the right of the point normally used. Keep this in mind when keying minutes of meetings.

COURTNEY SCHOOL JOURNALISM CLUB

Minutes of Meeting

Date: October 1, 19--
Time: 3:15 p.m.
Place: Journalism Room, Courtney School
Present: About 15 students in addition to the adviser, Mrs. Aquilar

1.   Mrs. Aquilar, the club adviser, presided. She introduced herself and the new and returning members of the newspaper staff.

2.   Last year's school paper editor, Robert Bailey, discussed the year's plans for the paper. It was decided by the group that the staff would put out six issues this school year. The theme "Reaching New Heights" was suggested and received a unanimous vote by the club members.

3.   The editor and adviser reviewed the assignments that would need to be done in order to complete the six issues of the school paper successfully. The editor assigned seven members of the club to be reporters and outlined their duties. The remaining members were assigned the support duties of selling, advertising, and preparing copy.

4.   Mrs. Aquilar made recommendations on deadline dates and times for each of the issues. These recommendations were accepted by the club members.

5.   A decision was made to hold all future meetings on the second Thursday of each month unless some special events required additional meetings to be called.

6.   There were three nominations for the position of editor for the coming school year. Virginia Smythe, a member of the club for two years, was elected. She was congratulated by all club members and Mrs. Aquilar.

7.   The meeting was adjourned at 4:00 p.m.

John Adams, Secretary

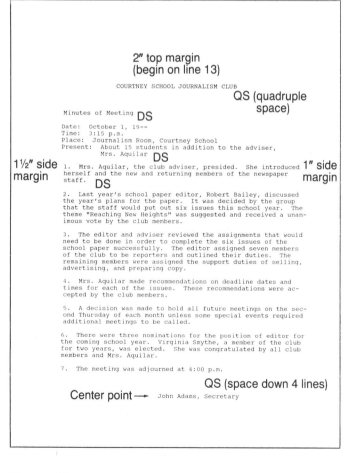

7 minutes

44a ● Keyboard Review

Directions: Key each sentence 3 times SS. DS between 3-line groups.

alphabet   I'm amazed Dave Kowing expects to qualify in the broad jump.

fig/sym   Hilary's check will be $246 when rates go from 7.8% to 9.1%.

adjacent keys   Sandra said a few more people were going there after dinner.

hyphen   Fifty-two east-west streets are two-way and six are one-way.

easy   It will pay them to take some time to plan for their visits.

   | 1 | 2 | 3 | 4 | 5 | 6 | 7 | 8 | 9 | 10 | 11 | 12 |

15 minutes

44b ● Paragraph Guided Writings

Directions: 1. Take a 1' writing on ¶ 1. Figure *gwam.* Add four words to your *gwam* for a new goal.
2. Take two 1' writings. Try to reach your new goal on each writing.

3. Take a 1' writing on the same ¶. Drop back two to four *gwam.* Your goal is to key the ¶ without errors.
4. Repeat Steps 1, 2, and 3 for the second and third ¶s.

all letters used   1.2 si

                                                 gwam 3'

	gwam 3'	
There can be no doubt that an information age is now	4	45
here in full force. In fact, it seems to expand so quickly	8	49
that most of us do not have time to adjust to any product	11	53
before a new one comes along.	13	54
No more than a few short years ago, the small computer	17	58
first appeared on desks across the land. Within three years	21	62
millions were in use, and now nearly half of our work force	25	66
is in some way involved with them.	28	69
In many cases, though, this new age has not brought order	31	73
to business nor has it lowered our work loads. We have come	36	77
to a point where people are so crazy they call to tell you	39	81
that your fax line is busy.	41	83

gwam 3' | 1 | 2 | 3 | 4 |

23 minutes

44c ● Formatting Problems: Personal Notes

Prepare to Format: Cut two sheets of 8½" by 11" paper in half. Beginning on line 4 (short side up), key your name and address on each sheet. Use clever arrangement of your name and address if you wish. Set off the return address with a line of hyphens as you did in 43d, Problem 3, on page 80. You will use these sheets in keying the following problems. (continued on next page)

Directions: Problem 2

Use a full sheet; 50-space line; follow Problem 1 directions.

COURTNEY SCHOOL ATHLETIC CLUB
Notice of Regular Meeting
October 12, 19--   3:45 p.m.
Conference Room
AGENDA
1. Approval of September 15 minutes
2. Report of the Treasurer, Alexis Nevel
3. Discussion of new business
    a. Need to plan fund-raisers
    b. Need to plan Annual Sports Banquet

LESSON 98

70-space line

5 minutes

98a ● Keyboard Review

Directions: Key each sentence three times SS. DS between 3-line groups.

key with a
flowing rhythm

alphabet	I know it is fully a more expensive job to organize or equip the dock.
figure	Since 1880, new inventions increased at a rate of 29 every 63 minutes.
shift key	Edmund Hillary and Tenzing Norkey scaled Mt. Everest in the Himalayas.
easy	It is often very helpful to be the one to know which way we are going.

| 1 | 2 | 3 | 4 | 5 | 6 | 7 | 8 | 9 | 10 | 11 | 12 | 13 | 14 |

10 minutes

98b ● Speed Builder

Directions: Take two 1' writings on each ¶; try to increase speed on the second writing. Figure *gwam.*

Alternate Procedure: Work for speed as you take one 5' writing on all three ¶s combined. Figure *gwam.*

all letters used   1.3 si

	gwam 1'		5'
Since the beginning of time, many forms of selling have gone on.	13	3	36
These sales were often paid for with a form of money or at times through	28	6	39
the exchange of goods. No matter how the seller might be paid, the key	42	8	41
item was being able to interest the buyer in the goods available.	55	11	44
In order to be the best in the sales field, the person selling must	14	14	47
keep in mind that you can never relax and just keep on doing things the	28	17	50
same way each day. If the seller fails to take changes in the needs and	43	20	53
wants of customers into account, the firm will surely fail.	54	22	55
Buyers who are not happy with the goods or services of a firm will	13	25	58
most of the time not tell the seller, but they will quickly seize the	27	27	60
chance to tell all of their friends or relatives. As a result, it is	41	30	63
very important for those in the sales field to know needs of customers.	55	33	66

gwam	1'	1	2	3	4	5	6	7	8	9	10	11	12	13	14
	5'			1				2				3			

44c, continued

Note: The lines in the problems are not set line for line as you will key them. Set margin stops properly; listen for the end-of-line signal.

Directions: Problem 1   Personal Note in Modified Block Style
1. Set margins for a 40-space line.
2. Key the personal note below in modified block style with blocked paragraphs and open punctuation. Use today's date and place the salutation on the 4th line space below the date.

Dear Indra

As secretary of the Drama Club at West Junior High School, I am pleased to announce that our annual free performances will be held on Wednesday, January 3, and Thursday, January 4.

Both performances will be given in the Little Theatre at 6 p.m.

All of our members hope to see a good turnout of students from Carson to enjoy the show.

Sincerely

Directions: Problem 2   Personal Note in Block Style
1. Set margins for a 40-space line.
2. Key the personal note below in block style with open punctuation. Use today's date.

Dear Julio

Thanks for sending me the extra set of prints. Your camera really does a great job. Of course, I don't want to take anything away from your skill as a photographer!

The pictures I took probably won't be nearly so good as yours, but then I used a camera that you throw away after the pictures have been developed. As soon as I finish this roll, I'll send copies of my best shots to you.

Good luck in the contest next week.

Sincerely

44d ● Extra Credit

Directions: Compose and key a reply to the personal note in Problem 1, explaining how many Carson students will attend. Use modified block style with indented paragraphs. Arrange your message neatly on the sheet; date the note three days from today.

LESSON 45

60-space line

5 minutes

45a ● Keyboard Review

Directions: Key each sentence 3 times SS. DS between 3-line groups.

alphabet   Jerry Diamond packed the fine quartz in twelve larger boxes.

fig/sym   Pam's cellular car phone cost $487 while mine was only $369.

easy   Their first goal is to make enough to own their own bicycle.

| 1 | 2 | 3 | 4 | 5 | 6 | 7 | 8 | 9 | 10 | 11 | 12 |

COURTNEY SCHOOL JOURNALISM CLUB
DS
Planning Meeting Notice
DS
October 1, 19--   3:15 p.m.
DS
Journalism Room
DS
AGENDA
DS
1. Introduction of adviser and staff

2. Discussion of school newspaper
    a. Completion dates
    b. The year's theme

3. Individual assignments
    a. Review of available assignments
    b. Duties required of each assignment
    c. Selection of student reporters
    d. Selection of support staff

4. Decision on deadline dates and times

5. Decision on future meeting dates

6. Selection of school newspaper editor

7. Adjournment by 4:00 p.m.

10 minutes

45b ● Timed Writings

Directions: 1. Take two 3′ writings on 44b, page 81. Proofread; circle errors.

2. Figure *gwam*; submit the better writing.

---

30 minutes

45c ● Formatting Problems: Postal Cards

Directions: Problem 1 Message

1. Insert a postal card or paper cut to size (5½″ × 3¼″) into your machine.

2. Set margin stops 4 spaces from each edge of the card. Set a tab stop at horizontal center.

3. Begin the date on line 3; then key the remaining lines as illustrated on the card.

```
 1
 2              begin 3 lines from top
 3                                        June 20, 19--
 4                                        ↑                    QS
 5  → 4 spaces                            └ center point
 6
 7      Dear Grandmother
 8                              DS
 9      Thank you very much for the check you sent for my
10      birthday.  You are certainly a generous lady.
11                                                      DS
12      I am planning to save the money and buy school
13      clothes with it this fall.  I'll let you know
14      what I get.  Have a good summer.
15                              DS
16              center point ——→ Cheryl
17
18
19
```

Directions: Problem 2 Address a Postal Card

1. Key the return address and the address of the recipient on the opposite side of the postal card you prepared in Problem 1.

2. Begin the return address on the second line from the top edge of the card and 3 spaces from the left edge.

3. Begin the address of the recipient about 2″ from the top of the card and 2″ from the left edge.

4. The 2-letter state abbreviations (keyed in capital letters without a period or space between) may be used, standard abbreviations may be used, or state names may be keyed in full.

Note: Addresses may be keyed in all caps with no punctuation (as illustrated here) or in both caps and lower case (as in the return address of the postal card). ZIP Code numbers are keyed two spaces after the 2-letter state abbreviation. The 2-letter state abbreviations are shown on page RG4.

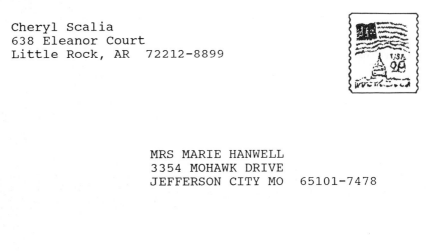

```
Cheryl Scalia
638 Eleanor Court
Little Rock, AR   72212-8899




            MRS MARIE HANWELL
            3354 MOHAWK DRIVE
            JEFFERSON CITY MO   65101-7478
```

LESSON 97

5 minutes

97a ● Keyboard Review

keep your eyes
on the copy
as you return

Directions: Key each sentence 3 times SS. DS between 3-line groups.

alphabet The six new big jet airliners flew quickly overhead at amazing speeds.

figure The sale of car phones grew from 68,945 in 1970 to 13,876,475 in 1990.

long words The prediction of future environment catastrophes appears pessimistic.

easy Many of the new jobs will be in the fields of theme and legal writing.

| 1 | 2 | 3 | 4 | 5 | 6 | 7 | 8 | 9 | 10 | 11 | 12 | 13 | 14 |

10 minutes

97b ● Control Ladder Paragraphs

Directions: 1. Take 1' writings on each ¶ in 96d, p. 171. Circle errors and figure *gwam*.
2. When you key a ¶ within the error limit specified by your teacher, move to the next ¶. Use control as you key this exercise.

97c ● Formatting Problems: Notices and Agendas of Meeting

30 minutes

Directions: Problem 1
1. On a full sheet, 50-space line, prepare the notice and agenda of a meeting from the copy below. Leave a 2" top margin; use the directions on the model, p. 173, as a guide for spacing copy.
2. The items in the third line (date and time) are to be keyed flush with left and right margins.

Note: To key an item flush with the right margin, tab to the right margin and backspace once for each character or space in the item. Begin keying where the backspacing ends.

Note: On some electronic machines and computers special function keys will automatically set up flush right margins for you.

COURTNEY SCHOOL JOURNALISM CLUB

Planning Meeting Notice

October 1, 19--   3:15 p.m.

Journalism Room

AGENDA

1. Introduction of adviser and staff

2. Discussion of school newspaper
    a. Completion dates
    b. The year's theme

3. Individual assignments
    a. Review of available assignments
    b. Duties required of each assignment
    c. Selection of student reporters
    d. Selection of support staff

4. Decision on deadline dates and times

5. Decision on future meeting dates

6. Selection of school newspaper editor

7. Adjournment by 4:00 p.m.

Directions: Problem 3   Postal Card in Modified Block Style

1. Prepare the following message on a postal card in modified block style. Use open punctuation (no punctuation after the salutation or complimentary close). SS the body of the message; use appropriate space between other message parts.

2. Use as the return address:

Rory Bannon
18 Hill Street
Your city, state, ZIP Code

3. Address the card to:

Miss Janine Ogas
829 North Kingston
Your city, state, ZIP code

Current date

Dear Janine

We are going to hold a rummage sale next Friday (use next Friday's date) at 4 p.m. Please bring clothing and small household items to the gym any day during the coming week.

We're counting on you to help make the sale a big success.

Rory Bannon
President, Pep Club

Directions: Problem 4   Postal Card in Block Style

1. Prepare the following message on a postal card in block style. Correct errors as indicated by the proofreader's marks.

2. Use as the return address:

Craig Vitale
3286 Wilson Avenue
Your city, state, ZIP Code

3. Address the card to:

Your name
Your street address
Your city, state, ZIP Code

Remember: When using the block style, begin the date and complimentary close at the left margin. Use open punctuation. SS the body of the message; use appropriate spacing between other parts of the message.

Use today's date

Dear *Use your name*

The student store has just placed∧orders *an* for 250 ninth-grade T-shirts. they come in several∧colors *bright* and contain the names of all dclass members. ~~They~~ *These shirts* ∧will be a real buy for only $10.75. ¶ By putting your name on the pre-order list∧ you can reserve yours for just $5. Sign up right away so your won't be left out.

Craig Vitale

45d ● Extra Credit

Directions: 1. Compose and key a reply to the message in Problem 4. Arrange the message neatly on a postal card.

2. Address the card to:

Craig Vitale
3286 Wilson Avenue
Your city, state, ZIP Code

3. Use your name and address for the return address.

96d ● Speed Ladder Paragraphs

Directions: 1. Take a 1' writing on ¶ 1 DS until you complete the ¶ in 1'.
2. When you complete ¶ 1 in 1', continue on to ¶ 2. Repeat this procedure as you try to complete each of the five ¶s in the given time.
3. Take three 1' writings on any ¶ you cannot finish in the given time.

all letters used 1.3 si

				gwam 5'

It may be hard to believe, but the average person spends more than — 3 | 52
two years of his/her lifetime talking on the telephone. This is the — 5 | 54
claim made by a group who has examined this form of voice communication. — 8 | 57

No one ever dreamed at the time of its invention that the telephone — 11 | 60
would become quite so popular and have such an impact on our social and — 14 | 63
our business lives. Who would have guessed that we would have computers — 17 | 66
using phone lines? — 18 | 67

Many people think that teenagers are the ones who spend the most — 20 | 69
time on the telephone. While this young group may use the telephone a — 23 | 72
lot more than they think, a large number of adults do spend their share — 26 | 75
of time on the line at work, and at home. — 27 | 76

Now, of course, the telephone can be used for a good deal more — 30 | 79
than just talking to someone. Phones enable computers to talk to one — 33 | 82
another. They help us send written messages as well as spoken ones. — 36 | 85
We can use them to do our banking and to pay our bills. — 38 | 87

As if all this is not amazing enough, consider the fact that the — 40 | 89
telephone can control the rest of our home appliances and serve as an — 43 | 92
intercom system. So far no one has been able to get one to walk the — 46 | 95
dog or run the bath water, but don't say it won't be done one of these — 49 | 98
days. — 49 | 98

gwam 5' | | 1 | | 2 | | 3 | |

96e ● Continuity Practice

Directions: Key the last paragraph of 96d as many times as you can in 5'.

Technique Goals: Work for continuous stroking, with eyes on copy, and with wrists and arms quiet.

LESSON 46

46a ● Keyboard Review

5 minutes

keep wrists
low and
still

Directions: Key each sentence 3 times SS. DS between 3-line groups.

alphabet Jake Hooper was not fazed by required large volume tax cuts.

fig/sym Key distances in figures: We drove 695 miles in 1 3/4 days.

easy They said she should get a bid from more than one rock band.

| 1 | 2 | 3 | 4 | 5 | 6 | 7 | 8 | 9 | 10 | 11 | 12 |

46b ● Language Arts Skills: Spelling and Proofreading Aid

5 minutes

keep fingers
deeply curved

Directions: Key each line 3 times. word as you key it.
SS. Study carefully the spelling of each

1 remittance laboratory signature proposal eligible sufficient

2 via cooperate analysis definite capacity develop commitments

3 tremendous beautiful essential consequently survey recommend

---

46c ● Timed Writings

15 minutes

Directions: 1. Take a 3' writing on the ¶s below. Figure *gwam.*

2. Take two 1' writings on each ¶; take the first for speed, the second for control.

3. Take another 3' writing on the ¶s below. Figure *gwam.* Compare the *gwam* and number of errors on this writing with your first 3' writing.

all letters used 1.2 si

	gwam 3'
Inventors the world over are hard at work churning out	4 | 45
all kinds of gizmos they think will improve the way we live.	8 | 49
Their goal is to help us save time, effort, or money.	11 | 52
We have been told for years that we will soon be talking	15 | 56
on video phones and going to work by air. Robots will take	19 | 60
care of the housework, they say. Some products succeed, of	23 | 64
course, while quite a few do not.	26 | 67
Take the picture phone, for example. Think what that	29 | 70
will do to your telephone habits. You might not answer so	33 | 74
quickly as you used to. You may want to let it ring several	37 | 78
times so you can adjust your tie or fix your hair first.	41 | 82

gwam 3' | 1 | 2 | 3 | 4 |

Unit 12 ▪ Keying for Club and Community Activities (Lessons 96–110)

Learning Goals:

1. To arrange and key a variety of written items used in club and community activities.

2. To develop further the necessary skills to use a typewriter and/or a computer as a tool for creative writing.

3. To learn to construct math signs by combining symbol keys.

General Directions

Use a 70-space line for all lessons in this unit (center − 35; center + 35 + 5) unless otherwise directed. SS sentences and drill lines; DS paragraphs. Your teacher will tell you whether or not you are to correct errors on the problems in this unit.

LESSON 96

5 minutes

96a ● Keyboard Review

Directions: Key each sentence three times SS. DS between 3-line groups.

keep wrists and elbows still

alphabet	Both larger sized computers make very quick jumps forward in new text.
figure	The principal locked rooms 24, 135, and 246, and opened rooms 8 and 9.
exa	I was exasperated and not exactly exalted by his exaggerated examples.
easy	When you write new themes, try to key your name the way you like best.

| 1 | 2 | 3 | 4 | 5 | 6 | 7 | 8 | 9 | 10 | 11 | 12 | 13 | 14 |

5 minutes

96b ● Making Times and Equal Signs

Times sign: Use a small letter *x* with a space before and after it.

Equal sign: Leave a space before and after the equal sign.

Directions: Key each sentence 3 times SS following the directions for making the *times* or *equal* signs. DS between 3-line groups.

1 The amount of interest is computed like this: $1,750 × .23 = $402.50.

2 You will be paid the minimum hourly rate: $4.25 × 35 hours = $148.75.

96c ● Language Arts Skills: Punctuation Guides (Semicolon) 10 minutes

Directions: The following are guides for the use of the semicolon and sentences that illustrate the use of those guides. Study each guide; then key the sentence(s) that illustrates the guide. Key each sentence or group of sentences twice SS; DS between groups.

think of the rules as you key the sentences

Use a semicolon between the clauses of a compound sentence when no conjunction is used.
The bus crash occurred at midnight; it was not reported until morning.
Take a careful look at the outline; you may wish to make some changes.

If a conjunction is used to join the clauses, use a comma between them.
There is little time left, but I will finish the projects on schedule.

Use a semicolon between the clauses of a compound sentence that are joined by such words as *also, however, therefore,* and *consequently.*
The surveys were very successful; consequently, we have a lot of data.
I plan to go ahead with the dance; however, it is subject to approval.

Use a semicolon to separate groups of words or figures if one or more of the groups contains a comma.
Sales were held in Houston, Texas; Washington, D.C.; and Reno, Nevada.

10 minutes

46d ● Technique Builder: Return Key

Directions: 1. Key the first line of the ¶ 3 times as your teacher gives the signal each 20". Return quickly; resume keying at once.

2. Repeat for lines 2, 3, 4, and 5.
3. Take a 1' writing on the entire ¶; DS without the call of the guide. Figure your *gwam*.

all letters used   1.2 si

	gwam 1'	20" guide
As amazing as it may sound, some health buffs now stand	11	33
in line at local fitness clubs just to climb stairs. We are	23	36
not talking about the kind required to transport you from one	36	36
floor to the next. These stairs are hooked up to machines	48	35
that remain still while you puff away on steps that move.	59	33

10 minutes

46e ● Language Arts Skills: Capitalization Guides

Directions: The following are capitalization guides and sentences that illustrate those guides.

Study each guide; key the line that illustrates the guide. Key each sentence twice SS; DS between 2-line groups.

keep eyes and mind on copy as you key

Capitalize the first word of a complete sentence.
English is spoken more widely today than any other language.

Capitalize the first word of a quoted sentence. (A period or comma is keyed before the ending quotation mark.)
It was Franklin who said, "A penny saved is a penny earned."

The names of school subjects, except languages and numbered courses, are not capitalized.
She is taking word processing, history, Math 10, and French.

Do not capitalize a quotation resumed within a sentence.
"When character is lost," a wise person said, "all is lost."

Capitalize the pronoun *I*, both alone and in contractions.
Unless I get there early, I'll have no chance to get a seat.

Capitalize titles of organizations, institutions, and buildings.
The Debate Club meets in the Fisk Building at Ripon College.

LESSON 47

60-space line

5 minutes

47a ● Keyboard Review

Directions: Key each sentence 3 times SS. DS between 3-line groups.

space quickly with down-and-in motion of thumb

alphabet Rex Fuji positively warned us smoking can be quite a hazard.

fig/sym Use their 800 number and order The Company We Keep ($12.95).

easy All of the big towns are right there at the end of the lake.

| 1 | 2 | 3 | 4 | 5 | 6 | 7 | 8 | 9 | 10 | 11 | 12 |

5 minutes | **95a ● Keyboard Review**

Directions: Key each sentence three times SS. DS between 3-line groups.

alphabet	Everybody expected a big kid my size to qualify for the javelin throw.
fig/sym	Cars that sold for $940 in the 1940's cost over $16,649 in the 1990's.
direct reaches	No doubt very many will obtain some piece of junk mail by Monday noon.
easy	It is your duty to try to win the games for your team and their firms.

| 1 | 2 | 3 | 4 | 5 | 6 | 7 | 8 | 9 | 10 | 11 | 12 | 13 | 14 |

---

10 minutes | **95b ● Timed Writings**

Directions: Take a 1' writing on 91c, page 164, with as few errors as possible. Take a 5' writing on the same ¶s. Circle errors and figure *gwam.*

---

30 minutes | **95c ● Formatting Problems: Writing a Report**

Directions: Problem 1   Title Page
Use the information at the right to format/key the title page for your leftbound report. If necessary, refer to 85c, page 155.

```
WRITING A REPORT

Your Name

Keyboarding II

Current Date
```

Directions: Problem 2   Bibliography
Format/key the bibliography for your leftbound report from the information given below. If necessary, refer to page 156. After you complete the bibliography, assemble your report. Place the title page on top, followed by the final outline, the body of the report, and the bibliography. Bind the pages at the left.

Bartky, Joyce and Yvonne Kuhlman. <u>Spectrum of English</u>. Encino: Glencoe Publishing Company, Inc., 1979.

Fraier, Jacob J., and Flora Morris Brown. <u>Effective English 7</u>. Morristown: Silver Burdette Company, 1985.

Glatthorn, Allan A. <u>Composition Skills</u>. Chicago: Science Research Associates, Inc., 1985.

Roberts, F. "A Revolution in Writing." <u>Parents</u>, October, 1983, p. 52.

Warriner, John E., and Sheila Laws Graham. <u>English Grammar and Composition, Second Course</u>. New York: Harcourt Brace Jovanovich, Inc., 1987.

Note: If you are using a computer, do not rekey the entire report; just make the necessary format changes.

95d ● Enrichment Activity

Directions: Problem 1
Format/key a short leftbound report based on the subject given in the outline in 87c, problem 2, page 159. Follow the rules given in the outline in 87c, problem 1, for keying a leftbound report.

Directions: Problem 2
Format/key the report you prepared in problem 1 except this time prepare it in an unbound report format.

5 minutes

47b ● Language Arts Skills: Keying from Dictation and Spelling Checkup

Directions: 1. Your teacher will dictate the words in 46b, page 85. Key the words from dictation.

2. Check your work for correct spelling. Rekey any words in which you made an error.

---

5 minutes

47c ● Continuity Practice from Rough Draft Copy

Directions: Key the ¶ at least twice DS. Make corrections as you work.

Listen for the end-of-line signal to know when to strike the return key.

all letters   1.2 si

words

While high/tech has equipped us with tools to handle   11

lots of ~~many~~ tough jobs, it has caused a few problems too. For ~~one~~   23

one thing, it gives us informatoin faster than we/can utilize   35

it. machines have done what they can do, *but* we have been   47

taxed to keep up with them.   52

---

5 minutes

47d ● Steps for Formatting Personal/Business Letters

Directions: Read the steps for formatting personal/business letters below. You will need this information when you key/

format the personal/business letters in 47e.

Step 1 Set your machine for single spacing.

Step 2 Set your margins. The margins vary according to the length of the letter.

Step 3 Space down to begin the return address. (The number of lines to space down varies with the length of the letter. The longer the letter, the fewer the number of spaces.) For a modified block style letter, start the return address at the center point of the paper. For a block style letter, start the return address at the left margin.

Step 4 Space down 4 times below the return address to the letter address.

Step 5 Begin the salutation a DS below the letter address.

Step 6 Begin the body of the letter a DS below the salutation. SS the paragraphs; DS between paragraphs.

Step 7 Begin the complimentary close a DS below the body of the letter. For a modified block style letter, start at the center point. For a block style letter, start at the left margin.

Step 8 Key the name of the writer on the 4th line space below the complimentary close. (The keyed name of the writer is optional.)

---

25 minutes

47e ● Formatting Problems: Personal/Business Letters
in Modified Block Style

Directions: Problem 1   Letter with Blocked Paragraphs, Open Punctuation

Key/format the letter on page 88. Use a full sheet, 50-space line, open punctuation. Follow the formatting steps given above as well as the directions given on the model letter, page 88.

Directions: Problem 2   Letter with Indented Paragraphs, Open Punctuation

Using a full sheet, 50-space line, open punctuation, key the letter in Problem 1 again. Indent the first line of each paragraph 5 spaces. Listen for the end-of-line signal to know when to return to the next line.

LESSON 94

5 minutes **94a ● Keyboard Review**

Directions: Key each sentence three times SS. DS between 3-line groups.

alphabet I quickly bought just one extra pass to watch from that very end zone.

fig/sym "All" of today's knowledge may likely increase (50%) by the year 2020.

adjacent keys We asked them to polish and weigh the brass pot prior to its delivery.

easy Kyle may not work for the firm until they do the audits they promised.

| 1 | 2 | 3 | 4 | 5 | 6 | 7 | 8 | 9 | 10 | 11 | 12 | 13 | 14 |

---

7 minutes **94b ● Language Arts Skills: Punctuation Guides for Commas**

Directions: The following are punctuation guides and sentences that illustrate the use of commas.

Study each guide; key the sentence that illustrates the guide. Key each sentence twice SS; DS between 2-line groups.

Use commas to set off interrupting words that are nonessential to the sentence.
The state income tax, however, will go into effect sometime next year.

Use a comma to set off interjections (yes, no, well) if there is a break in continuity.
Yes, all citizens of the state will be required to pay the income tax.

Use commas to set off the name of the person addressed.
The show, Jon, is next Friday. Carmella, do you have the new tickets?

Use commas to separate dates from years and cities from states.
An earthquake occurred October 17, 1989, in San Francisco, California.

---

8 minutes **94c ● Speed Builder**

Directions: 1. Take a 1' writing. The last word keyed will be your goal word.
2. Take a 5' writing with the return called after each minute. When the return is called, start the ¶ over again. Try to reach your goal each minute as the return is called.

all letters used   1.3 si

sit erect;
feet flat
on the floor

       •   4   •   8   •   12
The need to excel is very often present in all of us. That is why
  •   16   •   20   •   24
we quickly try to do the best on every job we undertake. Even though
 28   •   32   •   36   •   40
some duties appear to be breezes, it is important to prepare. All of
 •   44   •   48   •   52
us can excel in some duties, but it's unlikely that some will be able
 56   •   60
to excel in nearly all tasks.

---

25 minutes **94d ● Formatting Problem**

Directions: Continue keying the leftbound report as directed in 92c, page 165.

Keep margins and spacing uniform throughout the manuscript.

words

return address   center point   1328 Jerome Drive   2
                                      Plano, TX   75025-2271   8
                dateline   January 18, 19--   11

space down 4 times
(4 line spaces)

letter address   Mr. Jaime Magana   15
                     Alpha Office Systems   19
                     840 Sako Drive   22
                     Plano, TX   75023-1599   27
                                    DS

salutation   Dear Mr. Magana   30
                                  DS

body of   On behalf of the Computer Club members at Monroe   40
letter   Junior High School, I want to thank you for speaking   50
                 at our meeting last Thursday.   56
                                DS

You made a very complex subject clear and kept your   67
remarks entertaining at the same time.   Several of   77
the students told me they thought this program was   87
the best one we have had all year.   94
                                  DS

So far, 14 people have signed up for the field trip   105
to your store on Career Day.   We are looking forward   115
to seeing you again and to getting some hands-on   125
experience using the new software you described.   135
                                  DS

complimentary close   center point   Sincerely yours   138

space down 4 times
(4 line spaces)

keyed name   Miss Kelly Spencer   142

This style, with minor variations, is used in many personal/business letters.
Open punctuation is used; no marks of punctuation are used after the
salutation or complimentary close. A man need not use Mr. in his keyed or
handwritten name at the end of a letter. A woman may use her personal
title (Miss, Ms., or Mrs.) with her keyed name as a courtesy. This allows a
person to respond to a woman's letter using her preferred personal title.

92c, continued

The title page contains the name of the report and its writer. The bibliography contains titles of references that have been consulted.

It will pay you to learn how to write clear, interest-holding papers. It's not an easy job, but with a plan to guide you and some practice, you can turn out good work on your machine.

[1]John E. Warriner and Sheila Laws Graham, <u>English Grammar and Composition, Second Course,</u> (New York: Harcourt Brace Jovanovich, Inc., 1987), p. 376.

[2]Ibid., p. 377.

LESSON 93

5 minutes

93a ● Keyboard Review

Directions: Key each sentence three times SS. DS between 3-line groups.

alphabet Extras that just may quickly give us wins are briefer play zone codes.

fig/sym Roberto bought a CD player on May 5 for $213.04 with a discount (30%).

eve Do you ever wonder why every electric bill is higher for the evenings?

easy The money you will earn will depend on how well you prepare your work.

| 1 | 2 | 3 | 4 | 5 | 6 | 7 | 8 | 9 | 10 | 11 | 12 | 13 | 14 |

---

10 minutes

93b ● Speed Builder

Alternate Procedure:
Work for speed as you take one 5' writing on all three ¶s combined. Figure *gwam*.

Directions: Take two 1' writings on each ¶; try to increase speed on the second writing. Figure *gwam.*

all letters used 1.3 si

	gwam 1'	5'

Turning waste into building materials is a new process for reducing — 14 | 3 | 38

huge amounts of trash that every one of us discards each day. A new firm — 28 | 6 | 41

has developed a process that cuts up waste in very small parts and then — 42 | 8 | 43

adds water and clay. The ending mixture is then baked under quite high — 57 | 11 | 46

temperatures to form materials used to make light weight blocks. — 70 | 14 | 49

The heat used to make the blocks can be used to generate electric — 13 | 17 | 52

power at the same time. This extra does not cost any more. It appears — 28 | 19 | 54

to be a way to convert waste without adding any new hazards. If this — 42 | 22 | 57

develops, we will certainly be a long way ahead of where we are now in — 56 | 25 | 60

our efforts to use up the growing tons of waste. — 65 | 27 | 62

Who knows, the next home you notice may be constructed of blocks or — 14 | 30 | 65

other products that were just developed from the trash that every one of — 28 | 33 | 68

us discards every day of the week. Only the future holds the answer. — 42 | 35 | 70

gwam 1' | 1 | 2 | 3 | 4 | 5 | 6 | 7 | 8 | 9 | 10 | 11 | 12 | 13 | 14 |
     5' | | 1 | | | 2 | | | 3 | | |

---

30 minutes

93c ● Formatting Problem

Directions: Continue keying the leftbound report in 92c, page 165.

LESSON 48

5 minutes

48a ● Keyboard Review

Directions: Key each sentence 3 times SS. DS between 3-line groups.

alphabet Val Gumis will quickly explain the fire hazards on this job.

fig/sym Megan keyed a 5-minute writing on page 76 with 98% accuracy.

easy The right angle to use in solving problems is the try angle.

| 1 | 2 | 3 | 4 | 5 | 6 | 7 | 8 | 9 | 10 | 11 | 12 |

10 minutes

48b ● Paragraph Guided Writings

Directions: **1.** Take a 1′ writing on the ¶ below. Note the last word you keyed, make this your goal word.
2. Take three 1′ writings on the ¶. Try to reach your goal word as time is called. Key no faster or slower than it takes to reach your goal word.
3. Raise your goal by 4 words. Take 3 additional 1′ writings. Try to reach your new goal as time is called.

all letters used   1.2 si

One major use of the computer can be found in the world of art.   With its help experts can now analyze all the layers of paint that a finished work might contain.   It can give to them in an instant details that once would have required years to find.

30 minutes

48c ● Formatting Problems: Preparing a Personal/Business Letter and Small Envelope

Directions: **Problem 1   Letter with Blocked Paragraphs, Open Punctuation**

Key/format the letter below using a full sheet, 50-space line, open punctuation. Begin the return address on line 18; use today's date and your own address as the return address. Listen for the end-of-line signal to determine line endings. Sign the letter.

When you supply the information, 11 words are counted for the return address and date.

	words
	return address 11
	and date
Ms. Sonja Wilson	14
Vista Travel	17
Your city, state, and ZIP Code	23
Dear Ms. Wilson	26
(¶) When my parents returned home from their vacation,	36
they said your agency was planning to sponsor a	46
family cruise during the Easter holiday season.	56
(¶) My brother and I hope to interest them in taking us	66
on this cruise, but we need some help. If you will	77
please send some materials describing the special	87
family tour, we think we can get them to go.	95
Yours very truly	99

WRITING A REPORT

QS

Famous authors do not become great writers overnight. The process almost always begins with a desire to write about an idea, topic, or feeling that interests the writer. This strong desire is followed by a process that includes writing, starting over, rewriting, and perhaps coming out with a good page. Yes, many of our great writers probably had more paper in their wastebaskets than they had finished copy on their desks.

Most of us do not have any burning desire to become great literary geniuses. Even if we did, it is not likely that we could do so easily. The great writers whom we know about have worked long and hard at perfecting their writing skill. We can, however, learn how to write a short paper that is clear and interesting without having to master the skills of great authors. Let's see how you might go about this task.

Steps for Preparing a Report

Choose the right subject. To begin with, you need to select a subject you know something about. One authority says such a choice may be the most important decision you make in planning and writing your composition.[1] You can't write about the growing of figs unless you know how figs are grown. However, you can get information from books, from talks with fig growers, or from growing figs yourself.

Limit your subject. Don't try to cover too much ground in your paper. Young writers often butt their heads against this wall without getting anything more than a sore head for their trouble. As Warriner says, "Probably more student compositions turn out badly because their subjects are too broad than for any other reason."[2]

Narrow your subject down. Write about the kind of soil fig trees like or how figs are prepared for the market. You can't cover the whole life of a fig, from seedling to fig sauce, in two hundred words, no matter how skilled you become as a writer.

Prepare a preliminary outline. Jot down the major topics you expect to cover. This is the preliminary outline. It consists only of a number of topic headings. No subpoints need to be included.

Prepare bibliography cards. After you select a subject and prepare your preliminary outline, you must find out where you can obtain the information you need. For most students, books and articles will furnish the needed help.

As you find books and articles that appear to be helpful, write their titles on cards. On each card, write complete information about a single reference so the card can be used later to prepare the footnotes and bibliography for your paper.

Read and take notes. Start your reading. As you read, take notes. Record important facts, ideas, and quotations on note cards so that you can refer to them as you write your paper.

Each note card should be given a heading which describes the notes. Use one of the main headings of your preliminary outline, if you can, to identify each card. Write each note on a separate card. In every case, indicate the page number and reference from which the note was taken.

Prepare the final outline. When you have taken notes on all your readings, organize your cards in some order. This will usually be determined by the order of the points in the preliminary outline. You may find that some of the main points should now be changed. Try to group the cards under each major point into two or more subgroups. These will make up the subpoints of your outline.

Remember that an outline shows clearly what points are the most important as well as those that are less important. The Roman numerals show the chief ideas. The capital letters and Arabic numerals give details under the main points.

Steps for Writing a Report

Write the first draft. The first writing of a paper will usually not be the final one. Present the material you have collected. Don't worry too much about words, spelling, and keying mistakes.

Revise the first draft. When the first draft has been completed, check it for wording and mistakes. Mark your corrections with a pen or pencil. Careful writers read and correct their copy two or three times to make sure that their papers read well. It is recommended that you do this too.

Prepare the final copy. Good appearance in papers is important. Follow accepted rules for keying the final copy. Pay close attention to margins, placement of footnotes, and other similar details.

Prepare the title page and bibliography. Long, formal reports usually have a title page and bibliography.

(continued on next page)

48c, continued   **Directions: Problem 2   Addressing a Small Envelope**

1. Use a small envelope or paper cut to size (6½" × 3⅝").

2. Address the envelope for the letter you prepared in 47e, page 88. Follow the placement directions on the model envelope illustrated below.

3. Fold the letter and insert it in the envelope (if you are using an envelope). Follow the procedures for folding letters illustrated below.

```
Miss Kelly Spencer  ◄─── line 2
1328 Jerome Drive
Plano, TX  75025-2271
└ 3 spaces     └ 2 spaces
```

about 2 inches
(line 12)

about 2½ inches ────►
```
MR JAIME MAGANA
ALPHA OFFICE SYSTEMS
840 SAKO DRIVE
PLANO TX  75023-1599
        └ 2 spaces
```

1. Key the writer's name and return address in the upper left corner as shown in the illustration. Begin on the second line space from the top edge and 3 spaces from the left edge.

2. Key the receiver's name about 2 inches (line 12) from the top of the envelope. Start about 2½ inches from the left edge. Addresses may be keyed in all caps with no punctuation or in both caps and lower case.

3. Use block style and single spacing for all addresses. City and state names and ZIP Codes (see p. RG4 for ZIP Code abbreviations) must be placed on one line in that order.

4. The state name may be keyed in full, or it may be abbreviated using the standard abbreviation or, preferably, the 2-letter state abbreviation.

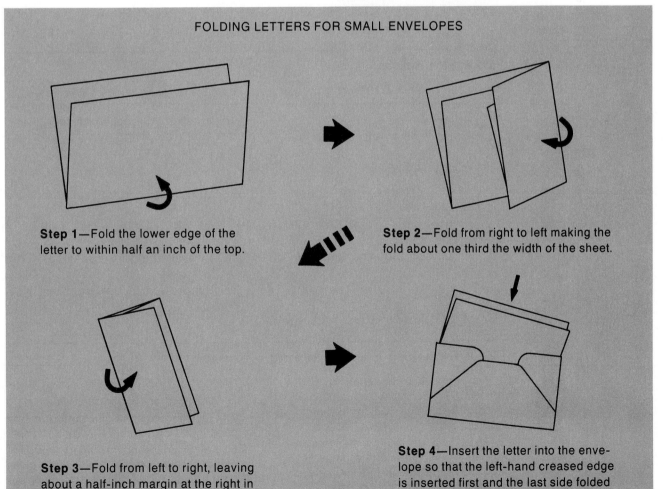

FOLDING LETTERS FOR SMALL ENVELOPES

Step 1—Fold the lower edge of the letter to within half an inch of the top.

Step 2—Fold from right to left making the fold about one third the width of the sheet.

Step 3—Fold from left to right, leaving about a half-inch margin at the right in order that the letter may be opened easily.

Step 4—Insert the letter into the envelope so that the left-hand creased edge is inserted first and the last side folded is toward the backside of the envelope.

10 minutes

91e ● Compose at Your Machine

Directions: 1. Key the following quotation and a short paragraph explaining what it means to you.
2. Using proofreader's marks, correct your printed copy.
3. Set a 60-space line. On a full sheet of paper, rekey the paragraph; leave a 2″ top margin.

Note: If you are using a computer, make your edited changes on the screen and print a final copy.

The mayor said, "Our environment will be in serious future difficulty."

LESSON 92

70-space line

5 minutes

92a ● Keyboard Review

Directions: Key each sentence three times SS. DS between 3-line groups.

alphabet The major quickly gave the extra field prizes to the best new winners.

figure If I subtract 3,460 from 4,337, I will get 877 for the correct answer.

shift Thomas Alva Edison started on many inventions in Menlo Park, New York.

easy It is our duty to be there when a new item is to be given to the town.

| 1 | 2 | 3 | 4 | 5 | 6 | 7 | 8 | 9 | 10 | 11 | 12 | 13 | 14 |

---

10 minutes

92b ● Skill Builder

Directions: 1. Take a 1′ writing on the ¶ below. The last word keyed will be your goal word.
2. Take a 5′ writing with the return called after each minute. When the return is called, start the ¶ over again. Try to reach your goal each minute as the return is called.

1.3 si

keep a steady flowing rhythm

If the latest reports are on target, it seems that there will be
two basic classes of jobs in the near future. One class will be in the
service industry and the other one in information managing. This may
mean that all of us will need to learn more about how to work with data
and how to work with people.

---

30 minutes

92c ● Formatting Problem: Writing a Report

Directions: 1. Key the report on pages 166 & 167 DS. Follow the directions given in 84b, page 153 for leftbound reports.
2. Refer to page 108 for assistance in formatting the two side headings in this report. The paragraph headings are indented 5 spaces and underlined.

Format as shown in the report on page 166.
3. All pages are to be numbered.
4. Place footnotes at the bottom of the page in which reference is made to them.
5. Key as much of the report as you can in the time given. You will be given time in Lessons 93 and 94 to complete the report.

(continued on next page)

Directions: Problem 3   Addressing Small Envelopes

1. Address envelopes for the four names and addresses listed below. Use small envelopes or paper cut to size (6½″ × 3⅝″).

2. Use your name and address as sender. Follow the spacing directions given on the model envelope on page 90.

Ms. Eileen Houtzer
1608 Ridge Road
Cheyenne, WY 82001-4703

Mr. Kevin E. Lollar
25 Fulton Avenue
Birmingham, AL 35217-8846

Custom Designers, Ltd.
84 Laurier E.
OTTAWA (ONTARIO)
CANADA
KIM 6N6

Mrs. Joanne Sanchez
1924 Poplar Lane
Louisville, KY 40299-7043

LESSON 49
60-space line

5 minutes

49a ● Keyboard Review

Directions: Key each sentence 3 times SS. DS between 3-line groups.

key with your fingers; keep wrists and arms still

alphabet   Jeff expects to have two dozen big aprons made very quickly.

fig/sym   Underline magazine titles: The Futurist, Vogue, and People.

easy   Their problem was to enter the figures right the first time.

| 1 | 2 | 3 | 4 | 5 | 6 | 7 | 8 | 9 | 10 | 11 | 12 |

10 minutes

49b ● Paragraph Guided Writings

Directions: 1. Take a 1′ writing on the ¶ below. Note the last word you keyed; make this your goal word.

2. Take three 1′ writings on the ¶. Try to reach your goal word as time is

called. Key no faster or slower than it takes to reach your goal word.

3. Raise your goal by 4 words. Take 3 additional 1′ writings. Try to reach your new goal as time is called.

use quick, crisp, short strokes

all letters used   1.2 si

To the child who has a new hammer, states an old maxim,
everything becomes a nail.   Some of us seem to apply this
law of the hammer when it comes to the computer.   In our zeal
to get things done quickly, we try to use it to perform tasks
for which it is just not well suited.

Mixed Punctuation: When using mixed punctuation, key a colon after the salutation and a comma after the complimentary close. All other parts are punctuated the same as in open punctuation.

49c ● Formatting Problems: Letters with Mixed Punctuation   30 minutes

Directions: Problem 1   Personal/Business Letter in Modified Block Style, Indented Paragraphs, Mixed punctuation

Key/format the letter on page 92. Use a full sheet, 50-space line, modified block style with indented ¶s and mixed

punctuation. Begin the return address on line 15. Address an envelope (or paper cut to size). If an envelope is used, fold and insert the letter.

91c ● Speed Ladder Paragraphs

Directions: Take a 1' writing on ¶ 1 DS. When you complete ¶ 1 in 1', repeat the procedure on succeeding ¶ s.

Take three 1' writings on any ¶ you do not finish in the time given.

Alternate Procedure: Work on control as you take a 1' writing on ¶ 1. Move to succeeding ¶ s when you complete each one within the error limit specified by your teacher. If time allows repeat any ¶ s in which you exceeded the error limit.

all letters used   1.3 si

		gwam 5'
For a long time the sports interests of our nation have stayed the	3	48
same. Recently, a sport that is old to most of the world is becoming	5	50
quite well liked by players in our nation.	7	52
Soccer, the world's most popular sport, may soon become one of our	10	55
nation's newest pastimes. Players on each team hit a round ball with	13	58
any body part except their hands. This proves quite exciting.	15	60
Many of us have read how fans can really get into the game. There	18	63
have been games in which fans have created riots when the home team is	21	66
losing. In Brazil the field has a moat on both sides to keep fans and	23	68
players apart.	24	69
Yet, the new sport has not yet taken over first place in our world	27	72
of sports. The fans in our country still support many of the old ball	30	75
games such as baseball, football, and basketball. Still it looks as if	32	77
soccer may soon end up a major sport.	34	79
It appears our current sports may be taking a back seat to the	36	81
game of soccer. What is to happen in the future will, of course, not	39	84
be decided for a few years. It will take a long time for our fans to	42	87
make a change. No matter when and how it occurs, it is likely to be	45	90
very exciting.	45	90

gwam 5' | 1 | 2 | 3 |

91d ● Correcting Errors: Spreading Letters

Directions: 1. Key the sentence as it appears with the error in *extra*.

2. Remove the incorrect word.

3. Move the carrier to the space where the e was keyed in exttra. Use either the half-backspace mechanism or the incremental back-spacer key,

whichever is on your machine, and strike the letter e.

4. Repeat this procedure to key xtra.

5. On a computer move the cursor to the space where the t was keyed in exttra and using the delete function key delete the t.

Error: Correct the exttra letter.

Correction: Correct the extra letter.

	words
2940 Stewart Road	4
Cedar Rapids, IA 52403-8896	9
April 24, 19--	12

Mr. Jeff Carlson, Manager — 18
Carlson's Calco Service — 22
87 Waconia Avenue — 26
Cedar Rapids, IA 52404-3679 — 32

use a colon after the salutation

Dear Mr. Carlson: — 35

Thank you for offering the facilities of your service station — 48 for our annual car wash on Saturday, May 1. — 57

We plan to have our members work in 4-hour shifts, be- — 67 ginning at 8 a.m. and ending at 8 p.m. Ten students will be — 80 assigned to each shift. — 85

You can depend on us to do a good job and to leave your — 96 station neat and clean. Please call me at 295-3966 if there is — 108 anything special we need to do to prepare for this important — 121 event. — 122

use a comma after the complimentary close

Sincerely yours, — 125

Angela Borrego, President — 130
Spanish Club — 133

Directions: Problem 2   Personal/Business Letter in Unarranged Form

Key/format the letter below on a full sheet, 50 space line. Use modified block style, indented ¶ s, mixed punctuation.

Begin the return address on line 16; use today's date. Address an envelope (or paper cut to size). Fold and insert the letter.

Return Address: **Mastin Middle School** | Tampa, FL 33647-2284 | Today's — 10 date | Letter Address: **Mr. Mark Cox** | President, Language Club | — 18 Dodds School | Tampa, FL 33605-0150 | Dear Mark: — 27

On Friday, March 9, a group of 24 students and one — 38 teacher from the Gymnasium Wolbeck is scheduled to arrive at — 50 the Tampa airport. They will be on our campus for two weeks. — 62 The German/American Partners program ends on March 24. — 73

We are holding a reception for them next Monday, March — 84 13, at 8:15 a.m. in our Little Theatre. Please let me know how — 97 many of your students will be able to join us in welcoming our — 110 European guests. — 113

Sincerely, | Ms. Kathryn Ricks — 119

90b, continued

Note Card 2

Heading: Planning the report
Notes: 1. Select a topic of interest.
2. Make a listing of information sources.
3. Check resources for important information.
4. Write key ideas.
Reference: Tompkins, p. 87.

Note Card 3

Heading: Completing the first outline
Notes: The first outline of a paper helps to finalize ideas and provides a map of how to put these ideas together to produce an organized report.
Reference: Piotrowski, p. 55.

---

15 minutes

90c ● Timed Writings

Directions: 1. Take one 1′ writing on each ¶ of 86d, page 157. Circle errors.

2. Take one 5′ writing on all five ¶s combined. Circle errors; figure *gwam*.

LESSON 91

70-space line

5 minutes

91a ● Keyboard Review

Directions: Key each sentence three times SS. DS between 3-line groups.

keep wrists and arms still

alphabet He was very glad and excited to win a bronze medal for the quick jump.

fig/sym Check #568 (dated July 8) was sent to Long & Smith Company early today.

adjacent keys The new engineer's performance, compared to others, was well prepared.

easy Do not tell others of their faults until you have no more of your own.

| 1 | 2 | 3 | 4 | 5 | 6 | 7 | 8 | 9 | 10 | 11 | 12 | 13 | 14 |

---

5 minutes

91b ● Language Arts Skills: Number Expression Guides

Directions: The following are fraction number guides and sentences that illustrate those guides. Study each guide; then key the sentence that illustrates the guide. Key each sentence twice SS; DS between 2-line groups.

Made fractions are used when the fraction is not on the keyboard.
"Made" fractions should be keyed in this way: 2/3, 1/5, 3/4, and 7/8.

Space between whole numbers and *made* fractions.
They needed 7 2/3 yards of wool and 6 1/2 yards of silk for their job.

Be uniform when you key fractions: ½ and ¼, but 1/2 and 2/5.
*If all fractions you need are located on the keyboard, key: ½ and ¼.

Note: Some computer and electronic keyboards do not contain fraction keys. When using these machines, you must construct all fractions.

LESSON 50

5 minutes

50a ● Keyboard Review

Directions: Key each sentence 3 times SS. DS between 3-line groups.

key steadily;
do not pause
between letters
or words

alphabet   Jack expects to be in Quincy for a visit with Zelda Goodman.

fig/sym   The 692 3/4 acres of land sold for more than $1,578 an acre.

easy   Make sure that the fuel is kept where there will be no risk.

| 1 | 2 | 3 | 4 | 5 | 6 | 7 | 8 | 9 | 10 | 11 | 12 |

5 minutes

50b ● Addressing a Large Envelope and Folding Letters for Insertion

Directions: Read the directions and study the illustrations below for addressing large envelopes and folding and inserting letters into large envelopes. You will need this information to prepare envelopes for letters you key for 50c, p. 94.

A large envelope (9½" × 4⅛") is usually prepared for business letters or for letters of more than one page. Key the writer's name and return address as you did on a small envelope (and as directed on the model at the right). Addresses may be keyed in all caps with no punctuation or in both caps and lower case with punctuation. Begin the name and address of the receiver 2½" from the top and 4" from the left edge of the envelope. Use block style and single spacing as you did for a small envelope (see page 90).

Ms. Julie Kamansky ←——— line 2
Park Junior High School
398 Rogers Road
Omaha, NE ↑ 68124-0011
└ 3 spaces └ 2 spaces

about 2½ inches
(line 15)

about 4 inches ————→ Mr. David Dondero
Dondero, Inc.
2319 Missouri Avenue
Omaha, NE ↑ 68107-2099
└ 2 spaces

FOLDING LETTERS FOR LARGE ENVELOPES

Step 1—Fold from bottom to top, making the fold slightly less than one third the length of the sheet.

Step 2—Fold the top down to within one half inch of the bottom fold.

Step 3—Insert the letter into the envelope with the last crease toward the bottom of the envelope and with the last fold up.

Bibliographical Card 2

Author:	Glatthorn, Allan A.
Title:	<u>Composition Skills</u>
Publisher:	Chicago: Science Research Associates, Inc., 1985
Short Description:	Explains composition process. Includes sentence and paragraph construction in writing the complete paper.
Library Call No.:	c 425.2028 G466

Bibliographical Card 3

Author:	Fraier, Jacob J. and Flora Morris Brown
Title:	<u>Effective English 7</u>
Publisher:	Morristown: Silver Burdette Company, 1985
Short Description:	Content includes grammar, usage, composition, speaking and listening, mechanics and reference.
Library Call No.:	c 372.602 K658

LESSON 90

70-space line

5 minutes

90a ● Keyboard Review

Directions: Key each sentence three times SS. DS between 3-line groups.

alphabet Victor's band may just win a quick prize for their next new love song.

figure More than 3,880 girls and 2,776 boys took the writing courses in 1992.

4th finger The play will open in April. Lloyd will stop playing most poor parts.

easy You can win the test only when you are the best at what you try to do.

| 1 | 2 | 3 | 4 | 5 | 6 | 7 | 8 | 9 | 10 | 11 | 12 | 13 | 14 |

25 minutes

Note cards contain ideas, facts, and quotations to be used in preparing the body of a report.

Note: If you are using a computer, rule the outline of the card size on your printer paper.

90b ● Formatting Problem: Note Cards

Directions: 1. Prepare the following note cards on 5" × 3" cards or paper cut to size. Key the first card from the illustration below, the second and third from the information that follows on page 163.

2. Begin the first entry a DS below the top edge of the card and 3 spaces from the left edge.

```
           ┌─ 3 spaces          DS
heading    │ Rules for making note cards
           │
notes        A note card should carry only one idea.

             The topic heading is placed in the upper left-
             hand corner and is usually taken from the
             preliminary outline.

             Reference to the source is placed in the lower
             left-hand corner of the card.
                                    DS
reference    Sigband, pp. 39-40.
```

(continued on next page)

50c ● Formatting Problems: Personal Business Letters in Block Style

Directions: Problem 1

Key/format the letter below using a full sheet, 50-space line, block style, open punctuation. Begin the return address on line 16 at the left margin. Sign the letter. Address a large envelope as shown on page 93.

Return Address: Park Junior High School| 398 Rogers Road| Omaha, NE 68124-0011| April 27, 19-- Letter Address: Mr. David Dondero| Dondero, Inc.| 2319 Missouri Avenue| Omaha, NE 68107-2099

Dear Mr. Dondero

As secretary of the Park Junior High School student body, I have the pleasure of welcoming you as one of the participants in our Job Fair on May 5. Mr. Lyons, our vice principal, has asked me to provide you with the information you will need.

Parking has been reserved in the faculty lot on the west side of the campus. Students will be stationed there to escort you to your room.

You are scheduled to speak to two different groups of students. Your morning session will begin at 10:15, and your afternoon session at 1:15. Each is planned for 45 minutes.

We appreciate your taking the time to help us.

Sincerely yours| Ms. Julie Kamansky| Student Body Secretary

Letter shown in block style:

begin return address at left margin

Park Junior High School
398 Rogers Road
Omaha, NE 68124-0011
April 27, 19--

Mr. David Dondero
Dondero, Inc.
2319 Missouri Avenue
Omaha, NE 68107-2099

Dear Mr. Dondero

As secretary of the Park Junior High School student body, I have the pleasure of welcoming you as one of the participants in our Job Fair on May 5. Mr. Lyons, our vice principal, has asked me to provide you with the information you will need.

Parking has been reserved in the faculty lot on the west side of the campus. Students will be stationed there to escort you to your room.

You are scheduled to speak to two different groups of students. Your morning session will begin at 10:15, and your afternoon session at 1:15. Each is planned for 45 minutes.

We appreciate your taking the time to help us.

begin closing lines at left margin

Sincerely yours

Ms. Julie Kamansky
Student Body Secretary

Directions: Problem 2

Key/format the letter below using a full sheet, 50-space line, block style, open punctuation. Begin the return address on line 16 at the left margin. Listen for the end-of-line signal to determine line endings. Sign the letter; address a large envelope; fold and insert the letter.

Return Address: 106 Chestnut Avenue| Kansas City, MO 64801-2357| February 17, 19--| Letter Address: Mrs. Loretta Carpenter| Midstates Office Equipment| 2525 Horseshoe Drive| Kansas City, MO 64804-3925| Dear Mrs. Carpenter

Your advertisement in last Tuesday's Herald caught the attention of me and my co-workers on our school newspaper staff.

According to the ad, your new LX 1400 electronic typewriter is equipped with full line correction and automatic centering. It also features a 50,000-word dictionary.

You mentioned that this machine is surprisingly affordable, but you did not include the price. Will you please let me know what this typewriter would cost us and whether we are entitled to any kind of school discount.

Yours very truly| Rick Tellier

5 minutes   **89a ● Keyboard Review**

Directions: Key each sentence three times SS. DS between 3-line groups.

alphabet   I quickly mixed and just played zooming tunes which were very big fun.

fig/sym   Your 1992 class trip (April 24-30) has been changed to November 25-30.

long reaches   Don must decide how curved fingers helped when keying special numbers.

easy   Both of us tried to audit all of the new firms with little or no help.

---

5 minutes   **89b ● Speed Ladder Sentences**

Directions: Key each sentence for 1'. Your teacher will call the guide at 15", 12", or 10" intervals. As time permits, repeat sentences on which you were not able to complete a line with the call of the guide.

	gwam	15" guide	12" guide	10" guide
space quickly with down-and-in motion of thumb 1 Always try to key with quick, sharp stroking.		36	45	54
2 Hold all your fingers curved and near to the keys.		40	50	60
3 Keep fingers and elbows very steady in all keyboarding.		44	55	66
4 Just plan to think and key the short, easy words as a whole.		48	60	72

| 1 | 2 | 3 | 4 | 5 | 6 | 7 | 8 | 9 | 10 | 11 | 12 |

---

35 minutes   **89c ● Formatting Problem: Bibliographical Cards**

Directions: 1. Prepare the following bibliographical cards on 5" × 3" cards or paper cut to size. Key the first card from the illustration below, the second and third from the information that follows on page 162.

2. Begin the first entry a DS below the top edge of the card and 3 spaces from the left edge.

Note: If you are using a computer, rule the outline of the card size on your printer paper.

Bibliographical cards contain information about references you will use in a report. The illustration at the right shows the type of information included.

author	┌─ 3 spaces DS │Houterman, Margaret M. DS
title	Computer Composing DS
publication information	Boston: Hewlett-Packard Co., 1987. DS
short description	Talks about the advantages of writing on the computer. Illustrates ideas on organizing thoughts and explains how to edit on a computer. DS
library call number	c 467.2667 H346

(continued on next page)

Lesson 89   **161**

15 minutes

50d ● Timed Writings

Directions: 1. Take two 3' writings on all paragraphs. Figure *gwam*.
2. Take two 1' writings on each ¶; take the first for speed, the second for control.

3. Take another 3' writing on all the paragraphs. Figure *gwam*. Compare your *gwam* and number of errors on this writing to those of your first 3' writing.

all letters used   1.2 si

	gwam 3'
You may not know what one of our major pastimes is these	4 | 45
days. It's going shopping. You will be amazed to learn that	8 | 49
adults spend six hours a week looking for things to buy.	12 | 53
This is more time than they spend at work in the garden	16 | 56
or in a chair with a book. It is way ahead of golf or time	20 | 60
with their kids. Only those hours spent in front of the tube	24 | 65
exceed those that are devoted to shopping.	27 | 68
No one is quite sure why all this is true, but here are	30 | 71
two possible reasons. Some people shop when they are bored.	34 | 75
Others treat this activity as a sport, to see if they can't	38 | 79
win out in a contest with the stores.	41 | 82

gwam 3' | 1 | 2 | 3 | 4 |

50e ● Extra-Credit

Directions: Problem 1

1. Key the timed writing in 50d as a short report. Provide a title; key the title in all capital letters, followed by a QS.

2. Use a 60-space line; center the entire report vertically on a full sheet; DS the body of the report.

Directions: Problem 2

1. Assume you are Loretta Carpenter in the letter in 50c, Problem 2, page 94. Write to Rick Tellier, telling him that the regular price of your electronic typewriter is $395.50. Schools are entitled to a 10% discount, making the net price $355.95.

2. Prepare the letter in modified block style, mixed punctuation. Date the letter May 15, 19--. Use personal titles as needed.

3. Address a small envelope (or paper cut to size). Fold and insert the letter if you are using an envelope.

Directions: Problem 3

1. Address large envelopes (or paper cut to size) for each of the addresses given in 48c, Problem 3, page 91.

2. Use your name and address as the sender on all the envelopes.

Lesson 50

88c ● Formatting Problems: Outlines

Starting with this lesson, you will prepare some of the materials needed for the leftbound report that you will key in Lessons 92–95. A preliminary outline, bibliography cards, note cards, and a final outline are usually prepared before a report is written. Lessons 88, 89, and 90 will give you practice in preparing these items. With your teacher's approval, keep all items that pertain to this report until completion at the end of this unit.

Directions: Problem 1   Preliminary Outline (General Listing of Topics to be Used in a Report)

1. Set margins for a 40-space line.
2. On a full sheet of paper, key the outline in exact vertical center.

3. Center the heading. QS below heading; DS all items.

STEPS IN WRITING THE FORMAL REPORT

Note: Since final outline will be bound with the report, use center point for leftbound report.

1. Select a subject.
2. Write preliminary outline.
3. Choose reference materials.
4. Read and take notes.
5. Write final outline.

6. Write first draft.
7. Edit and revise first draft.
8. Write final copy.
9. Write title page and bibliography.
10. Proofread entire final report.

Problem 2   Final Outline for a Leftbound Report
Use a 2" top margin, 60-space line.
Leave 1½" left margin; 1" right margin.

Center the heading over the copy. Refer to 57d, page 106, if necessary.

WRITING A REPORT

I. STEPS TO TAKE BEFORE WRITING A REPORT
   A. Choose the right subject.
      1. Choose a topic that intrigues you.
      2. Choose a topic about which you know something.
   B. Limit your subject.
   C. Prepare a preliminary outline.
      1. Jot down the major points only.
      2. This outline acts as a guide in your search for information.
   D. Prepare bibliography cards.
      1. The cards should contain information on your readings.
      2. The data recorded should be complete and accurate.
   E. Read and take notes.
      1. Use note cards.
      2. Record important facts, opinions, and quotations.
   F. Prepare the final outline.
      1. Organize the information collected.
      2. Group note cards under topics used in the preliminary outline.

II. STEPS TO TAKE IN WRITING THE REPORT
   A. Write the first draft.
      1. The explanations should be clear, complete, to the point, and accurate.
      2. The sentences should be in logical order.
      3. Illustrate points by references to personal experiences.
      4. Compare your topic with one that is more familiar to the reader.
   B. Revise the first draft.
      1. Check the first draft for wording, spelling, and typographical errors.
      2. Make pencil or pen corrections.
   C. Prepare the final copy.
      1. Good appearance is important.
      2. Use standard rules on arrangement of report.
   D. Prepare the title page and bibliography.
      1. A title page contains the name of the report, the writer's name, and the date.
      2. The bibliography names the references consulted.

Unit 8 ▪ Keying Reports and Outlines (Lessons 51–60)

Learning Goals:

1. To format poems in both exact and reading positions using the vertical centering shortcut method.
2. To format a short report or theme in correct form.
3. To format a two-page theme with side margins specified in inches.
4. To format class notes, sentence and topic outlines, and book reviews.
5. To key correctly words that are commonly misspelled.
6. To apply capitalization guides in keying sentences.
7. To key from rough draft containing common proofreader's marks.
8. To increase keying skill by further refining basic techniques.

General Directions

Use a 60-space line, unless otherwise directed, for all lessons in this unit (center − 30; center + 30 + 5). SS sentences and drill lines; DS between repeated groups of lines. DS paragraph copy.

Your instructor will tell you if you are to correct errors in formatting problems.

LESSON 51

5 minutes

51a ● Keyboard Review

Directions: Key each sentence three times SS. DS between 3-line groups.

keep fingers
deeply curved

alphabet I quite expected June was a lazy time for living back there.
fig/sym She said that 80.6% of her 34 car trips were under 15 miles.
easy He may sign his name on both of the forms if he has a proxy.

| 1 | 2 | 3 | 4 | 5 | 6 | 7 | 8 | 9 | 10 | 11 | 12 |

---

5 minutes

51b ● Language Arts Skills: Spelling and Proofreading Aid

Directions: Key each line three times SS. DS between 3-line groups.

1 decision parcel ordinary maintenance canceled serious choose
2 belief familiar across wholly experience responsible visible
3 absence eighth congratulate immediate committee incidentally

---

12 minutes

51c ● Paragraph Guided Writings

Directions: 1. Take a 1′ writing to establish a goal rate.
2. Take two additional 1′ writings, trying to reach your goal word just as time is called.

3. Add four words to your original goal. Take three 1′ writings, trying to reach your new goal on each timing. Your teacher may call the quarter- or half-minute guide.

all letters   1.3 si

keep your eyes
on the copy

Quite a few baseball pitchers have been injured while
off the mound and outside the batter's box. They have been
hurt sneezing, pulling up a sock, and kicking a door. One
of them even caught his finger in a pinball machine.

87c, continued   **Directions: Problem 2   Sentence Outline**
Set a 60-space line; set tab stops as in Problem 1. Leave a 2″ top margin.

DETERMINING CAREER INTERESTS

I. MAKE AN INVENTORY OF STRENGTHS
  A. Working indoors or outdoors?
  B. Working with people or alone?
  C. Concentrating or oriented to action?

II. LEARN ABOUT JOBS
  A. Read about jobs.
  B. Talk to people with same jobs.

III. OBSERVE PEOPLE DOING JOBS
  A. Ask to observe.
  B. Observe a typical day.
  C. Ask questions.
    1. Learn job duties.
    2. Learn all the job requirements.
  D. Judge what you have learned.

LESSON 88
70-space line

5 minutes   **88a ● Keyboard Review**

Directions: Key each sentence three times SS. DS between 3-line groups.

keep arms and wrists quiet

alphabet	Seven troop trucks quenched a major gas fire ablaze yet at a new exit.
figure	It is expected by the year 2034 that there will be 679 new car models.
shift	The early automobiles carried the names Ford, Hudson, Dodge, and Nash.
easy	Most of them on the new team did not go to the party until much later.

| 1 | 2 | 3 | 4 | 5 | 6 | 7 | 8 | 9 | 10 | 11 | 12 | 13 | 14 |

---

10 minutes   **88b ● Speed Builder**

Directions: Take two 1′ writings on each ¶; try to increase speed on the second writing. Figure *gwam.*

Alternate Procedure: Work for speed as you take one 5′ writing on all three ¶s combined. Figure *gwam.*

all letters used   1.3 si

gwam 1′ 5′

keep your eyes on the copy

Long distance travel has changed quite a bit from the days when 13 | 3 | 34
people traveled long days in a stagecoach just to get from one town to 27 | 5 | 36
another.   The roads were rough, and the ride was not exactly pleasant. 41 | 8 | 39

Trains made quite a difference in the comfort and speed of travel, 13 | 11 | 42
and they could go just about anywhere that there were tracks to ride on. 28 | 14 | 45
From steam engines to diesels the ride kept getting longer and better. 43 | 17 | 48
In a shorter time you could now travel from the East to the West Coast. 57 | 20 | 51

The airplane really changed travel.   The first planes were not as 13 | 22 | 53
comfortable as the trains, but they were a lot quicker and did not have 28 | 25 | 56
to depend on tracks or roads.   The move from propellers to jets made a 42 | 28 | 59
recognizable difference in travel time from one city to the next. 55 | 31 | 62

gwam 1′ | 1 | 2 | 3 | 4 | 5 | 6 | 7 | 8 | 9 | 10 | 11 | 12 | 13 | 14 |
     5′ | | 1 | | | 2 | | | 3 | |

51d ● Technique Builder: Stroking

use quick,
sharp strokes

Directions: Key each line three times SS. DS between 3-line groups.

one-hand   we saw | we saw him | we saw him jump | we are | we are here | you are

balanced-hand   He and she own half of the firm that makes their big robots.

direct reach   My Uncle Brad understood he was to bring my unique umbrella.

| 1 | 2 | 3 | 4 | 5 | 6 | 7 | 8 | 9 | 10 | 11 | 12 |

---

15 minutes

51e ● Timed Writings

Directions: **1.** Take two 1′ writings on each ¶. Figure *gwam.*
2. Take 2′ and 3′ writings on all three ¶s combined. Compare your 2′ rate to the longer writing.

If you complete a writing before time is called, rekey the copy until you are told to stop. To figure *gwam,* add the last number in the column to the number of words in the second writing.

all letters 1.3 si

gwam 2′ | 3′

All through history stories have been told about strange   6 | 4
events that no one has ever been able to explain. There have   12 | 8
been reports of objects falling from the sky and of all kinds   18 | 12
of liquids oozing from the ground.   22 | 14

More than a hundred years ago someone claimed to have   27 | 18
discovered a toad inside a chunk of coal. A more recent yarn   33 | 22
tells about a bald farmer who began to grow hair again after   39 | 26
a cow licked his scalp.   42 | 28

One person who keeps track of these things has a room   47 | 31
jammed with books describing them. Folders spill from filing   53 | 36
cabinets full of tales you and I would be hard pressed to   59 | 40
believe. He needs a computer to sort them all out.   64 | 43

| gwam 2′ | 1 | 2 | 3 | 4 | 5 | 6 | |
| 3′ | 1 | 2 | 3 | 4 | |

LESSON 52

60-space line

52a ● Keyboard Review

5 minutes

keep wrists and
elbows quiet

Directions: Key each sentence three times SS. DS between 3-line groups.

alphabet   Bob was asked to quote from every zany jingle except theirs.

fig/sym   Use a diagonal for "made" fractions such as 2 7/8 or 15 3/4.

easy   They will spend half of their profit to pay for this emblem.

| 1 | 2 | 3 | 4 | 5 | 6 | 7 | 8 | 9 | 10 | 11 | 12 |

5 minutes **87a ● Keyboard Review**

Directions: Key each sentence three times SS. DS between 3-line groups.

alphabet A geography quiz must first be taken by Jack and Val before next week.

figure Nearly 35 of the 6,720 tourists passed through all 27 of the tunnels.

direct reaches Before the ceremony began, my brother checked twice to find the music.

easy Way high above in the sky the sun is very bright and is also very hot.

| 1 | 2 | 3 | 4 | 5 | 6 | 7 | 8 | 9 | 10 | 11 | 12 | 13 | 14 |

10 minutes **87b ● Skill Builder**

Directions: **1.** Take a 1' writing on the ¶ below. The last word keyed will be your goal word.
2. Take a 5' writing with the return called after each minute. When the return is called, start the ¶ over again. Try to reach your goal each minute as the return is called.

all letters used   1.3 si

                                                                          gwam 5'

use a quick carrier return

Sound has come a long way since being first recorded on a large   3 | 15

record. It moved from the waxed disc to a slowly moving tape that could   5 | 17

be played at different speeds. From the tape format the music craze   8 | 20

quickly jumped to the audio disc, which has a very good sound in a small   11 | 23

package that is great to hear.   12 | 24

gwam 5' | 1 | 2 | 3 |

30 minutes **87c ● Formatting Problems: Formatting/Keying Outlines**

Directions: Problem 1   Topic Outline
1. Set a 60-space line. Clear all tab stops; set 3 tab stops of 4 spaces each beginning at the left margin.

2. Leave a 2" top margin; center the heading. If necessary, refer to 57d, page 106.

FORMATTING LEFTBOUND REPORTS

I. MARGINS
    A. Left Margin of 1½ Inches
    B. Right Margin of 1 Inch
    C. Bottom Margin of 1 Inch
    D. Top Margin of First Page: Line 13
    E. Top Margin of Subsequent Pages of 1 Inch
        1. At least 2 lines of paragraph at bottom of page
        2. At least 2 lines of paragraph carried forward to new page

II. SPACING
    A. Quadruple Space Below Title
    B. Double Space Contents of Report
    C. Single Space Quoted Materials of 4 Lines or More, Footnotes, and Bibliographical Items

III. PAGE NUMBERS
    A. Centered ½ Inch From Bottom of First Page or Omit Number
    B. Aligned with Right Margin 1 Inch (6 Line Spaces) from Top for All Other Pages

(continued on next page)

5 minutes

52b ● Language Arts Skills: Keying from Dictation; Spelling Checkup

Directions: Key the words in 51b, page 96, from your teacher's dictation.

Check for correct spelling. Rekey any words in which you made an error.

5 minutes

52c ● Paragraph Skill Builder from Rough Draft

Directions: Key the ¶ once for practice; then take three 1' writings. Circle your errors. Figure *gwam*.

Compare your best rate with the highest rate reached in 51c, page 96.

all letters used   1.2 si

gwam 1'

For years we have expected science to create the products   11 | 57

that could be used just once one time and then quickly tossed thrown out.   23 | 69

they included everything from razor blades to paper plates.   35 | 81

Now our are biggest problem is to find a place to throw them.   46 | 92

5 minutes

52d ● Vertical Centering: Backspace from Center Method

1. Insert paper to line 33 (vertical center of a piece of paper 11" long). Roll cylinder back (toward you) one line space for each two lines in the copy to be keyed. This will place the copy in exact vertical center.

2. To key a problem off-center or in *reading position,* roll cylinder back two

extra line spaces.

3. Another centering method is to fold the paper from top to bottom and make a slight crease at the right edge. The crease will be at the vertical center (line 33). Insert the paper to the crease; roll the cylinder back one line space for each two lines in the copy.

25 minutes

52e ● Formatting Problems: Exact Vertical Center and Reading Position

Problem 1   Exact Vertical Centering
Directions: 1. Set a 40-space line.
2. Key the poem line for line in exact vertical center position using a full sheet of paper.
3. Center the heading horizontally. Review horizontal centering on page 69 if necessary.
4. Place the author's name even with the right margin.

Problem 2   Reading Position
Directions: 1. Key the poem in reading position.
2. All other directions are the same as in Problem 1.

HOW TALL?
                              DS
Will growing tall as I grow up
eventually mean more
than inches marked in pencil on
the kitchen closet door?
                              DS
Will I stand straight and bump my head
where satellites abound
but still touch earth, with both feet
firmly planted on the ground?
                              DS
Will my hands close on comets, will
I really stretch that far,
a tingle in my fingers as
I touch a distant star?
                              DS
                              --Nancy Breen

86d ● Speed Ladder Paragraphs

Directions: Take a 1' writing on ¶ 1 DS. When you complete ¶ 1 in 1', repeat procedure on succeeding ¶ s.

Take three 1' writings on any ¶ you do not finish in the time given.

Alternate Procedure: Work on control as you take a 1' writing on ¶ 1. Move to succeeding ¶ s when you complete each one within the error limit specified by your teacher. If time allows, repeat any ¶ s in which you exceeded the error limit.

all letters used   1.3 si

	gwam 5'	
Many interviews fail before they start. They do not work because	3	47
the person interviewing has not spent time getting ready. The time a	5	49
person spends in getting ready is a key factor.	7	50
The first step in preparing for the interview is to gather as much	10	54
information as you can about the firm. Find out what the company makes	13	57
or sells, and where its major plants and outlets are located.	15	60
When you arrive at the firm, keep in mind that first impressions	18	62
are very important. You should go to the interview by yourself. Once	21	65
you are there, try to relax and be at ease. Be alert and try to act	24	68
self confident.	24	68
You should have already planned ahead and as a result be all set	27	71
to answer almost any question you may be asked. Respond to all the ques-	30	74
tions with interest and zest. Be careful of your grammar and of the	32	77
way in which you pronounce words.	34	78
At the end of the interview, be sure to ask some questions to show	37	81
the interviewer you did plan for the day and are interested in the job	39	83
which is being offered. Say you will be very glad to furnish all other	42	86
facts that will be of some help to the interviewer.	44	88

gwam 5' | 1 | 2 | 3 |

86e ● Language Arts Skills: Number Expression Guides Review

Directions: The first sentence gives the rule; the other sentences illustrate the rule. Key each sentence twice SS. DS between 2-line groups.

1 All numbers used at the beginning of a sentence must be keyed in full.

2 Twenty-two of the personal computers were working at the end of class.

3 Eighteen barrels of the chemical were shipped from Chicago to Detroit.

LESSON 53

5 minutes

53a ● Keyboard Review

Directions: Key each sentence three times SS. DS between 3-line groups.

return carrier
quickly

alphabet Phil Singer wanted Liza to fly Jack to Quebec next November.

fig/sym Even sums like $580 or $476 don't require decimals or zeros.

easy He has to learn to handle those kinds of problems right now.

| 1 | 2 | 3 | 4 | 5 | 6 | 7 | 8 | 9 | 10 | 11 | 12 |

10 minutes

53b ● Paragraph Guided Writings

Directions: 1. Take a 1' writing to establish a goal rate.

2. Take two additional 1' writings, trying to reach your goal word just as time is called.

3. Add four words to your original goal. Take three 1' writings, trying to reach your new goal on each timing. Your teacher may call the quarter- or half-minutes.

all letters
1.3 si

People don't just blow balloons up for parties any more. They ride in them too. The riding ones, like their smaller cousins, come in various sizes and colors. Some are as large as jets. Liquid propane is used to make the air hot, and the excess heat is let out through vents at the top.

30 minutes

53c ● Formatting Problems: One-Page Report

Directions: 1. Key the report on page 100 using a 60-space line DS.

2. Begin on line 13; center the heading horizontally. QS follows heading.

LESSON 54

5 minutes

54a ● Keyboard Review

Directions: Key each sentence three times SS. DS between 3-line groups.

alphabet We might require five dozen packing boxes for our July crop.

symbol Place added information (such as a date) within parentheses.

easy We bought some more land down the lane from their big house.

| 1 | 2 | 3 | 4 | 5 | 6 | 7 | 8 | 9 | 10 | 11 | 12 |

5 minutes

Keep your eyes
on the copy

54b ● Technique Builder: Stroking

Directions: Key each line three times SS. DS between 3-line groups.

one-hand Barbara was served extra water. Jim swears Jill beat Lynn.

weak fingers After passing the quiz, we happily asked for pizza and pop.

double letters All three Mississippi schools offer bookkeeping/accounting.

| 1 | 2 | 3 | 4 | 5 | 6 | 7 | 8 | 9 | 10 | 11 | 12 |

85c, continued

BIBLIOGRAPHY

QS

indent
5 spaces → Croyderman, Elizabeth C. <u>Using the Thesaurus</u>. Knoxville: Barston
and Company, 1987.

margin ↓

DS

Laughlin, R. M. "Fun in the Word Factory: Experiences with the
Dictionary." <u>Language Arts</u> (March, 1988), pp. 319-21.

DS

Marston, John M. <u>Ginn Elements of Good English</u>. Lexington: Ginn
and Company, 1984.

DS

Pollock, Thomas Clark, and Richard L. Loughlin. <u>The Macmillan English
Series</u>. New York: Macmillan, Inc., 1983.

LESSON 86

70-space line

5 minutes | **86a ● Keyboard Review**

Directions: Key each sentence three times SS. DS between 3-line groups.

alphabet Just as we all half realized, all experts must be very quick and good.

figure George Bush was inaugurated as our 41st President on January 20, 1989.

double letters All letters need to be discussed before supplying necessary approvals.

easy I will learn to like the work that must be done to be the team winner.

| 1 | 2 | 3 | 4 | 5 | 6 | 7 | 8 | 9 | 10 | 11 | 12 | 13 | 14 |

---

8 minutes | **86b ● Correcting Errors: Squeezing Letters**

Directions: 1. Key the first sentence as it appears below.

3. Use the same procedure to key and correct the next sentence with an error.

2. On electric or electronic typewriters erase or lift off the incorrect word and move your position indicator two spaces after the word been; use the half-back-space mechanism or the incremental back-spacer, whichever is on your machine.

 Note: On a computer it may only be necessary to use the insert function to add the additional letter to the word needing the correction.

Error: A letter has been mitted at the beginning of a word.
Correction: A letter has been omitted at the beginning of a word.

Error: A letter has bee omitted at the end of a word.
Correction: A letter has been omitted at the end of a word.

---

5 minutes | **86c ● Speed Builder from Script**

Directions: Key the ¶ below as many times as you can in the given time.

all letters used   1.3 si   words

If you want to be successful, you must go after each task   12
with zeal and interest. It is great to be relaxed, but you   25
need to be sure that you are still working to the very best of   37
your ability. Just always be quite sure that you are putting   49
your "best foot forward" in all that you attempt to do.   60

KEYING A SHORT REPORT

QS

Short reports of one page or less may be formatted with a   16

60-space line. If the number of lines can be counted easily,   29

center the copy vertically; if not, use a standard margin of 2   42

inches (12 line spaces) at the top.   49

Double spacing is usually used for reports and book re-   61

views. Class notes and minutes are usually single spaced to   73

provide better groupings of information.   81

Every report should have a heading that is keyed in all   94

capital letters. It is separated from the body by a quadruple   107

space.   108

Unbound or topbound reports or papers are usually for-   120

matted with side margins of 1 inch. When the paper is to be   132

bound at the left, however, an extra one-half inch must be   144

provided in the left margin for binding.   152

The heading is placed 2 inches from the top of the first   165

page. All pages after the first have a top margin of 1 inch   177

except for topbound reports. If the report is to be topbound,   190

leave an extra one-half inch for binding. The bottom margin   203

should not be less than 1 inch.   209

One-page report

LESSON 85

5 minutes   **85a ● Keyboard Review**

Directions: Key each sentence three times SS. DS between 3-line groups.

keep fingers
deeply curved

alphabet   A friend's new craze was just to move extra quickly to buy autographs.

figure   Nearly 3,643,557 fans were on hand to welcome their 1990-91 champions.

4th finger   People are being quickly sent to aid the poor citizens in their ports.

easy   A key item is to know how to spend your money and still save a little.

| 1 | 2 | 3 | 4 | 5 | 6 | 7 | 8 | 9 | 10 | 11 | 12 | 13 | 14 |

---

15 minutes   **85b ● Timed Writings**

Directions: Take a 1' writing on each ¶ on 81d, page 147. Circle errors. Figure *gwam.* Take one 5' writing on all five ¶s combined. Circle errors. Figure *gwam.*

---

25 minutes   **85c ● Formatting Problems**

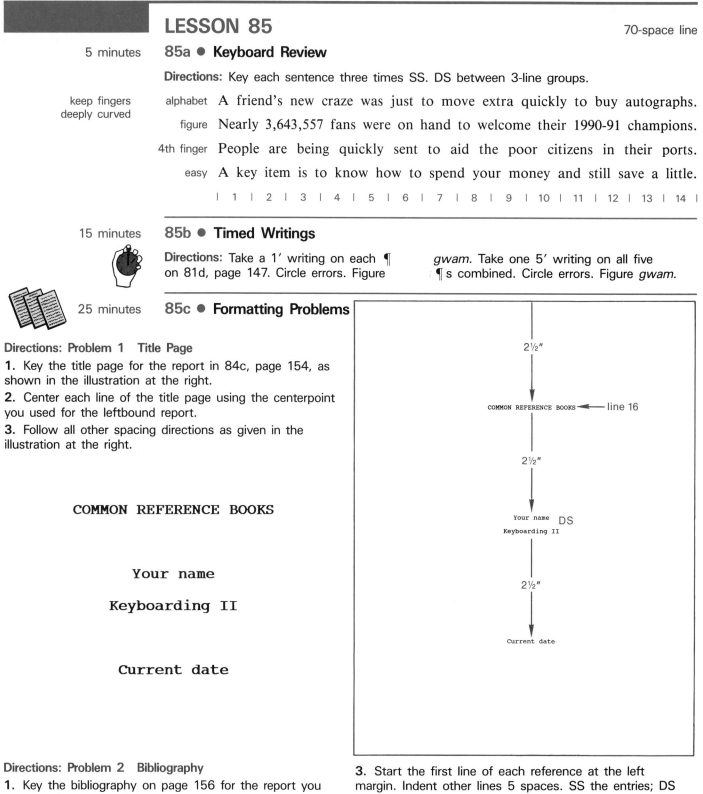

Directions: Problem 1   Title Page

1. Key the title page for the report in 84c, page 154, as shown in the illustration at the right.

2. Center each line of the title page using the centerpoint you used for the leftbound report.

3. Follow all other spacing directions as given in the illustration at the right.

COMMON REFERENCE BOOKS

Your name

Keyboarding II

Current date

2½"

COMMON REFERENCE BOOKS ◄─── line 16

2½"

Your name   DS
Keyboarding II

2½"

Current date

Directions: Problem 2   Bibliography

1. Key the bibliography on page 156 for the report you keyed in 84c, page 154.

2. Use the same top and side margins used for page 1 of the report. Center the heading over the line of writing.

3. Start the first line of each reference at the left margin. Indent other lines 5 spaces. SS the entries; DS between entries.

4. Place the title page, report, and bibliography in the proper order. Staple together at the left side.

(continued on next page)

54c ● Language Arts Skills: Spelling and Proofreading Aid

Directions: Key each line three times SS. DS between 3-line groups.

1 accept independent liable promptly appearance column fulfill

2 occasion explanation affect color vehicle budget unnecessary

3 summary guidance temporary favorable possibility approximate

54d ● Learn to Make Carbon Copies (optional)

Directions: Before copying machines became commonly used, extra copies were often prepared with carbon paper as follows:

Step 1 Place the carbon paper (with glossy side down) on a sheet of plain paper. The paper on which you will prepare the original is then laid on top of the carbon paper.

Step 2 Place the sheets between the cylinder and the paper table (glossy side of carbon facing you). Roll into the typewriter. The dull surface of the carbon should be facing you.

Step 3 Refer to page xvi for erasing on carbon copies.

sit erect;
keep your eyes
on the copy

Your teacher will tell you
if you are to prepare
carbon copies.

54e ● Formatting Problem: Short Report

Directions: Key the unbound report below on a 60-space line DS. Use a 2" top margin (begin on line 13). Center the heading horizontally. Your teacher will tell you whether to prepare a carbon copy.

words

HOW TO GET BETTER USE FROM YOUR PERSONAL COMPUTER　10

QS

One of the most helpful computers available today is a　21
personalized model that we carry along with us wherever we go. It's　35
better in many ways than the most expensive electronic device, and its　49
contents cannot be tapped by some mischievous hacker.　60

This remarkable computer is our memory, a powerful machine　72
that we seldom use efficiently to process information.　83

One psychologist has pointed out that both humans and　94
computers require the use of software as well as hardware. Our brain　108
structure makes up the hardware; the processes we can control are the　121
software.　124

Here are two hints for developing the software of your memory.　136
First, when you read, don't read the material several times and then　150
underline it. Instead read it just once, stopping now and then to　164
summarize the key points in your own words. Second, when you are　177
introduced to someone for the first time, make sure you understand　190
how to spell and pronounce the new name. Recall the name　201
immediately and visualize its spelling. A few minutes later think of　215
the name again, trying to associate it with other friends you know.　229

Make the best possible use of your memory. It is your own　240
personal computer, and you will still need it in the information age.　254

Directions: Key the 2-page leftbound report below DS. Refer to the directions in 84b and 84c, page 153, for assistance. (Do not number the first page of this report.)

COMMON REFERENCE BOOKS

QS

words

All throughout our lives we will need to use reference books to aid us in   19
our speaking and writing tasks. Two of the most commonly used reference   34
texts are the dictionary and the thesaurus. We need to examine each one to get   50
a much clearer understanding of their value.   59

The first English dictionary was not written until the early 1600's. It was   74
more than 200 years later, in 1828, when Webster first published his two-volume   90
American Dictionary of the English Language (Pollock and Loughlin, 1973, 23).   105

A dictionary provides a reliable way of getting answers to many different   120
kinds of questions about words. The major function of the dictionary, of course,   137
is to promote accuracy in spelling, pronunciation, and word division.   150

While the dictionary is the main source used by most writers to check   164
spelling, another source is available to individuals who use word processing   180
computer software. All a writer needs to do when using such a package is to   195
depress the correct computer function key, and the software will indicate words   211
misspelled and, in addition, suggest the correct spelling. A list of words that   227
are similar to the word indicated will appear, and all the writer has to do is   243
select the correct one. The computer will make the changes in the copy without   259
the writer having to rekey the word. Even the good proofreader can benefit   274
from this kind of checking. Many software packages will also suggest the point   290
at which words are to be divided. We have come a long way since that first   306
dictionary in the 1600's.   311

The thesaurus has a different purpose than the dictionary. The thesaurus   325
goes one step further than providing meanings of words--it finds words that   341
express an idea that the writer has in mind (Croyderman, 1987, 121). The   355
thesaurus provides the reader with word definitions and synonyms. These   370
synonyms help the writer use a variety of words to express a thought. Again,   386
computer software packages can be used to help you find the best word to   400
express an idea.   403

QS

REFERENCES   405

QS

Croyderman, Elizabeth C. Using the Thesaurus. Knoxville: Barston and Com-   420
    pany, 1987.   423

DS

Pollock, Thomas Clark, and Richard L. Loughlin. The Macmillan English Series.   438
    New York: Macmillan, Inc., 1973.   445

5 minutes

55a ● Keyboard Review

Directions: Key each sentence three times SS. DS between 3-line groups.

alphabet Max delivered the wrong size pack to Jeff quite by accident.

symbol You may wish to use "c/o" for the abbreviation "in care of."

easy Both of them asked to take their autos to the new body shop.

| 1 | 2 | 3 | 4 | 5 | 6 | 7 | 8 | 9 | 10 | 11 | 12 |

---

15 minutes

55b ● Timed Writings

Directions: 1. Take two 1' writings on each ¶. Figure *gwam*.
2. Take 2' and 3' writings on all three

¶ s combined. Compare your 2' rate to the longer writing.

all letters used   1.3 si

	gwam 2'	3'
After years of research, we now use robots to do some	6	4
jobs that used to require a human being. They have been used	12	8
for sentries along a track, for example. If its sensors pick	18	12
up an intruder, its sirens sound and quartz lights flash.	24	16
You can even purchase a home robot that will move around	29	20
a smooth uncrowded floor and deliver a cart or tray to one	35	24
specified spot. If you want your dumb waiter to walk up a	41	27
flight of stairs, however, you are asking a little too much.	47	32
Walking on two legs is one thing that no robots are yet	53	35
able to do. Nor can they recognize a face or understand a	59	39
natural language. While robots can do some types of work,	65	43
they must still learn to solve problems and make decisions	70	47
if they expect to mimic human skills.	74	49

gwam 2'	1	2	3	4	5	6	
3'	1		2		3		4

If you complete a writing before time is called, rekey the copy until you are told to stop. To figure gwam, *add the last number in the column to the number of words on the second writing.*

---

25 minutes

There are 10 pica spaces per inch; 12 elite spaces per inch.

55c ● Formatting Problems: Two-Page Report

Directions: 1. Key the unbound report on page 103 DS (refer to page 100 for directions on preparing unbound reports).
2. Leave a 2" top margin above the heading on the first page (begin on line 13). Leave 1" bottom and side margins.

3. Center the heading horizontally (refer to 40c, page 73 to find center point). QS below the heading.

4. Place the page number 2 at the right-hand margin on line 6 of the second page; continue keying report on line 8.

LESSON 84

5 minutes

84a ● Keyboard Review

Directions: Key each sentence three times SS. DS between 3-line groups.

sit erect;
keep feet
flat on floor

alphabet   Rex must have just delivered the wrong size of pack quite by accident.

fig/sym   They saved on item #4–81, which weighed more than 435# before packing.

adjacent keys   As they recommended, her warehouse was closed long before you knew it.

easy   It is not easy to be on time if you do not make plans early every day.

| 1 | 2 | 3 | 4 | 5 | 6 | 7 | 8 | 9 | 10 | 11 | 12 | 13 | 14 |

10 minutes

84b ● Learn to Key Two-Page Leftbound Reports

Directions: 1. For the first page of a leftbound report, leave a 2″ top margin; leave a 1″ top margin on all succeeding pages.

2. Leave a 1½″ left margin and a 1″ right margin. The bottom margin should be approximately 1″.

3. Find your new center point by adding the figures at the left and right margins and dividing by 2. Backspace from this point to center the heading.

4. If the first page is numbered (optional), center the number one-half inch from the bottom. Other page numbers are placed on the sixth line from the top and aligned with the right margin.

5. At least 2 lines of a paragraph must appear at the bottom of a page, and at least 2 lines of a new paragraph should be carried forward to a new page.

On page 151, you learned to document sources by using footnotes. The form of documentation shown here is the reference citation.

84c ● Learn to Format/Key Reference Citations

30 minutes

Step 1 After keying the quoted material, place within parentheses the author's last name, date of publication, and page number of the cited material as shown in the example below.

Step 2 At the end of the report, QS and center the word ''References,'' QS and key in alphabetical order (by authors' last names) each complete reference.

16	plan to pay all charges when due. This plan will save many dollars in	51
15		52
14	the course of a lifetime" (Phillips, 1988, 59).	53
13		54
12	QS	55
11		56
10	REFERENCES	57
9		58
8	QS	59
7		60
6	Phillips, Patricia A. "Using Credit Wisely And Effectively." <u>The Credit</u>	61
5	<u>Journal</u>, October 1988, 59.	62
4		63
3		64

55c, continued

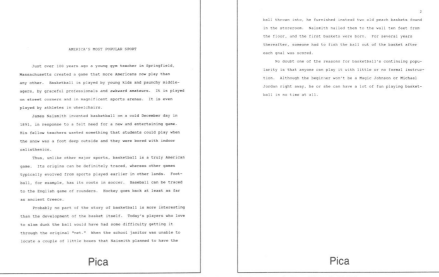

Pica

Pica

AMERICA'S MOST POPULAR SPORT

Just over 100 years ago a young gym teacher in Springfield, Massachusetts created a game that more Americans now play than any other. Basketball is played by young kids and paunchy middle-agers, by graceful professionals and awkward amateurs. It is played on street corners and in magnificent sports arenas. It is even played by athletes in wheelchairs.

James Naismith invented basketball on a cold December day in 1891, in response to a felt need for a new and entertaining game. His fellow teachers wanted something that students could play when the snow was a foot deep outside and they were bored with indoor calisthenics.

Thus, unlike other major sports, basketball is a truly American game. Its origins can be definitely traced, whereas other games typically evolved from sports played earlier in other lands. Football, for example, has its roots in soccer. Baseball can be traced to the English game of rounders. Hockey goes back at least as far as ancient Greece.

Probably no part of the story of basketball is more interesting than the development of the basket itself. Today's players who love to slam dunk the ball would have had some difficulty getting it through the original "net." When the school janitor was unable to locate a couple of little boxes that Naismith planned to have the ball thrown into, he furnished instead two old peach baskets found in the storeroom. Naismith nailed them to the wall ten feet from the floor, and the first baskets were born. For several years thereafter, someone had to fish the ball out of the basket after each goal was scored.

No doubt one of the reasons for basketball's continuing popularity is that anyone can play it with little or no formal instruction. Although the beginner won't be a Magic Johnson or Michael Jordan right away, he or she can have a lot of fun playing basketball in no time at all.

Elite

Elite

O. J. Simpson

QS

Two events marked the coming of age of the American Football League in January, 1969. One was Joe Namath's leading the New York Jets to a Super Bowl victory over the National Football League. The other was the Buffalo Bills' signing of Orenthal Simpson, better known to most as O. J. Simpson. He had just led his university, Southern California, to the No. 1 ranking team in the country.

DS

Orenthal James Simpson, a cousin of Ernie Banks, the first baseman of the Chicago Cubs, was born in San Francisco, California, on July 9, 1947. His unusual first name was suggested to his mother by an aunt, who Simpson has said, "then turned around and gave her own kids very common names like Stanley, Stewart, and Pam."[1]

DS

Simpson's participation in sports began at a field near his home. His running ability became evident at Everett Junior High School, when he broke the school record for the 60-yard dash. In high school he was placed as a tackle on the football team until the coach discovered his speed in running. He was then moved to full-back, and in that position he won all-city honors in his senior year.

DS

DS

[1]Ray Hill, _Complete O. J. Simpson_ (New York: Random House, 1975), p. 21.

approximately 1″

LESSON 56

60-space line

5 minutes **56a** ● **Keyboard Review**

Directions: Key each sentence three times SS. DS between 3-line groups.

alphabet	These new drug czars firmly backed every major export quota.
fig/sym	All 7 of the 4-door cars had 59.8 cubic feet of cargo space.
easy	The students wanted to visit all the towns shown on the map.

| 1 | 2 | 3 | 4 | 5 | 6 | 7 | 8 | 9 | 10 | 11 | 12 |

---

10 minutes **56b** ● **Paragraph Guided Writings**

Directions: **1.** Take a 1′ writing to establish a goal rate.
2. Take two additional 1′ writings. Try to reach your goal word as time is called.

3. Add four words to your original goal. Take three 1′ writings, trying to reach your new goal on each timing. Your teacher may call the quarter- or half-minute guides.

all letters 1.3 si

        Whether you drop out of school or not has little to do
with the size of your brain.   Yet we do know that one out of
every five or six eighth graders is at serious risk of not
getting through high school.   Major causes include being
home alone quite a bit and having limited language skills.

---

15 minutes **56c** ● **Timed Writings**

Directions: **1.** Take two 1′ writings on each ¶. Figure *gwam*.
2. Take 2′ and 3′ writings on both ¶s combined. If you complete a writing

before time is called, repeat until you are told to stop.
3. Figure *gwam*. Compare your 2′ rate to the longer writing.

all letters used 1.3 si

gwam 2′ | 3′

	gwam 2′	3′
Getting some exercise didn't used to be a very big deal.	6	4
You could walk around the block or dig in the yard. At most,	12	8
all you really had to have was a pair of jogging shoes plus	18	12
a healthy supply of willpower.	21	14
Staying in shape is not the same now. The new exercise	27	18
devices are well equipped with lights, buzzers, screens, and	33	22
readouts. They measure your heart rate, tell you to speed up	39	26
or slow down, and furnish electronic cheers when you're done.	45	30

gwam 2′	1	2	3	4	5	6	
3′	1		2		3		4

83b ● Learn to Key Superscripts and Subscripts

Directions: 1. For placement of a superscript (superior number), press the paper down key (14).

2. Key the figure or symbol, then press the paper up key (13) to return to original position.

3. For a subscript, press the paper up key (13).

4. Key the subscript, then press the paper down key (14) to return to original position.

5. Key each sentence below two times SS. DS between the 2-line groups.

Note: Some microcomputers have special function keys that can automatically set codes for superscripts and subscripts to be printed. If your machine cannot key these figures, place figure between two diagonals with no spaces before or after figure: /2/. Check your machine manual.

Key superscripts one-half space above a line: kg/m^3, Masters[4].

Key subscripts one-half space below a line: H_2O, CU_3N_2, CU_6H_6.

83c ● Steps in Formatting Reports with Footnotes

Note: Short quotations appear within the copy.

Directions: Read the steps below for formatting reports with footnotes. You will need to include footnotes in a report if you use statements or direct quotations from books or articles. The traditional way to document sources is to key in footnote form complete information about the references from which the materials were taken.

Step 1 Key a superior number immediately following the material in the report which will be documented by a footnote.

Step 2 Draw a light pencil mark on your paper to mark the 1″ bottom margin. Space up 2 or 3 lines from that mark for each footnote. If 2 or more footnotes will be on the page, leave an extra line space for a DS between each of the footnotes. Then space up an additional 2 lines and draw a second light pencil mark. This is where you will key the divider line that separates the footnotes from the body of the report.

Step 3 After completing the last line of the report that will appear on the page, DS; then use the underscore key to key a 1½″ divider line (15 spaces pica; 18 spaces elite) at the point where you have your second pencil mark.

Step 4 After keying the divider line, DS, indent 5 spaces, and key the footnote reference. Key each footnote SS; DS between footnotes.

Step 5 On a partially filled page, the footnotes may appear at the bottom of the page, or they may begin a DS below the last line of the report.

by an aunt, who Simpson has said, "then turned around and gave her

own kids very common names like Stanley, Stewart, and Pam."[1]
                                                        DS

_____
                    DS
[1]Ray Hill, Complete O. J. Simpson, (New York: Random House, 1975), p. 21.

83d ● Formatting Problem: Unbound Report With Footnotes

Directions: Key the first page of the unbound report as illustrated on page 152. Follow the directions on the illustration. If necessary, refer to page 100.

(continued on next page)

56d ● Language Arts Skills: Composing at the Keyboard

Directions: Key answers to each question below. Use complete sentences.

If time permits, correct any sentences in which you made errors.

Questions:

1. Name a nationally prominent person in politics and the office that person holds or has held.
2. Name one of the United States senators from your state.
3. Name the capital city of the state in which you are now living.
4. What nationally prominent person would you most like to meet in person? Why?

---

10 minutes

56e ● Language Arts Skills: Capitalization Guides

Directions: The following are capitalization guides and sentences that illustrate those guides. Study each guide.

Key the sentences that illustrate the guides twice SS; DS between 2-line groups.

use a quick, firm reach to the shift key

Capitalize days, months, years, and holidays; but not seasons.
Next fall we won't observe Labor Day on Monday, September 1.

Capitalize names of rivers, oceans, and mountains.
I saw the Columbia River, Mount Hood, and the Pacific Ocean.

Capitalize North, South, etc., when they name particular parts of the country, but not when they refer to directions.
People living in the South had to drive west to the meeting.

Capitalize names of religious groups, political parties, nations, nationalities, and races.
The Democrats meet in New Orleans, a city with French roots.

Capitalize all proper names.
Jo gave Kim a Japanese watch and a Hawaiian shirt from Maui.

Capitalize the names of stars, planets, and constellations except sun, moon or earth, unless they are used with astronomical names.
We studied the Sun and the Moon as well as Jupiter and Mars.

Capitalize a title when used with a person's name.
She heard Mayor Bradley, Senator Dole, and Justice O'Connor.

LESSON 57

60-space line

5 minutes

57a ● Keyboard Review

Directions: Key each sentence three times SS. DS between 3-line groups.

alphabet   The quiz kept Jim and Dick Law busy for six very long hours.

fig/sym   Sandra's score was 76%, Sean's was 85%, and Cindy's was 91%.

easy   He knows you can locate all eight of the islands on the map.

| 1 | 2 | 3 | 4 | 5 | 6 | 7 | 8 | 9 | 10 | 11 | 12 |

Directions: Problem 2   Unbound Report with Indented Items

1. Key the unbound report below on a 60-space line DS. Clear all tab stops; set a 5-space ¶ indention. Leave a 2″ top margin.

2. Indent numbered items 5 spaces from the left margin SS. DS between items.

3. Use a spread heading. QS below heading.

Guide for Indented Items
Indent numbered items 5 spaces from the left margin SS. DS between items.
  Key Figure 1 at the ¶ indention point, and reset the left margin at this point.
  After you complete the item, DS. Key Figure 2, key the period, space twice, and complete the item. Repeat the process for Items 3 and 4.

Note: On some electronic typewriters and on microcomputers, special function keys will allow you to indent appropriately. Check the manual that comes with your machine.
  Return to original settings for margins and spacing to complete the report.

J O B   I N T E R V I E W I N G   T I P S

Getting the job you want both now and in the future may require your successful participation in an interview.   Next to an application form the interview is the tool most often used by an employer in selecting the right job applicant.

Applying the following tips on job interviewing may very well make the difference in getting the job you want.

1.   Prepare before you go to the interview. Find out all you can about the company at which you are applying. Check a library for reports and other information about the firm. Ask friends and relatives for more information.

2.   Plan what you will wear to the interview. The way you look will have a key role in the outcome of the interview. Conservative clothes that are neatly pressed are the best bet.

3.   Practice for the interview. Find out the kind of questions that might be asked and practice the answers that you will give.

4.   Follow up on the interview. Always write a thank you letter to the employer after the interview. Offer to provide more information if necessary.

Your efforts in preparing for the interview and your follow up will make the difference between you and other candidates.   Plan ahead to be successful.

LESSON 83

70-space line

5 minutes   **83a ● Keyboard Review**

Directions: Key each line three times SS. DS between 3-line groups.

alphabet The jury may even want a full extra dozen required copies of big pack.

figure Mary made 432 copies of the article before the 6:40 deadline on May 8.

combination be alert, be careful, be on time, be cheerful, be friends, be thrifty.

easy Plan to be first to get on the train when you leave for your new trip.

| 1 | 2 | 3 | 4 | 5 | 6 | 7 | 8 | 9 | 10 | 11 | 12 | 13 | 14 |

5 minutes

57b ● Language Arts Skills: Spelling and Proofreading Aid

Directions: Key each line three times SS. DS between 3-line groups.

1 statue preparation foreign already quality listen economical
2 occupy receive piece dining judgment grateful emphasis loose
3 freight surprise competent weather language succeed campaign

---

5 minutes

57c ● Skill Comparison

Directions: 1. Take a 1′ writing on the goal sentence. Figure *gwam.*
2. Take a 1′ writing on each of the other sentences.

3. Try to match or exceed your goal sentence *gwam* on each of the other sentences.

keep wrists and elbows still

		words
goal sentence	Everyone needs very good sight to see his or her own faults.	12
one-hand	Get him a few cases of free milk. Jim gave up a great seat.	12
script	*Some think that a bird in the hand is worth two in the bush.*	12
rough draft	try not to talk when you mouth is full or you head is emtpy.	12

---

30 minutes

57d ● Learn to Format Outlines

Problem 1   Sentence Outline

Always use complete sentences in a sentence outline. Each entry is followed by a period.

Directions: 1. Use a 60-space line. Clear all tab stops; set 3 tab stops of 4 spaces each beginning at the left margin.
2. Center the outline vertically in reading position (2 line spaces above center point).

Center the heading horizontally.

3. Key the problem line for line; indent, space, capitalize, and punctuate exactly as shown.

```
                        GUIDES FOR STUDYING
                                        QS

left margin →I.  STUDYING IS A SKILL, LIKE READING AND WRITING.
  2 spaces                                               DS
1st tab stop →A.  Learn how to study.
             B.  Develop correct study habits through practice.
                                                              DS
use margin release;
backspace one time →II.  OBSERVE THESE GUIDES IN DEVELOPING STUDYING SKILLS.
                                                               DS
             A.  Set up a schedule with definite study periods.
2d tab stop →1.  Do not let anything change this schedule.
             2.  Find a quiet place to study.
             3.  Have needed materials available before you start.
             4.  Start at once; don't find excuses for delaying.
             B.  Study with a purpose.
             1.  Copy your assignments accurately; know what you
3d tab stop →are to do.
             2.  Search for ideas; think as you read or solve
                 problems.
             C.  Practice remembering the main points of a lesson.
             1.  Ask yourself questions on what you have studied.
             2.  Take brief notes.
```

continued on next page

leave 2″ top margin

A WHALE OF A TALE

QS

1″ left margin

1″ right margin

Whales have become one of the hottest items on the list of conservationists. Their efforts in terms of saving the whale population have been successful and exciting. Not since the seventeenth century has the population of whales been holding its own or growing.

DS

This statement reverses centuries of decline for the animals caused through their extensive killing by whalers for over 400 years. Because of the value of whale oil, whalers have prospected for whales in every ocean of the world; and many species have been hunted to near extinction.

DS

The optimism by conservationists is based on the latest survey of whale populations. It is important to note that whale counting has become a more sophisticated science in recent years, and the higher numbers may, in part, reflect that fact. Regardless, a quick species-by-species count shows that many of the great whales are doing better. In fact, in the past decade, it has now become evident that the recovery of the West Coast gray whale is complete.

DS

Conservationists and a great many other individuals are hoping that efforts to save the whale population will grow.

approximately 1″

57d, continued

Omit end-of-line periods when using the Topic Outline format.

Problem 2   Topic Outline

Directions: Key the topic outline below on a 40-space line DS. QS after the heading. Refer to Problem 1 for formatting directions.

LEARNING TO WRITE SUMMARIES

I. REASONS FOR SUMMARIZING
   A. Getting Ideas From Your Lessons
   B. Expressing Ideas Concisely
II. GUIDES FOR WRITING SUMMARIES
   A. Reading the Lesson
   B. Finding the Central Idea
   C. Finding Supporting Ideas
   D. Writing Down Ideas
     1. Writing briefly
     2. Using nouns and verbs
     3. Using your own words
   E. Editing Your First Draft
     1. Eliminating minor details
     2. Arranging ideas in order
     3. Omitting your own opinions
   F. Writing Summary in Final Form
     1. Using proper form
     2. Writing or keying neatly

LESSON 58

60-space line

5 minutes

58a ● Keyboard Review

Directions: Key each sentence three times SS. DS between 3-line groups.

alphabet   Hal G. Kumpf also said it was just six above zero in Quincy.

symbol   The guard screamed out, "Don't you dare park in that space!"

easy   I know for sure when items are for sale on the market shelf.

10 minutes

58b ● Paragraph Guided Writings

Directions: Take three 1' writings on each ¶ below. Try to make no more than three errors on the first writing; one error on the second; no errors on the third. Compare *gwam* on the three writings of each ¶.

all letters   1.3 si

gwam 3'

keep your eyes on the copy

The subject of life span is one that the experts know   4 | 40

quite a bit about. Not only do they know that women the   7 | 43

world over live longer than men do, but they realize that   11 | 47

this fact is not unique to human beings. The same thing is   15 | 51

true for almost every other species of mammal.   18 | 55

Just why females are the stronger sex is not so clear.   22 | 58

Some people say long life is due to genetic causes. Others   26 | 62

think that women tend to take better care of themselves.   30 | 66

There may be some truth in all the theories, whether they   34 | 70

are based on biology or behavior.   36 | 72

gwam 3' | 1 | 2 | 3 | 4 |

81e ● Right Margin Alignment on a Computer

Directions: 1. Key the following items in a play program. Use a 60-space line, aligning the names of the actors at the right margin. Use DS and center the title.

2. Use the flush right alignment feature of your machine. Refer to your equipment user's guide.

3. Center the problem vertically on the screen.

 Note: Most software will allow you to format automatically items in line (flush) with the right margin.

CAST

The Postman   Pat Spaulding

The Teacher   John Reichs

The Judge   Mary Beth Ryan

LESSON 82

70-space line

5 minutes

82a ● Keyboard Review

Directions: Key each sentence three times SS. DS between 3-line groups.

keep fingers deeply curved

alphabet Six dozen packages of quilts were just moved and sent by this factory.

figure The new address is 137 East 12th Street; our phone number is 555–6766.

o, i This ratio of pilots on radio and television was opposed to revisions.

easy Their old team was too tired to run that way again for four more days.

| 1 | 2 | 3 | 4 | 5 | 6 | 7 | 8 | 9 | 10 | 11 | 12 | 13 | 14 |

10 minutes

82b ● Control Ladder Paragraphs

Directions: 1. Take 1' writings on each ¶ in 81d, page 147. Circle errors and figure *gwam*.

2. When you key a ¶ within the error limit specified by your teacher, move to the next ¶. Use control as you key this exercise.

30 minutes

82c ● Formatting Problems: Unbound Reports

Directions: Problem 1   One-Page Report
Key the report on the next page on a 60-space line DS. Leave a 2″ top margin (begin on line 13). Refer to page 100, Keying a Short Report.

58c ● Learn to Format Class Notes

Directions: 1. Key the class notes below. Space as indicated by the colored notations on the copy.
2. Assume these notes will be placed in a notebook. Use leftbound report form.
3. Place the date even with the right margin on line 7. Center the heading 1″ below the date (center point will be three spaces to the right of the usual center point).
4. Clear all tab stops. Set two 4-space tab stops from the left margin.

Today's Date

TAKING NOTES
QS

left margin → <u>Notes on What You Hear</u>
DS
1st tab stop → 1. Don't try to write everything down. Get only the
important facts and ideas.
2 spaces DS
2. Relate what you know to what you hear. In this way you
2d tab stop → will get a better understanding of the topics
discussed.

3. If the speaker says something is important, put it
down.

4. If the speaker dwells on a fact or point, put it down.
DS

<u>Notes on What You Read</u>

1. Get the major points in mind by reading an article that
gives you a broad view of the subject in which you are
interested.

2. Summarize. Don't try to copy everything you read.

3. If a statement is made that you wish to quote, put
quotation marks around it. Get the complete source.
DS

<u>Preparing Notes in Final Form</u>

1. If you have taken the notes hurriedly, the sooner you
key them in final form, the better.

2. Key your notes in complete sentences. Add details that
you remember from your reading or from listening to a
discussion so that your notes will be meaningful to you
when you read them later.

3. Key your notes in good form. Space them so they will be
easy to read. Put a heading on them. Date them.

T A B L E O F C O N T E N T S

DINNER MENU

FOOTBALL SCHEDULE

MUSICAL SELECTIONS

20 minutes **81d ● Speed Ladder Paragraphs**

Directions: 1. Take a 1′ writing on ¶ 1 DS.
2. When you complete ¶ 1 in 1′, continue on to ¶ 2. Repeat this

procedure as you try to complete each of the five ¶ s in the given time.
3. Take three 1′ writings on any ¶ you cannot finish in the time given.

all letters used   1.3 si

gwam 5′

| | 4 | 8 | 12 | | |
| In both business and personal life it is quite important to be able | | | | 3 | 47 |

In both business and personal life it is quite important to be able   3 | 47
to send messages from one person to another.   If you can't talk face to   6 | 50
face, words must be sent some other way.   7 | 51

A long time ago the only way to get or send messages was to write   10 | 54
a letter and wait a long time for a return.   Voice communication that   13 | 57
used the phone and the radio speeded up the process a great deal.   15 | 59

While computers were at first developed just to process and store   18 | 62
data for tasks in science, changes have taken place.   At present one of   21 | 65
the primary uses of computers in the workplace and in the home is to   23 | 67
process words.   24 | 68

In fact, the use of word processing software has become the most   27 | 71
common application of today's computers.   This software has become so   29 | 74
popular because it has made it very easy to key, edit, and store words.   32 | 76
The words can then be processed.   34 | 78

The text that has been stored on a floppy or hard disk can now be   36 | 80
sent to the reader in a number of ways.   It can, of course, be sent to   39 | 83
a printer to produce a hard copy.   It can also be zoomed to a second   42 | 86
computer through a phone modem and be read on the spot.   44 | 88

gwam 5′ | 1 | 2 | 3 |

LESSON 59

5 minutes

59a ● Keyboard Review

Directions: Key each sentence three times SS. DS between 3-line groups.

key without pauses

alphabet   Kim required only five major exercises with the big trapeze.

symbol   She delivered my papers (Los Angeles Times) in half an hour.

easy   See if they can do most of their work on these new machines.

| 1 | 2 | 3 | 4 | 5 | 6 | 7 | 8 | 9 | 10 | 11 | 12 |

5 minutes

59b ● Language Arts Skills: Dictation and Spelling Checkup

Directions: 1. Your teacher will dictate the words in 57b, page 106. Key the words from dictation.

2. Check your work for correct spelling. Rekey any words in which you made an error.

5 minutes

59c ● Skill Comparison

keep your fingers deeply curved

Directions: 1. Take a 1' writing on the easy sentence. Figure *gwam*.
2. Take a 1' writing on each of the other sentences.

3. Try to match or exceed your goal sentence *gwam* on each of the other sentences.

words

easy   Their firms did not wish to take such a big risk right then. 12

direct reach   Bryan brought a number of my many friends to hear the music. 12

script   *Eight of the girls might visit both the towns and the lakes.* 12

rough draft   ~~They~~ *Those* who pull on teh oars ~~do not~~ *don't* have time to rock the boat. 12

30 minutes

59d ● Language Arts Skills

Problem 1   Capitalization

Directions: 1. Use a 60-space line and key the problem below on a full sheet of paper DS.
2. Use a 2" top margin and center the heading horizontally.
3. Correct any word that needs capitalization (refer to rules on page 105 if necessary).

APPLYING THE CAPITALIZATION RULES

1 i live in tucson in the winter and in chicago in the summer.
2 classes will be held at east junior high school next monday.
3 our october guest speaker is mayor dinkins of new york city.
4 all the delegates from africa and india could speak english.
5 both republicans and democrats supported the idaho proposal.
6 ms. cox said, "please return my copy of tom sawyer on time."
7 the lions club meets at the hotel cortez every tuesday noon.
8 all spanish visitors toured the south near atlanta, georgia.
9 just past lane middle school you will see gates junior high.
10 i think the pyrenees mountains lie between france and spain.
11 dr. handell spoke of exciting space trips to venus and mars.
12 the muddy mississippi river empties into the gulf of mexico.

(continued on next page)

Unit 11 ■ Keying School Papers (Lessons 81–95)

Learning Goals:

1. To arrange and key a variety of short reports, and a formal report with title page, footnotes, and bibliography.

2. To key related materials, such as outlines and bibliographical and note cards.

3. To develop additional basic skills, such as horizontal and vertical paper alignment, keying spread headings, and correcting errors by squeezing and spreading or replacing and inserting letters.

General Directions

Use a 70-space line for all lessons in this unit (center – 35; center + 35 + 5) unless otherwise directed. SS sentences and drill lines. DS paragraph copy.

Your teacher will tell you whether or not you are to correct errors on the problems in this unit and if you are to follow the procedures in this unit for correcting errors by "squeezing" and "spreading" letters and keying insertions.

LESSON 81

5 minutes   **81a ● Keyboard Review**

Directions: Key each sentence three times SS. DS between 3-line groups.

use quick,
sharp strokes

alphabet	Excited crowds enjoy big trapeze events and frequently want them back.
figure	The Pacific Ocean's depth of 35,958 feet makes it the world's deepest.
shift	Gene and Carl Kaminski, John Burns, and Billy M. Joel are on the team.
easy	The signs were easy to see if you were there near the top of the hill.

| 1 | 2 | 3 | 4 | 5 | 6 | 7 | 8 | 9 | 10 | 11 | 12 | 13 | 14 |

10 minutes   **81b ● Alignment of Paper: Horizontal and Vertical**

It may be necessary to reinsert paper to correct an error. The following drill will help you align your paper correctly.

Directions: 1. Insert paper and key this sentence:

I will align copy with skill.

2. Move the carrier so a word containing "i" or "I" is directly above a vertical line on the aligning scale (No. 33).

3. Note the relationship of the vertical line to the center of the letter. Note also the relationship of the top of the aligning scale to the bottom of the letters.

4. Remove paper; reinsert it. Use the variable line spacer (No. 34) to align the letters correctly in relation to the top of the aligning scale. Use the paper release lever (No. 7) to move the paper to the left or right until the lines on the scale are brought into alignment with the letters "i" and "I".

5. Rekey the sentence over the first writing, making any necessary adjustments.

6. Repeat the problem if time permits.

Note: If you are using a computer, complete 81e, page 148, in place of this assignment.

10 minutes   **81c ● Keying "Spread" Headings**

Directions: 1. Backspace from center one space for each letter, character, or space in a spread heading. Do not backspace for the last character or space in the line.

2. Key the heading. Space once between letters and three times between words.

3. The first heading on the following page is formatted correctly. Center and spread each of the other headings.

Problem 2   Topic Outline
Directions: 1. Key the outline below on a 60-space line. Use a 2″ top margin.

2. Follow the directions on the model outline. If necessary, refer to 57d, pages 106 and 107.

Key all strokes within circled lines in all CAPS.

(General) Directions for Writing a Book Review) — *Caps*

 I. (Items to ~~be~~ Included in Review) — *Caps*
             and Name
     A. Title ∧of Author
     B. central Theme of Book
     C. Some of the Important People
     D. Setting for the Story
     E. Brief Summary of Some Incidents
     F. Comments on and Opinion of the Book ~~Itself~~

 II. (General Guides ~~which are~~ to be Followed) — *Caps*
                         #
     A. Should Arouse Reader's Interest
     B. Should be Well Written   *Support*
     C. Should Contain examples to ∧comments

III. (Keying Guides to be Observed) — *Caps*

     A. Keyed in Report Form ∧*at*
     B. Quadruple Space After ~~the~~ Title; all Other ~~Material~~ *Copy*
         Double Spaced
     C. center heading over copy

LESSON 60

5 minutes

60a ● Keyboard Review

Directions: Key each sentence three times SS. DS between 3-line groups.

alphabet Jack Walder bought five exquisite topaz pins in Mexico City.

fig/sym Mr. Kim's students raised $685.70 during the 1992-93 season.

easy He thinks he will be there to see them when the plane lands.

| 1 | 2 | 3 | 4 | 5 | 6 | 7 | 8 | 9 | 10 | 11 | 12 |

---

10 minutes

60b ● Timed Writings

Directions: Take two 3′ writings on 58b, page 107. Figure *gwam*.

Submit the better writing.

---

30 minutes

60c ● Formatting Problem: Book Review

Directions: 1. Key the book review on page 111 in the format of a leftbound report DS.
2. Center the heading over the copy. Use a 2″ top margin. Follow the spacing as indicated in the model. As explained

on page 100, leftbound reports should have a left margin of 1½ inches and a right margin of 1 inch.
3. Clear all tab stops. Set a 5-space tab stop for indentation.

(continued on next page)

LESSON 80

5 minutes **80a ● Keyboard Review**

Directions: Key each sentence three times SS. DS between 3-line groups.

alphabet	Toxic waste is a major problem all good citizens have to face quickly.
fig/sym	The larger Lake Victoria has 26,828 square miles or 43 271 kilometers.
adjacent keys	We said the captain was astonished to see several sailors fast asleep.
easy	Now is the time to be sure to set your new goals for your school year.

| 1 | 2 | 3 | 4 | 5 | 6 | 7 | 8 | 9 | 10 | 11 | 12 | 13 | 14 |

---

15 minutes **80b ● Timed Writings**

Directions: 1. Take a 1' writing on each ¶ in 76d, page 138. Circle errors. Figure *gwam*.

2. Take a 5' writing on all five ¶s combined as you work for control. Circle errors. Figure *gwam*.

---

25 minutes **80c ● Formatting Problem: Club Schedule**

Directions: Key the club schedule below on a half sheet (long side up). Center the main heading 1" from the top. DS the entries. Leave eight spaces between columns. You may need to review the steps for arranging tables, page 114 and the steps for centering columnar headings, page 123.

STUDENT ACTIVITIES SCHEDULE

Month	Event	Leader
October	Homecoming Game	Coach Jim Jones
November	Talent Show	Betty Foster
December	Student-Faculty Game	Alicia Foster
February	Annual School Dance	William Funaro
March	Student Council Sale	Consuelo Blanco
April	Spring School Play	Richard Rogers
May	Magazine Sale	Issah Jones
June	Awards Banquet	Barbara Dobbs

80d ● Extra-Credit Activities

Directions: Problem 1

Assume that you needed more information on a product you planned to buy soon. On a half sheet of paper (short side up), compose/format a letter to a business firm requesting information about the item.

Directions: Problem 2

Key/format the letter in Problem 1, page 142, in modified block style with mixed punctuation on 8½ x 11" paper.

Directions: Problem 3

Key/format the letter in Problem 1, page 140, in block style with open punctuation on a full sheet of paper.

words

BOOK REVIEW: THE CALL OF THE WILD   7
DS

THE AUTHOR: Jack London   12
QS

This story relates the adventures of a very strong and intel-   24

ligent dog named Buck. Kidnapped from his comfortable California   37

home, he is transported to the Klondike and trained to work as a sled   51

dog. Buck learns very quickly to perform superbly in this rugged en-   65

vironment and to survive under extremely harsh conditions. He be-   79

comes admired and respected by many different people who recognize   92

his strength and courage.   97

Although Buck comes under the control of several different mas-   110

ters, he becomes truly devoted to only one of them. John Thornton,   124

who saves Buck's life when he is being mistreated, is repaid later   137

when the dog pulls him from a raging river. In one of the book's   150

most famous scenes, Buck wins a large bet for Thornton by pulling a   164

half-ton sled a distance of 100 yards.   172

THE CALL OF THE WILD offers the reader graphic descriptions of   184

the conditions under which the sled dogs lived. It contains many ex-   198

citing scenes. Anyone who considers reading this book should real-   212

ize, however, that it is not for the softhearted. It includes vivid   226

accounts of confrontations between the animals, as well as between   239

the dogs and those who handled them.   246

60d ● Extra Credit

Problem 1   Unbound Report
Directions: Key the two ¶ s in 58b, page 107 in unbound report form. Supply an appropriate heading.

Problem 2   Leftbound Report
Directions: Key the two ¶ s in 56c, page 104 in leftbound report form. Supply an appropriate heading.

79c, continued

Enclosure Notation Guide: An enclosure notation is used when an attachment is sent with the letter. Key the enclosure notation at the left margin a double space below the keyed name of the sender.

Use the plural *Enclosures* if two or more items will be enclosed.

Format/Key Totals: After keying a column of figures to be totaled, key an underline directly under the last line in the column as long as the total and the $.

Double space to key the word "Total"; indent three spaces from the left margin.

Directions: Problem 2   Order Letter in Block Style with Open Punctuation

1. Format/key the letter below on a 50-space line. Begin the return address on line 15; leave four spaces between the date and the inside address.
2. Use a 40-space line for the table within the letter. (Indent five spaces from the right and left margins. To determine the tab stop for the second column, backspace 6 spaces from your new right margin.)

Return address: 3230 Beacon Lane | Lexington, KY 40504-1923 | August 15, 19--

Recipient's address: Sampson & Sons, Inc. | 397 Almont Highway | Midland, MI 48612-1289 | Ladies and Gentlemen

(¶) Please send me the following computer supplies that were advertised in the July issue of *Computer News*.   I understand that if I order these supplies now they will arrive in time for the fall opening of school.

12	#741 Printer ribbons	$39.95
10	#45 DD microdisks	15.50
1	#20 Pin feed paper	21.99
1	#87 Dust cover	18.50
	Total	$95.94

(¶) Enclosed is my check for $95.94. I presume all shipping costs are included in the order prices. Sincerely yours | Bill House | Enclosure

Directions: Problem 3   Order Form

1. Using the order form included in your workbook (WB, p. 159), key the copy below exactly as it appears in the illustration at the right.
2. Use the variable line spacer to adjust the paper correctly for each line of copy.

Alternate Suggestion: If a workbook is not available, or if you are using a computer, order the items below by order letter similar to the one you keyed in Problem 2, above.

Order No.: 107   Ship via: Parcel Post

To: The Cabinet Shop
1980 Moore Street
Rogers, MN 55374-1495

Quantity	Cat. No.	Description	Price	Total
3	B241-1	Corner posts	3.95	11.85
4	D412-5	Hinges, semi-concealed	1.75	7.00
24	B125-0	Wood pegs	.32	7.68
				$26.53

Date: 5/23/--   Purchasing Agent: Marie Jarvis

The Attic Shop
3724 Vine Street Lima, OH 45804-2985
419-242-3905

To: The Cabinet Shop
1980 Moore Street
Rogers, MN 55374-1495

Order No. 107

Ship via Parcel Post

Quantity	Cat. No.	Description	Price	Total
3	B241-1	Corner Posts	3 95	11 85
4	D412-5	Hinges, semiconcealed	1 75	7 00
24	B125-0	Wood pegs	32	7 68
				$26 53

Date 5/23/--   Purchasing Agent Marie Jarvis

Unit 9 ■ Learning to Key Tables (Lessons 61–70)

Learning Goals:

1. To format tables that present information clearly and attractively.

2. To format a report including a short table.

3. To continue development of language arts skills—including spelling, proofreading, composing, and punctuation.

4. To continue refinement of stroking and operating techniques through meaningful practice.

General Directions

Use a 60-space line, unless otherwise directed, for all lessons in this unit (center – 30; center + 30 + 5). SS sentences and drill lines. DS between repeated groups of lines and paragraph copy. Set machine for a 5-space paragraph indention. Your teacher will tell you whether or not to correct errors when keying problems.

LESSON 61

5 minutes

61a ● Keyboard Review

Directions: Key each sentence three times SS. DS between 3-line groups.

keep wrists and elbows quiet

alphabet	We have quoted him fairly as a recognized junk bonds expert.
fig/sym	Leave 18 spaces (elite) for the left margin of 1 1/2 inches.
easy	It looks as if six or eight giant signs were then torn down.

| 1 | 2 | 3 | 4 | 5 | 6 | 7 | 8 | 9 | 10 | 11 | 12 |

5 minutes

61b ● Fluency Practice

Directions: Key each line 3 times SS. DS between 3-line groups.

1 to use| to use the| to use this| to get| to get this| to get that
2 for their| their plan| for their plans| their use| for their use
3 when the| when they| want this| want their| when they want their
4 if the| if the one| if they| if they want| if they want that one

| 1 | 2 | 3 | 4 | 5 | 6 | 7 | 8 | 9 | 10 | 11 | 12 |

10 minutes

61c ● Technique Builder: Stroking

keep your eyes on the copy

Directions: Key each line three times SS. DS between 3-line groups.

hyphen	Joan Lucas-Homan installed high-quality, low-volume faucets.
double letters	Manny Dunne will keep that fellow from passing the football.
direct reaches	Under no circumstances can my younger brother receive money.
one-hand	Teresa read up only on car races. Dad bragged on my grades.
balanced-hand	She paid the rich man for half of the fish kept at the dock.
combination	We got the rebate as a reward for the work that we did then.

| 1 | 2 | 3 | 4 | 5 | 6 | 7 | 8 | 9 | 10 | 11 | 12 |

5 minutes

61d ● Skill Comparison

Directions: Key 57c, page 106, as directed.

LESSON 79

5 minutes **79a ● Keyboard Review**

Directions: Key each sentence three times SS. DS between 3-line groups.

keep wrists and elbows quiet

alphabet	The judge was quick to penalize the six boys for moving the green car.
fig/sym	New subscriptions cost $8.47 for 39 weeks and only $9.60 for 52 weeks.
long words	Their organization's new constitution includes a number of paragraphs.
easy	The problem they have right now is caused by the slant of their hands.

| 1 | 2 | 3 | 4 | 5 | 6 | 7 | 8 | 9 | 10 | 11 | 12 | 13 | 14 |

10 minutes **79b ● Language Arts Skills: Punctuation Guides**

Directions: The following are punctuation guides and sentences that illustrate those guides. Study each guide; then key the line that illustrates the guide. Key each sentence twice SS; DS between 2-line groups.

Use a comma after each item in a series, except the last one.
Most students hope someday to own, drive, and care for their new cars.

Use a comma to separate consecutive adjectives when the *and* has been omitted.
The coach gave out uniforms to the excited, eager members of the team.

Use a comma to separate a dependent clause that precedes the main clause.
When you have special writing assignments, I will want to review them.

Use a comma to separate two complete clauses separated by *and, but, for, or, so, yet.*
He was hoping to do well in the typing class, but he did not practice.

Use a comma to set off day from year, city from state, and hundreds from thousands.
A March 5, 1991, meeting was attended by 2,115 members in Berea, Ohio.

Use a comma to set off a short direct quotation from the rest of the sentence.
His teacher stated, "All your assignments must be in by the deadline."

30 minutes **79c ● Formatting Problems**

Directions: Problem 1 Keying on Ruled Lines

1. Key three horizontal lines 30 spaces wide with the underline key DS. Remove the paper from the machine.

2. Reinsert paper and use the variable line spacer to align the paper.

3. Use the backspace-from-center method to center the first line. Set your left margin at the point where the backspacing is completed. Key each line as shown below.

4. Compare your copy with the example to check alignment. Only a slight space should separate the letters from the underline.

Note: If you are using a computer, format this problem by keying the three lines by using the automatic underlining feature of your software.

Mr. William R. Keskey

17239 Dean Avenue

Boston, MA 02187-0255

(continued on next page)

61e ● Paragraph Guided Writings

Directions: 1. Take one 3' writing on the ¶s below. Circle errors; figure *gwam*.
2. Key each circled word three times along with the words that precede and follow it.

3. Take two 1' writings on each ¶. Try to add 4 words to your 3' rate. Figure *gwam*.
4. Key another 3' writing. Figure *gwam* and circle errors. Compare with your first 3' writing.

all letters used   1.3 si

gwam 3'

strike each key
with quick,
sharp strokes

		gwam 3'
As is the case with many of our major discoveries, the	4	55
exact origin of ice cream is not known. The cold, hard fact	8	59
of the matter is that no one knows for sure who should get	12	63
the credit for inventing this frozen delight.	15	66
We do know, however, that enough ice cream is produced	18	70
in this country alone to allow each and every one of us to	22	74
consume more than a dozen quarts a year. It is a safe bet,	26	78
of course, that kids of all ages are doing their level best	30	82
to keep this average right up there.	33	85
The flavors people like the best are pretty well known.	37	88
Vanilla, as you might guess, outsells chocolate by about four	41	92
to one. Strawberry has dropped clear down to eighth place.	45	97
You will not be surprised to hear that dill pickle and kidney	49	101
bean are not on the list of favorites.	52	103

gwam 3' | 1 | 2 | 3 | 4 |

---

5 minutes   **61f ● Control Practice**

Directions: 1. Key the last ¶ in 61e as many times as you can in the time that remains.

2. Circle your errors. Place a check mark in the margin of each ¶ in which you made no more than one error.

LESSON 62

60-space line

5 minutes   **62a ● Keyboard Review**

Directions: Key each sentence three times SS; DS between 3-line groups.

alphabet Peggy Klem was acquitted of tax evasion by the dozen jurors.
fig/sym A & R Mfg. has been on E. 76th St. for 58 years (1934–1992).
easy The firms will not pay us for the pens if they are worn out.
       | 1 | 2 | 3 | 4 | 5 | 6 | 7 | 8 | 9 | 10 | 11 | 12 |

25 minutes   **78d ● Formatting Problems: Personal/Business Letters**

Directions: Problem 1   Block Style Application with Open Punctuation

1. Key the letter below as illustrated at the right. Use a full sheet, block style, open punctuation, 60-space line.
2. Begin the return address on line 15. Follow other spacing directions as

shown on the model.
3. Address a small envelope (or paper cut to size). If an envelope is used, fold and insert the letter.

Return address: 1927 Council Street | Fremont, NE 68025-6543 | April 22, 19--

Recipient's address: Ms. Luisa Moreno | The Fremont Daily | 17 South Pine Avenue | Fremont, NE 68025-5640 |
Dear Ms. Moreno

This letter is in response to your advertisement in Sunday's issue of the Fremont Daily. That advertisement did indicate that you were now looking for 14- to 16-year-old students to work part time after school trying to get new customers for your newspaper. I would like to apply for this job.

Next fall I will be in the tenth grade at Carver Middle School and am 15 years of age. A job such as the one you advertised would help me gain good work experience and allow me to earn some money for a college education.

I do have some experience which was gained by working in the school office. Mr. Paul Marks, school principal, has given me permission to use him as a reference. He indicated that he would be glad to furnish a letter of recommendation.

I am available to come in for an interview any day after school. My home phone number is 555-4781.

Sincerely yours | Roberta Miles

```
begin on
line 15   1927 Council Street
          Fremont, NE  68025-6543
          April 22, 19--
                    space down
                    4 times
          Ms. Luisa Moreno
          The Fremont Daily
          17 South Pine Avenue
          Fremont, NE  68025-5640
                                  DS
          Dear Ms. Moreno
                          DS
          This letter is in response to your advertisement in Sunday's
          issue of the Fremont Daily.  That advertisement did indicate
          that you were now looking for 14- to 16-year-old students to
          work part time after school trying to get new customers for
          your newspaper.  I would like to apply for this job.
                                                              DS
          Next fall I will be in the tenth grade at Carver Middle School
          and am 15 years of age.  A job such as the one you advertised
          would help me gain good work experience and allow me to earn
          some money for a college education.
                                             DS
          I do have some experience which was gained by working in the
          school office.  Mr. Paul Marks, school principal, has given
          me permission to use him as a reference.  He indicated that
          he would be glad to furnish a letter of recommendation.
                                                                 DS
          I am available to come in for an interview any day after
          school.  My home phone number in 555-4781.
                                                     DS
          Sincerely yours

          Roberta Miles       space down
          Roberta Miles       4 times
```

Directions: Problem 2   Block Style Thank You Letter With Open Punctuation

1. Key the letter below in block style, open punctuation, 50-space line.
2. Date the letter May 18, 19--. Begin the return address (use the return

address given in Problem 1) on line 18. Also use recipient's address given in Problem 1. Follow other spacing directions as shown on the model above.

Dear Ms. Moreno | Thank you very much for interviewing me on Monday afternoon.

The duties of the job you described sound quite interesting. I like the idea of being able to work with other employees who are my age. Also, the opportunity to win bonus trips is exciting.

I will be able to start working on May 6. Again, my home phone is 555-4781.

Sincerely yours | Roberta Miles

62b ● Sentence Guided Writings

Directions: 1. Take 1' writings on each sentence SS. Try to reach the end of the sentence as the guide is called.
2. Your instructor will call the return each 15" or 12" to guide you. If you complete each sentence as the guide is called, you will key the sentence four times with the 15" call of the guide or five times with the 12" call of the guide.
3. Figure *gwam* and circle errors.

	gwam	15" guide	12" guide
1 A new world era has now begun.		24	30
2 Today's economy is global in scope.		28	35
3 Products come from many different lands.		32	40
4 Be aware of the changes happening around you.		36	45
5 These trends will greatly influence your own life.		40	50
6 An information age requires a well educated work force.		44	55
7 You should continue to work hard to upgrade your job skills.		48	60

| 1 | 2 | 3 | 4 | 5 | 6 | 7 | 8 | 9 | 10 | 11 | 12 |

---

5 minutes

62c ● Steps in Arranging Tables: Horizontal Placement

Step 1 Insert paper into the machine with left edge at "0."

Step 2 Move the left and right margin stops to the ends of the scale. Clear all tab stops.

Step 3 Move the printing point to the center of the paper.

Step 4 Determine spacing between the columns (if a specific number of spaces is not given).

Step 5 Spot the longest word or entry in each column.

Step 6 From the center of your paper, backspace once for each 2 letters, figures, spaces or punctuation marks in each column. If you have an extra character in any column, add that character to the first character of the next column. If one space is left over after backspacing for all the columns, disregard it.

Step 7 Backspace once for every 2 spaces to be left between the columns. If one space is left over, disregard it.

Step 8 Set the left margin at the point at which you stop backspacing. This is the point where the first column will start.

Step 9 Space forward once for each letter, figure, space or punctuation mark in the longest entry in the first column and once for each space between Columns 1 and 2. Set a tab stop for the second column. Continue in this way until stops have been set for each column.

---

25 minutes

There are 33 line spaces on a half sheet of paper.

62d ● Formatting Problems: Two-Column Tables

Directions: Problem 1

1. Center the table on page 115 horizontally and vertically on a half sheet of paper.

2. Vertical placement directions for this problem are given in the table. This table is placed in exact vertical center.

3. Center the heading over the columnar entries. Leave 12 spaces between columns. Set the left margin stop for the first column, as directed above.

4. Space forward once for each letter and space in Column 1. Then space forward 12 spaces for the space between columns. Set a tab stop.

(continued on next page)

LESSON 78

70-space line

5 minutes **78a ● Keyboard Review**

Directions: Key each sentence three times SS. DS between 3-line groups.

keep your eyes
on the copy

alphabet We realize that even a good ex-jockey must pass qualify before racing.

fig/sym Check #14983 for the amount of $174.50 was for the 24 printer ribbons.

o, i A ratio of anxious seniors outside an office of the station was great.

easy You might train yourself to think just as you train yourself to write.

| | 1 | 2 | 3 | 4 | 5 | 6 | 7 | 8 | 9 | 10 | 11 | 12 | 13 | 14 |

---

10 minutes **78b ● Speed Builder**

Directions: Take two 1' writings on each ¶; try to increase speed on the second writing. Figure *gwam*.

Alternate Procedure: Work for speed as you take one 5' writing on all three ¶ s combined. Figure *gwam*.

all letters used 1.4 si

gwam 1' | 5'

keep fingers
deeply curved

One of the major early reasons that a typewriter was invented was 13 | 3 | 35
the need to be able to write with speed in a readable form. To be able 28 | 6 | 38
to get thoughts down quickly and in a form that is easy to read is still 42 | 8 | 41
a goal that needs to be recognized. 49 | 10 | 42

Some people think that the need to input data with speed does not 13 | 13 | 45
exist since we are now using computers. These people are wrong. The 27 | 15 | 48
ability to key data with speed and accuracy is even more critical today 42 | 18 | 51
than it was in the early years of typing. 50 | 20 | 52

What good are the high speeds with which a computer can process 13 | 23 | 55
data and help make decisions if the person entering the data is slow and 27 | 25 | 58
is not accurate? Your skill in keying data is very key to future suc- 41 | 28 | 61
cess in business and the use of any writing device with a keyboard at 55 | 31 | 64
home. Work hard to build your skill. 63 | 33 | 65

gwam 1' | 1 | 2 | 3 | 4 | 5 | 6 | 7 | 8 | 9 | 10 | 11 | 12 | 13 | 14 |
5' | 1 | 2 | 3 |

---

5 minutes **78c ● Skill Builder**

Directions: Take two 1' writings on each sentence. Figure *gwam*.

Work for speed as you key this exercise.

keep arms and
wrists quiet

1 Those who learn from their failures can make their names in the world.

2 Your keying skills will improve if you practice them in the right way.

| | 1 | 2 | 3 | 4 | 5 | 6 | 7 | 8 | 9 | 10 | 11 | 12 | 13 | 14 |

```
 3
 4
 5
 6
 7                              Begin on line 10
 8
 9
10                    OUTSTANDING  STUDENT  AWARDS
11                                                        DS
12        Deborah Chaffee                 Academics
13                                                        DS
14        Stan Ledermann                  Athletics
15
16        Manuel Guerrero                 Drama
17
18        Willie S. Fuller             Instrumental Music   Longest item
19
20 Longest item Gloria Anne Podolsky      Journalism
21
22        Elizabeth Nielsen               Service
23        ↑                               ↑
24     Left margin                      Tab
25              20               12      |         18
26        |                       |      |                    |
27
28
29
```

Simple two-column table

62d, continued **Directions: Problem 2**

1. Key the table in Problem 1. Add Allison Leung, who won the Vocal Music award, to the list of students.
2. Place the table on a full sheet of paper in reading position. Use the backspace from center method for vertical centering. Refer to 52d, page 98, if necessary.
3. Center the heading. Leave 16 spaces between columns.

LESSON 63

60-space line

5 minutes **63a ● Keyboard Review**

Directions: Key each sentence three times SS. DS between 3-line groups.

alphabet Please pack my boxes with five dozen jugs of liquid varnish.

fig/sym Dale is almost 5′8″, Anne is 5′10″, and Jose is nearly 6′2″.

easy They thought there should be goals at each end of the field.

| 1 | 2 | 3 | 4 | 5 | 6 | 7 | 8 | 9 | 10 | 11 | 12 |

77c ● Formatting Problems: Personal/Business Letters

Directions: Problem 1   Modified Block Style Letter with Open Punctuation

1. Key the letter below as illustrated at the right. Use a full sheet, modified block style, open punctuation, 50-space line.

2. Begin the return address on line 18. Follow other spacing directions as shown on the model.

3. After you have finished, address a small envelope or paper cut to size (6½" x 3⅝") for the letter. Fold the letter and insert it in the envelope if you are using one. (Refer to 48c, page 90 for placement and folding instructions.)

Return address: 1821 Raleigh Road | Napa, CA 94558-3312 | Today's date

Recipient's address: Ms. Jane Stacey | Northern Bank & Trust | 3947 Spruce Street | Napa, CA 94558-2787 Dear Ms. Stacey

Our school paper is planning to publish an article on savings accounts for young investors. I understand there are a number of different ways that students in our school could begin a savings program that would grow in value.

Would you please send me any materials or information that would be of interest in the article on savings that I plan to write. I will be sure to send you a copy of the article as soon as it is published in our school paper.

Sincerely yours | Toshi Kato

centerpoint

begin on line 18

```
1821 Raleigh Road
Napa, CA  94558-3312
Today's Date
```
space down
4 times

```
Ms. Jane Stacey
Northern Bank & Trust
3947 Spruce Street
Napa, CA  94558-2787

Dear Ms. Stacey   DS
                DS
Our school paper is planning to publish an article
on savings accounts for young investors.  I under-
stand there are a number of different ways that
students in our school could begin a savings program
that would grow in value.  DS

Would you please send me any materials or information
that would be of interest in the article on savings
that I plan to write.  I will be sure to send you a
copy of the article as soon as it is published in our
school paper.   DS

                Sincerely yours   space down
                Toshi Kato        4 times

                Toshi Kato
```

Directions: Problem 2   Modified Block Style Letter with Open Punctuation

1. Key the letter below in modified block, open punctuation. Use your own address and today's date in the return address.

2. Follow all other directions as given in Problem 1.

Return address: Your address | Today's date | Recipient's address: Mr. James Funaro | 201 Villa Way | Seattle, WA 98109-1009 | Dear Mr. Funaro

I recently read an article indicating that you are a former typing champion who reached record speeds on one-hour timed writings.

Our keyboarding class at Seattle Junior High School is currently working on a variety of exercises and drills designed to build strong keyboarding skills. As you know, it is not always easy to attain high speeds with good accuracy.

Mr. Funaro, you could be of great help to us if you would come to our keyboarding class and demonstrate your championship skills. If this is possible, please write me at the above address.

Sincerely | Sign your name

63b ● **Skill Comparison**

Directions: 1. Take two 1' writings on the easy sentence SS. Figure *gwam*.
2. Take two 1' writings on each of the other sentences.

3. Try to match or exceed your *easy* sentence *gwam* on each of the other sentences.

words

easy   She said that their big problems are due to a lack of goals.   12

fig/sym   Our Model 368 (about $25,000) has a high-performance engine.   12

script   *It's hard to climb a ladder with your hands in your pockets.*   12

rough draft   ~~When~~ *If* the going seems to easy you may well be going down hill.   12

---

5 minutes   **63c** ● **Language Arts Skills: Spelling and Proofreading Aid**

Directions: Key each line three times SS. DS between 3-line groups.

1   bureau February partial forty governor miscellaneous process
2   between niece participate battery ceiling graduate permanent
3   address lose recognize nephew courteous family exceed memory

---

25 minutes   **63d** ● **Formatting Problems: Centering Two-Column Tables**

Directions: Problem 1
1. Key the table below on a half sheet of paper DS. Use the exact vertical centering method.

2. Center the headings horizontally. Leave 12 spaces between columns.

POPULATION PROJECTIONS
DS
(State Rank by 2000)
DS

California (1)	South Dakota (46)
Texas (2)	Alaska (47)
New York (3)	North Dakota (48)
Florida (4)	Vermont (49)
Illinois (5)	Wyoming (50)

Directions: Problem 2
1. Key the table below in reading position on a half sheet of paper DS.

2. Center the headings horizontally. Leave 10 spaces between columns.

THE THROWAWAY SOCIETY
DS
Billions Thrown Away Every Year
DS

Plastic bottles	91
Plastic bags	25
Disposable diapers	18
Razors and blades	2
Pens	1

Note: Indent from tab stop for shorter items

76e ● Language Arts Skills: Punctuation Guides
Period, Question Mark, and Exclamation Point

Directions: Each of the punctuation guides below is followed by a sentence that illustrates it. Study each guide; then key the sentence that illustrates the guide. Key each sentence twice SS. DS between 2-line groups.

Note: A space follows each period after initials. No space is needed after a period within an abbreviation. Space once after a period that ends an abbreviation unless that period ends a sentence, in which case, space twice.

Use a period after a sentence making a statement or giving a command.
Sheena told the class that it must support the school teams this year.

Use a period after an initial.
The A. J. Foss Company named Hector A. Sanchez to succeed May B. Hoyt.

Do not use a period after a nickname.
Al told me that he and Ed would meet with Jennifer later that morning.

Use a period after most abbreviations.
Mr. Bob Smith worked full time for the Jones Corp. in Washington, D.C.

Use a question mark after a direct question.
Will there be enough tickets for all of us to attend their first game?

Use a period after requests and indirect questions.
I wonder whether we all can go. Will you be sure to let me know soon.

Use an exclamation mark to express strong or sudden feeling.
Congratulations! You came in first in the event! You can really run!

LESSON 77

70-space line

77a ● Keyboard Review

5 minutes

Directions: Key each sentence three times SS. DS between 3-line groups.

keep feet flat on the floor

alphabet   We made expensive jacks of high quality, but they were the wrong size.

fig/sym   The Jones & Lauglin Co. sold 21,000 new units in the 100+ degree heat.

direct reach   My batter must do better than a certain grounded player on that bench.

easy   Did the girl in the auto signal to make the right turn on time or not?

| 1 | 2 | 3 | 4 | 5 | 6 | 7 | 8 | 9 | 10 | 11 | 12 | 13 | 14 |

77b ● Skill Builder

10 minutes

Directions: 1. Take a 1' writing. The last word keyed will be your goal word.
2. Take a 5' writing with the return called after each minute. When the return is called, start the paragraph over again. Try to reach your goal each minute as the return is called.

return quickly   1.3 si

A cork tree plays a key role in our everyday lives. Yet, its very importance is little recognized. The bark of this tree is used in quite a number of common household products. Cork is used in many useful items such as shoe soles, sports helmets, and floor coverings. It is strong, but light enough to float.

LESSON 64

5 minutes

64a ● Keyboard Review

Directions: Key each sentence three times SS. DS between 3-line groups.

alphabet Tammy Planck will squeeze five or six juicy oranges by hand.

fig/sym We sent a check for $56.80 to Box #174 on February 23, 1992.

easy They came with the chain to see if we had made a first down.

| 1 | 2 | 3 | 4 | 5 | 6 | 7 | 8 | 9 | 10 | 11 | 12 |

---

5 minutes

64b ● Language Arts Skills: Keying from Dictation and Spelling Checkup

Directions: 1. Your teacher will dictate the words in 63c, page 116. Key the words from dictation.

2. Check your work for correct spelling. Rekey any words in which you made an error.

---

10 minutes

64c ● Sentence Guided Writings

Directions: 1. Try to key each sentence in 62b, page 114, four times in 1' without error.

2. Your teacher will call the return each 15" to guide you.

64d ● Formatting Problems: Tables With Subheadings   25 minutes

Directions: Problem 1

Key the table directly below in exact vertical and horizontal center on a full sheet of paper. DS between main and subheading and between subheading and body. DS entries in columns. Leave 18 spaces between columns.

Directions: Problem 2

Key the table directly below in reading position. Center horizontally on a full sheet of paper. DS between main and subheadings; DS between subheadings and body. DS entries in columns. Leave 12 spaces between columns.

FAVORITE COMICS
DS
Strip and Cartoonist
DS

BC	Johnny Hart
Beetle Bailey	Mort Walker
Blondie	Chic Young
Broom Hilda	Russell Myers
Calvin and Hobbes	Bill Watterson
Cathy	Cathy Guisewite
Dennis the Menace	Hank Ketcham
Doonesbury	Garry Trudeau
The Family Circus	Bil Keane
The Far Side	Gary Larson
Garfield	Jim Davis
Jump Start	Robb Armstrong
Momma	Mell Lazarus
Peanuts	Charles Schulz
Spiderman	Stan Lee

STATE NICKNAMES
DS
Fifteen Largest U.S. States
DS

Alaska	Last Frontier
Arizona	Grand Canyon
California	Golden
Colorado	Centennial
Idaho	Gem
Kansas	Sunflower
Nebraska	Cornhusker
Nevada	Sagebrush
New Mexico	Sunshine
Minnesota	Gopher
Montana	Treasure
Oregon	Beaver
Texas	Lone Star
Utah	Beehive
Wyoming	Equality

76c ● Technique Builder: Stroking

Directions: Key each sentence 3 times SS. DS between 3-line groups.

1 A team should know that a winner never quits and a quitter never wins.

2 Remember, you can never possibly win any races if you never start one.

3 Winning is everything, and it is way ahead of what is in second place.

4 Try never to confuse keeping your chin up with sticking your neck out.

| 1 | 2 | 3 | 4 | 5 | 6 | 7 | 8 | 9 | 10 | 11 | 12 | 13 | 14 |

76d ● Speed Ladder Paragraphs

Directions: 1. Take 1' writings on ¶ 1 DS until you complete the ¶ in 1'. 2. When you complete ¶ 1 in 1', continue on to ¶ 2. Repeat this procedure as you try to complete each of the five ¶ s in the given time.

all letters used   1.3 si

gwam 5'

Most students worry about two things when they are planning their school schedules--preparing for college and getting a good job. Both of these concerns are important, yet taxing.   3 | 47 ... 6 | 50 ... 7 | 51

One way to get ready to deal with these concerns is to attempt to get as many facts as possible about your interests. Try hard to find out what new course of study might be needed to reach your goal.   10 | 54 ... 13 | 57 ... 15 | 59

There is no quick way to get those facts you will need to make a good career decision. You can't just breeze through the reading of some textbooks or go around asking a few general questions. You must be ready to plan.   18 | 62 ... 21 | 65 ... 23 | 67 ... 24 | 68

Your plan should include a good deal of reading and a good deal of question asking. Your school and local libraries will have a number of books and other writings on how to find out your interests. Teachers and counselors are helpful too.   27 | 71 ... 30 | 74 ... 32 | 76 ... 34 | 78

Once you have determined what your interests are, you will need to decide what school of study you will need to support your interests. Two more sources of help in making this decision are your friends and relatives who have already made their career choices.   36 | 80 ... 39 | 83 ... 42 | 86 ... 44 | 88

gwam 5' | 1 | 2 | 3 |

5 minutes   **65a ● Keyboard Review**

Directions: Key each sentence three times SS. DS between 3-line groups.

alphabet   Four experts quickly amazed the crowd by juggling five axes.

fig/sym   Two tickets (priced at $18.75 each) will be offered for $35.

easy   Please have them fix the sign on the left side of the shelf.

| 1 | 2 | 3 | 4 | 5 | 6 | 7 | 8 | 9 | 10 | 11 | 12 |

---

10 minutes   **65b ● Technique Builder: Stroking**

Directions: Key each sentence 3 times SS. DS between 3-line groups.

home row   Dad dashed ahead just as there was a flash at Jake's garage.

1st finger   The hungry youngsters went right by without stopping to buy.

2d finger   Dick Duke, it was said, did check the deeds before deciding.

3d finger   L. W. Lo saw six old people mop, wax, and polish all floors.

double letters   Ann will discuss all three letters when the committee meets.

| 1 | 2 | 3 | 4 | 5 | 6 | 7 | 8 | 9 | 10 | 11 | 12 |

---

10 minutes   **65c ● Timed Writings**

Directions: Take two 3′ writings on all three ¶s combined. Circle errors. Figure   *gwam.* Submit the better of the two writings.

keep wrists and arms still

all letters used 1.3 si   *gwam 3′*

	gwam 3′	
The idea of flying flags is quite old. Their use can	4	51
be traced to ancient times, when soldiers fixed some kind of	8	55
emblem to long poles. Doing this enabled them to see where	12	59
their leader was as they followed him into battle.	15	62
Our country, as do all nations of the world, flies the	19	66
flag as a symbol of its people. The importance of such a	23	70
symbol to our citizens can be judged by the fact that flag	27	74
sales have been increasing in recent years.	30	77
Their size and design keep changing. One of the largest	33	80
flags ever attempted was larger than a football field and had	38	84
stars that were more than ten feet across. Whether they are	42	89
large or small, flags express an eloquent message for the	45	92
nation they represent.	47	94

gwam 3′ | 1 | 2 | 3 | 4 |

75c, continued

Directions: Problem 2   Modified Block Style with Open Punctuation

1. Set margins for a 40-space line.

2. On a half sheet of paper (short side up), key the personal letter below.

3. As you did in Problem 1, follow spacing directions as given in the model.

Return address: 209 East Dean | Ogden, UT 84404-3522 | May 21, 19--

Recipient's address: Miss Barbara Cubor | 1801 Willow Court | Ogden, UT 84404-3412 | Dear Barbara

Congratulations to you on your election as president of the student council of North Ogden High School.

As editor of the Ogden Community News I am pleased to welcome you to the special group of high school students that will be honored by our newspaper on June 5 at Balsy Auditorium.

I know that you will do an excellent job for your school and your fellow students. I look forward to meeting you in person on June 5.

Sincerely | sign your name

LESSON 76

70-space line

5 minutes

76a ● Keyboard Review

Directions: Key each sentence three times SS. DS between 3-line groups.

alphabet George played very quaint music that was the craze from old jukeboxes.

fig/sym Diaz bought 6 dozen eggs @$1.39 in the new store for a total of $8.34.

e, i Their friends tried to unite to find issues while mine remained quiet.

easy When you play to win, it is not easy to lose your games by a few runs.

| 1 | 2 | 3 | 4 | 5 | 6 | 7 | 8 | 9 | 10 | 11 | 12 | 13 | 14 |

---

10 minutes

76b ● Speed Ladder Sentences

Directions: Key each sentence for 1'. Your teacher will call the guide at 15", 12", or 10" intervals. As time permits, repeat sentences on which you were not able to complete a line with the call of the guide.

	15" guide	12" guide	10" guide
1 You should always plan a long way ahead.	32	40	48
2 Great planning makes it easy to reach a goal.	36	45	54
3 Choose your career first and then make your plans.	40	50	60
4 When you plan, you will find that you have new talents.	44	55	66
5 Your new talents will grow into a career if you choose well.	48	60	72
6 Look at all fields that you think will fit your skills and plans.	52	65	78
7 If a time comes to make a final choice, you will be happy you planned.	56	70	84

| 1 | 2 | 3 | 4 | 5 | 6 | 7 | 8 | 9 | 10 | 11 | 12 | 13 | 14 |

65d ● Formatting Problems: Tables

Directions: Problem 1   Three-Column Table
1. Key the table below in reading position on a full sheet of paper.
2. DS columnar entries; leave six spaces between the columns.
3. Refer to page 114, if necessary.

FAMOUS DISABILITIES
DS

Ludwig Beethoven	Composer	Deaf
Robert S. Dole	U.S. Senator	Amputation/arm
Helen Keller	Educator	Blind/deaf
John F. Kennedy	U.S. President	Bad back
Mary Tyler Moore	Actress	Diabetic
Ronald Reagan	U.S. President	Hard of hearing
Franklin D. Roosevelt	U.S. President	Polio/wheelchair
Mel Tillis	Singer	Stutter
Stevie Wonder	Singer	Blind

Directions: Problem 2   Two-Column Table from Script
1. Key the table below in exact vertical center on a half sheet of paper.
2. SS the columnar entries; leave 8 spaces between columns.

INTERESTING FACTS
DS

Largest state	Alaska
Smallest state	Rhode Island
Tallest building	Sears Tower, Chicago
Longest river	Mississippi-Missouri
Oldest national park	Yellowstone
Easternmost city	Eastport, Maine
Westernmost city	Lihue, Kauai
Highest mountain peak	Mt. McKinley, Alaska
Highest waterfall	Yosemite Falls
Lowest point	Death Valley, California
Highest city	Climax, Colorado
Southernmost city	Hilo, Hawaii
Northernmost city	Barrow, Alaska

75c ● Formatting Problem: Personal Letters

Directions: Problem 1   Modified Block Style With Open Punctuation

1. Key the letter below as illustrated at the right on half-size stationery (5½ × 8½"), or use a half sheet of paper (short side up). Set a 40-space line.

2. Use modified block style and open punctuation with 5-space paragraph indentions.

3. Begin the return address on line 9. Follow other spacing directions as shown on the model. Sign your name.

Return address: **2879 Roland Drive** | **Tulsa, OK 74104-2028** | **October 17, 19--**

Recipient's address: **Mr. Roger Vanderlan** | **786 Davenport Circle** | **Tulsa, OK 74104-1813** | **Dear Mr. Vanderlan**

Thank you very much for your help in researching the history of the computer in the business office.

As you indicated, the development of the modern computer was very rapid. From huge machines that took up an entire room to units that fit on an office desk took less than fifty years to accomplish.

Thank you again for your help and please let me know if I may be of help to you in the future.

Sincerely yours | sign your name

Note: A personal letter requires only the signature of the sender. Do not key your name.

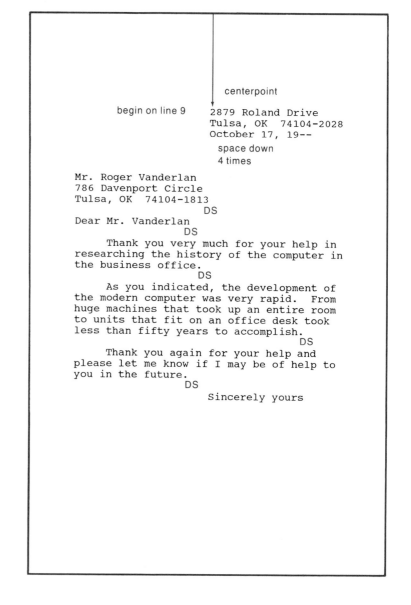

LESSON 66

5 minutes   **66a ● Keyboard Review**

Directions: Key each sentence three times SS. DS between 3-line groups.

alphabet   Jim was very excited by that big, powerful Santa Cruz quake.

fig/sym   All prices--except on Model 1927--will increase 5.6% June 4.

easy   I asked them to print their names to the right of the title.

| 1 | 2 | 3 | 4 | 5 | 6 | 7 | 8 | 9 | 10 | 11 | 12 |

---

5 minutes   **66b ● Language Arts Skills: Capitalization Guides**

Directions: The following are capitalization guides and sentences that illustrate those guides. Study each guide. Key the sentences that illustrate the guides twice SS; DS between 2-line groups.

Capitalize the principal words in titles of articles and plays, except short prepositions, conjunctions, or articles.

Our teacher read "The Planet-Sensitive Art of the Nineties."

We saw "The Grapes of Wrath" on the stage while in New York.

Capitalize or underscore the complete title of a book.

MEGATRENDS 2000 predicts what may happen in the years ahead.

I have the library's copy of Wilbur Smith's A Sparrow Falls.

---

15 minutes   **66c ● Sentence Guided Writings**

Directions: 1. Take 1' writings on each sentence SS. Try to key each sentence four times within the minute without error.

2. Your instructor will call the return each 15" to guide you.
3. Figure *gwam* and circle errors.

15" guide

gwam

1   Key all these facts carefully.   24

2   A fact is a statement that is true.   28

3   Television helps make the world smaller.   32

4   English is now becoming a universal language.   36

5   Today you are truly living in the information age.   40

6   Computers are a real force driving change in the world.   44

7   *They certainly affect the ways in which all of us live.*   44

8   Talking to someone almost anywhere on earth is quite simple.   48

9   *Even words in written form can now be transmitted instantly.*   48

74d ● Formatting Problems: Postal Cards

Directions: Problem 1

1. Insert a postal card or paper cut to size (5½ " × 3¼ ") into your machine.

2. Set margin stops 4 spaces from each edge of the card. Set a tab stop at

horizontal center.

3. Begin the date on line 3. DS below the date. DS between ¶s; QS to key name. Key the address on the opposite side of the card.

March 19, 19--
DS

Congratulations! You have been selected to represent your school in the annual Borden Speech Contest.   As a result, it will be necessary for you to be present at the WEXL TV studios on Wednesday, April 14.
DS

The event will begin at 7:00 p.m.   Our best wishes for your future success.
QS

Mr. Luis Garcia

Address the postal card to:

MS OKI SAGA | 655 BEACH STREET | FLUSHING NY 11356-8421

Addresses may be keyed in all caps with no punctuation or in caps and lower case with punctuation.

Directions: Problem 2

Key the message in Problem 1 on

postal cards. Use an appropriate salutation. Address the postal cards to:

1. MS LINDA STOCKBRIDGE
    918 SOUTH BROADWAY
    LOS ANGELES CA 90015-1618

2. MR YUAN SHENG
    ROUTE 2
    MIAMI FL 33132-1611

LESSON 75

70-space line

5 minutes

75a ● Keyboard Review

Directions: Key each line three times SS. DS between 3-line groups.

alphabet Jones knew exactly why he received a bad grade on that final map quiz.

fig/sym Maria bought 8# of the nails on January 25 and paid $7.62 for the lot.

br braid bright brag break bran brake brought brush brat brood bring bred

easy Try to stay even with all your work, and you will surely make the top.

| 1 | 2 | 3 | 4 | 5 | 6 | 7 | 8 | 9 | 10 | 11 | 12 | 13 | 14 |

15 minutes

75b ● Timed Writings

Directions: 1. Take one 1' writing on each ¶ on 71b, page 130. Circle errors.

2. Take one 5' writing on all four ¶s combined. Circle errors; figure *gwam*.

66d ● Paragraph Guided Writings

Directions: **1.** Take one 3' writing on the ¶s below. Circle all errors. Figure *gwam*.
2. Key each circled word three times with the word that precedes and follows it.

3. Take two 1' writings on each ¶. Try to increase your speed. Figure *gwam* and circle errors.

all letters used   1.3 si

gwam 3''

keep your wrists
low and still

Down through the years, humans have always found a need   4 | 50
to exchange written messages with those who live some distance   8 | 54
away. The first record of a system for doing this goes back   12 | 58
to the days of bronze tablets carried on horseback.   16 | 62

Our own mail service has evolved from the era of the   19 | 65
pony express to the jet age. To handle the expanding volume,   23 | 70
equipment is used that reads zip codes to direct a piece of   27 | 74
mail to one section of a block or one certain building.   31 | 77

No one knows how we will be sending written notes to   34 | 81
each other in the future. Today many firms use some form of   38 | 85
electronic mail, where their letters are sent by means of   42 | 89
telephone lines and no written copies are transported at all.   46 | 93

gwam 3' | 1 | 2 | 3 | 4 |

---

5 minutes **66e ● Control Practice**

Directions: **1.** Key the last ¶ in 66d above as many times as you can in the time that remains.

2. Circle your errors. Place a check mark in the margin of each ¶ in which you made no more than one error.

LESSON 67

60-space line

5 minutes **67a ● Keyboard Review**

Directions: Key each sentence three times SS. DS between 3-line groups.

alphabet The quiz show Jack Palm entered had six girls and five boys.
fig/sym Janine ran the 100-yard dash (91.4 meters) in less than 15".
easy Kate tossed the ball right to him as she ran down the court.

| 1 | 2 | 3 | 4 | 5 | 6 | 7 | 8 | 9 | 10 | 11 | 12 |

73d ● Enrichment Activities

Directions: Key the paragraph below using a 50-space line. If you finish a word within the next 3 strokes after the end-of-line warning, do so; if not, apply the guides on page RG11.

Note: On a microcomputer and on some electronic typewriters, end the first line after "ver" by inserting a hyphen and striking return; divide words on other lines, if necessary, to prevent an uneven right margin.

> To center your copy on the writing page ver-
> tically, you must know the number of lines in your
> copy and the number of lines available on the page.
> If you plan to center horizontally, set your tab at
> the center point of paper and backspace once for
> every 2 characters or spaces.

LESSON 74

70-space line

5 minutes **74a ● Keyboard Review**

Directions: Key each line three times SS. DS between 3-line groups.

alphabet Wax on the airbag did not faze Jo, who was very quick to mop it clean.

fig/sym Most of the 180 students scored 70 or better on 90% of #7 test series.

combination to the rest, to the sea, to the inn, to the keyboard, to the new pupil

easy It is easy to do well if you do your best every time and in all cases.

| 1 | 2 | 3 | 4 | 5 | 6 | 7 | 8 | 9 | 10 | 11 | 12 | 13 | 14 |

---

5 minutes **74b ● Control Builder**

Directions: 1. Take a 1' writing on each ¶ in 73b, page 132. Circle errors. Figure *gwam*.

2. Work for control as you key this exercise.

---

5 minutes **74c ● Language Arts Skills: Number Expression Guide**

Directions: The following are examples of number expressions. The first line gives the rule; the remaining lines illustrate it.

Key each sentence three times SS; DS between each 3-line group.

Note: When referring to the time of day, spell out the hour with *o'clock;* use figures with *a.m.* or *p.m.*

1 With "o'clock," spell out the hour.   Use figures with "a.m." or "p.m."

2 They will arrive in the morning sometime between five and six o'clock.

3 The sun will rise as early as 4:55 a.m., and it could set at 8:17 p.m.

67b ● Language Arts Skills: Spelling and Proofreading Aid

Directions: Key each line three times SS. DS between 3-line groups.

1 machinery endeavor faculty assistant ninth necessity equally

2 appropriate ninety knowledge career truly pamphlet Wednesday

3 doctor completely enthusiasm since occur accurate beneficial

5 minutes

67c ● Paragraph Guided Writings

Directions: 1. Take a 1' writing on ¶ 1, 66d, page 121. Figure *gwam*. Add four words to your *gwam* for a new goal. **2.** Take three 1' writings on the same ¶.

Try to reach your goal on each writing. The quarter- or half-minutes will be called to guide you.

30 minutes

67d ● Formatting Problem: Four-Column Table

Directions: 1. Key the table below in reading position on a full sheet of paper. **2.** SS the columnar entries; leave six spaces between the columns.

Refer to page 114 for help in setting the left margin stop for the first column and tab stops for the second, third, and fourth columns.

TWO-LETTER ABBREVIATIONS FOR THE STATES
DS
Recommended by the U.S. Postal Service
DS

Alabama	AL	Montana	MT
Alaska	AK	Nebraska	NE
Arizona	AZ	Nevada	NV
Arkansas	AR	New Hampshire	NH
California	CA	New Jersey	NJ
Colorado	CO	New Mexico	NM
Connecticut	CT	New York	NY
Delaware	DE	North Carolina	NC
Florida	FL	North Dakota	ND
Georgia	GA	Ohio	OH
Hawaii	HI	Oklahoma	OK
Idaho	ID	Oregon	OR
Illinois	IL	Pennsylvania	PA
Indiana	IN	Rhode Island	RI
Iowa	IA	South Carolina	SC
Kansas	KS	South Dakota	SD
Kentucky	KY	Tennessee	TN
Louisiana	LA	Texas	TX
Maine	ME	Utah	UT
Maryland	MD	Vermont	VT
Massachusetts	MA	Virginia	VA
Michigan	MI	Washington	WA
Minnesota	MN	West Virginia	WV
Mississippi	MS	Wisconsin	WI
Missouri	MO	Wyoming	WY

Directions: Problem 1
Informal Invitation

1. Key the informal invitation shown in the model illustration at the right on a half sheet of paper, (short side up). You may also use 4½″ × 5½″ stationery for personal notes such as informal invitations.

2. Leave a 2″ top margin. Set a 40-space line and a 5-space tab stop for indented paragraphs.

3. Use modified block style, open punctuation. Begin the return address, dateline, and complimentary close at the horizontal center of the paper.

4. Begin the salutation on the 4th line space below the date. Sign the letter.

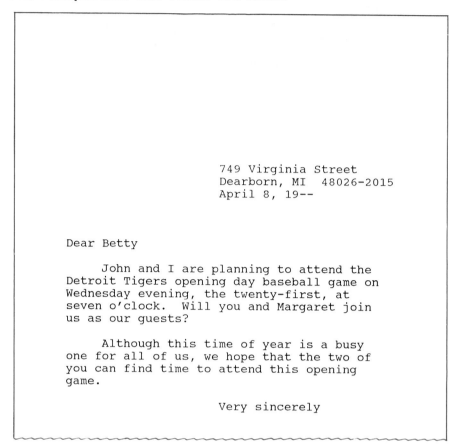

```
                          749 Virginia Street
                          Dearborn, MI  48026-2015
                          April 8, 19--


Dear Betty

     John and I are planning to attend the
Detroit Tigers opening day baseball game on
Wednesday evening, the twenty-first, at
seven o'clock.  Will you and Margaret join
us as our guests?

     Although this time of year is a busy
one for all of us, we hope that the two of
you can find time to attend this opening
game.

                          Very sincerely
```

Directions: Problem 2   Informal Acceptance
Key the informal acceptance below as directed in Problem 1.

Return Address: **1822 Dean Avenue** | **Detroit, MI 48212-6238** | Today's date
Dear Bill

Margaret and I are pleased to accept your generous invitation to attend the opening day ballgame with you and John next Wednesday evening. We are particularly interested in seeing the new stadium.

We are delighted that you thought of us and will plan on meeting you at gate 12 just before seven.

Sincerely | Betty

Directions: Problem 3   Thank You Note
Key the thank you note below as directed in Problem 1.

Return Address: **425 Ryan Road** | **St. Paul, MN 55110-2105** | Today's date
Dear Carmella

The party at your new house was the perfect way to end a weekend. It was really great to spend the evening with you and our former and new classmates.

Again, thank you very much for planning such a nice party and for including me.

Sincerely | Sign your name

LESSON 68

5 minutes   **68a** ● **Keyboard Review**

Directions: Key each sentence three times SS. DS between 3-line groups.

alphabet   Gail required me to fix every brown jacket with new zippers.

fig/sym   On April 1 the Cota-Lee extension changed from 2530 to 6847.

easy   I know she can see most of the fish if she sits on the dock.

| 1 | 2 | 3 | 4 | 5 | 6 | 7 | 8 | 9 | 10 | 11 | 12 |

---

5 minutes   **68b** ● **Skill Comparison**

Directions: 1. Take a 1' writing on the *easy* sentence. Figure *gwam*.

2. Take a 1' writing on each of the other sentences.

3. Try to match or exceed your *easy* sentence *gwam* on each of the other sentences.

words

do not pause between words

easy   She did not want us to visit with the rich widow on the bus.   12

script   *You know that when the going gets tough the tough get going.*   12

rough draft   one who was a shallow thinker never leaves a deep impression.   12

---

5 minutes   **68c** ● **Language Arts Skills: Keying from Dictation and Spelling Checkup**

Directions: 1. Your teacher will dictate the words in 67b, page 122. Key the words from dictation.

2. Check your work for correct spelling. Rekey any words in which you made an error.

---

5 minutes   **68d** ● **Centering Column Headings**

Directions: Study these steps for centering headings over columns in a table.

Step 1 Set the printing point or cursor at the point a column is to begin.

Step 2 Space forward 1 space for each 2 spaces in the longest line in that column.

Step 3 From that point, backspace once for each 2 spaces in the columnar heading.

Step 4 Key the heading. It will be centered over the column.

Note: If a column heading is longer than any item in the column, use the heading as the longest item in the column to figure the point to begin the column.

---

25 minutes   **68e** ● **Formatting Problems: Learn to Center Column Headings**

Directions: Problem 1 Practice Problem

1. Insert a sheet of practice paper. The two entries below are the longest items in each of two columns in a table.

2. Center the longest entries horizontally on your paper, leaving six spaces between the columns.

3. Following the steps given in 68d above, center the headings two spaces above the entries.

4. Then key the entries under the column headings.

Column Headings	Date	Chairperson
	DS	DS
Longest entries	September 20	Kimberly Mitchell

(continued on next page)

72c, continued

Directions: Problem 2   Invitation
Key the invitation below in exact vertical center using a half sheet of paper (long side up.)

MEET YOUR CANDIDATE NIGHT

You are invited to the gym
to meet officer candidates
Monday, October 7, 3:30 p.m.
Riverview School Gymnasium

Directions: Problem 3   Announcement
Key the announcement below in reading position using a full sheet of paper.

BASKETBALL TRYOUTS

Saturday, March 21--1:00 p.m.
Farwell School Gymnasium
Bring your equipment
Sign up in Room 7 before Tuesday

LESSON 73

5 minutes   **73a ● Keyboard Review**

Directions: Key each sentence three times SS. DS between 3-line groups.

alphabet   Just do not pull the gym fire alarm except when a blaze is very quick.

fig/sym   High density disks are $1.50 each or sell for $12.80 for a pack of 10.

long words   Language often flounders where a population is uninformed about books.

easy   I know that one way to get rid of old enemies is to make them friends.

| 1 | 2 | 3 | 4 | 5 | 6 | 7 | 8 | 9 | 10 | 11 | 12 | 13 | 14 |

10 minutes   **73b ● Speed Builder**

Directions: Take two 1' writings on each ¶; try to increase speed on the second writing. Figure *gwam.*

Alternate Procedure: Work for speed as you take one 5' writing on all three ¶s combined. Figure *gwam.*

all letters used   1.3 si   *gwam* 1'   5'

keep fingers curved and upright

	1'	5'
Writing for a school paper can be fun and an excellent way to learn	14	3 | 36
more about what is happening in your school and with fellow students.	28	6 | 39
It is also a way to build better writing and keying skills. There are	42	8 | 42
a number of things that you can do to get on the writing team.	55	11 | 44
If you would like to work on your school paper, you must first find	14	14 | 47
out who sponsors it. Next, you should attempt to make a contact with	28	16 | 50
that person to see what is required to serve on the paper. You may be	42	19 | 53
required to compose an article to discover just what skills you have.	56	22 | 56
If you are assigned to a school paper, you should not relax. While	14	25 | 58
writing may appear quite easy to you, it is not a breeze. Care must be	28	28 | 61
taken to write skillfully and with correctness. Plan on putting some	42	31 | 64
extra time on tasks that you are given, and you will be a good writer.	56	33 | 67

gwam 1' | 1 | 2 | 3 | 4 | 5 | 6 | 7 | 8 | 9 | 10 | 11 | 12 | 13 | 14 |
5' | 1 | 2 | 3 |

68e, continued

Directions: Problem 2 Table with Columnar Headings

1. Key the table below in exact vertical center on a half sheet of paper. Center horizontally.

2. SS the columnar entries, as shown. Leave 12 spaces between columns.

3. DS after each heading. Center the columnar headings over the entries. Refer to 68d, page 123 if necessary.

Note: Space the main and subheading as you did in previous problems.

INTERNATIONAL CLUB
DS
Regular Meeting Schedule
DS

Date	Chairperson
DS	DS
September 20	Yolanda Lopez
October 18	Scott Nelson
November 15	Paula Wanchik
January 17	Robert Sakata
February 14	Kimberly Mitchell
March 14	Steven Casperson
April 18	Lor Van Cheng

LESSON 69

60-space line

5 minutes

69a ● Keyboard Review

Directions: Key each sentence three times SS. DS between 3-line groups.

use quick, sharp strokes

alphabet Barney knew when Jacque played the fine new sax Roz gave me.

fig/sym Asia's Mount Everest (5 1/2 miles high) was climbed in 1953.

easy All of us think she would be wise to visit the island today.

| 1 | 2 | 3 | 4 | 5 | 6 | 7 | 8 | 9 | 10 | 11 | 12 |

---

10 minutes

69b ● Language Arts Skills: Composing at the Keyboard

Directions: Compose answers to as many of the questions below as time permits. Use complete sentences as you key your answers.

1. What is your favorite song?
2. Which singer do you like best?
3. What is your favorite subject in school?
4. What is the capital of your state?
5. What do you enjoy doing most in your spare time?
6. What event is celebrated on July 4?
7. Who is the governor of your state?
8. What was the event that made Charles Lindbergh famous?

71d ● Language Arts Skills: Spacing Guides

Directions: Each of the spacing guides below is followed by a sentence that illustrates it.

Study the guides; key each line that illustrates the guide two times SS. DS between 2-line groups.

Space twice after a period at the end of a sentence.
Listen very carefully. Instructions are important. Display interest.

Space once after a semicolon or comma.
The day of the game has been changed; however, the teams are the same.

Space twice after a question mark at the end of a sentence.
What is the day? Who is the new teacher? Who will play at the dance?

Space twice after a colon except when stating time.
A good spelling rule to remember is: If you are not sure, look it up.

Space twice after an exclamation mark that ends a sentence.
Always try to do better! Look what you are doing! Please plan ahead!

Key the dash with two hyphens. Do not space before or after.
A computer is not super smart--it only knows what you want it to know.

LESSON 72

72a ● Keyboard Review

Directions: Key each sentence three times SS. DS between 3-line groups.

alphabet The breeze was very full, making the old pro box kite just go quickly.

fig/sym The 28 students in homeroom 91 earned more than 50% of the top grades.

shift key The Americans from Washington, D.C., earned impressive English scores.

easy Our boss said that it can be a lot of fun to ride a new bus every day.

| 1 | 2 | 3 | 4 | 5 | 6 | 7 | 8 | 9 | 10 | 11 | 12 | 13 | 14 |

72b ● Control Ladder Paragraphs

Directions: 1. Take 1' writings on each ¶ in 71b, page 130. Circle errors and figure *gwam*.

2. When you key a ¶ within the error limit specified by your teacher, move to the next ¶. Use control as you key this exercise.

72c ● Formatting Problems

Directions: Problem 1 Announcement
Key the copy below in exact vertical center using a half sheet of paper (long side up). DS below the heading; DS between all other lines.

ANNOUNCING

First Annual Career Day

Guidance and Placement Department

Riverview Middle School

Friday, May 19, 8:00 p.m.

(continued on next page)

30 minutes

69c ● Formatting Problems: Table with Columnar Headings

Directions: Problem 1

1. Key the table below in reading position on a full sheet of paper.
2. DS columnar entries; leave six spaces between columns.
3. Center the columnar headings over the columns.

MOST VALUABLE BASEBALL CARDS

DS

Year	Player	$ Value
1951	Mickey Mantle	6,300
1954	Ted Williams	4,200
1952	Eddie Matthews	2,800
1951	Willie Mays	2,000
1952	Roy Campanella	2,000
1967	Tom Seaver	1,750
1954	Hank Aaron	1,400
1955	Roberto Clemente	1,400
1948	Duke Snider	1,250
1955	Sandy Koufax	1,000
1949	Jackie Robinson	1,000
1975	Robin Yount	210
1984	Kirby Puckett	150
1975	George Brett	140
1980	Rickey Henderson	115
1972	Carlton Fisk	115
1984	Roger Clemons	90
1977	Dale Murphy	80
1984	Don Mattingly	70
1983	Darryl Strawberry	65
1986	Jose Canseco	50

Note: Indent from tab stop for shorter items.

Directions: Problem 2

1. Key the table above, listing only the first 11 players. Place it in exact vertical center on a half sheet of paper.
2. SS columnar entries; leave eight spaces between columns.
3. Center the columnar headings over the entries.

LESSON 70

60-space line

5 minutes

70a ● Keyboard Review

Directions: Key each sentence three times SS. DS between 3-line groups.

alphabet Jeff Long experienced a quick shave with my razor and brush.

fig/sym Luis said, "To get the answer, add 6 1/2, 9 5/8, and 7 3/4."

easy Jena took the lead early in the race and thus won the title.

| 1 | 2 | 3 | 4 | 5 | 6 | 7 | 8 | 9 | 10 | 11 | 12 |

71b ● Speed Ladder Paragraphs

Directions: 1. Take a 1' writing on ¶ 1 DS until you complete the ¶ in 1'.
2. When you complete ¶ 1 in 1', continue on to ¶ 2. Repeat this procedure as you try to complete each of the four ¶s in the given time.
3. Take three 1' writings on any ¶ you cannot finish in the time given.

all letters used   1.3 si

gwam 5'

use quick
sharp strokes

		gwam 5'
Today there is a great deal of concern about our diet. A large	3	36
part of our population has become very puzzled over what foods they	5	39
eat and how they may affect their future health.	7	41
The concern over a good diet has not relaxed. The press has been	10	44
letting the public know what is good for a healthy diet. Food chains	13	46
are selling new products to meet the demands for good nutrition.	15	49
Medical experts have known for quite a long time that what we eat	18	51
does make a major difference. They cite research which is quick to point	21	54
out that foods high in fat and salt contribute to higher rates of heart	24	57
disease.	24	58
Most people develop their eating habits during the time they are	27	60
in school. Now may be the time for you to check out your eating hab-	29	63
its. It is easy to do, and it may surprise you how your diet can make	32	66
a very big difference in your life.	34	67

gwam 5' | 1 | 2 | 3 |

71c ● Learn to Divide Words

Beginning with this lesson, you will be formatting copy that appears in lines either longer or shorter than those for which your margin is set.

It will be necessary for you to listen for the line-end signal and to divide long words correctly to keep fairly even right margins.

Note: On some electronic typewriters and on computers, the writing line will "wrap around" automatically to the next line when you reach your right margin. Check with your teacher or equipment and software manual for word-division procedures.

Directions: 1. Read and study the word-division guides on page RG11.

2. As time permits, key a word which is an example of each guide given on the page but is *not* on the list. Divide each word correctly.

3. When dividing a word at the end of a line, use a hyphen and finish the word on the next line.

4. If you are uncertain about the division of a word, use a dictionary or a word-division manual.

70b ● Sentence Guided Writings

Directions: 1. Take 1' writings on each sentence. Try to key the sentence four times within the minute.

2. Your instructor will call the return each 15 seconds to guide you.

3. Figure *gwam* and circle errors.

		15" guide	*gwam*	words
1	Do you sit erect in the seat as you key?	32		8
2	Do you look at the copy and not your fingers?	36		9
3	Do you strike each key with a quick, sharp stroke?	40		10
4	Do you think and key every easy combination as a whole?	44		11
5	Do you hold the wrists low and quiet as you strike the keys?	48		12

| 1 | 2 | 3 | 4 | 5 | 6 | 7 | 8 | 9 | 10 | 11 | 12 |

70c ● Timed Writings

Directions: 1. Key two 1' writings on each ¶ DS. Check the one on which you made the better rate; then check the one on which you made fewer errors.

2. Take two 3' writings on all three ¶s combined. Circle errors. Figure *gwam*. Submit the better of the two writings.

all letters used   1.3 si

	gwam 3'
The one thing that most of us never have quite enough of	4	57
is time. At least that's the excuse we usually fall back on	8	61
whenever we do not get a job finished as soon as we or the boss	12	65
wanted. Time is a precious commodity that always seems to be	16	69
in short supply.	17	70
Time is so important that several different methods have	21	74
been devised for keeping track of it. For hundreds of years	25	78
one of the most common ways of measuring time was to use the	29	82
sun. A second method was to see how long it took for sand to	33	86
flow between two glass bulbs.	35	88
Whether we use such primitive means of telling time or	39	92
rely on modern clocks and watches, the time available for us	43	96
remains constant. No matter how rich or poor we might be, or	47	100
what time zone we live in, the number of hours in each day stays	52	105
exactly the same.	53	106

gwam 3' | 1 | 2 | 3 | 4 |

Each Lesson in Cycle 3 provides materials to help you improve the basic skills you have learned in previous lessons. In addition, you may want to preview some of the problems you will prepare by using the following summary.

Announcements, invitations, and thank you notes, pages 131–133.
Letters in semibusiness form, pages 136–137.
Personal/business letters, pages 140–142.
Orders and order letters, page 144.
Themes and reports, including outlines, footnotes, title pages, bibliographies, and note cards, pages 148–169.
Agenda and minutes, pages 172–175.
Club tickets and membership cards, page 176.
Postal cards, pages 177–178.
Bar graphs, pages 180–181.
School organization budget, pages 182–183.
Programs of meetings, pages 184–186.
Bulletin board notices, page 189.
Articles and stories for the school newspaper, pages 190–192.
Student-writer's style guide, pages 194–198.

Basic Skills Improvement: One lesson in each group of five covers technique and skill building. These lessons are designed to help you improve your speed and accuracy.

Language Arts Development: Drills stressing capitalization, punctuation, and number expression guides appear throughout this cycle. These drills will help you improve the quality of all your written work.

Measurement: Timed writings are given in each lesson to aid you in checking your keying speed and accuracy. Use Unit 14 as a check on your understanding of the different types of problems in this cycle.

Extra-Credit Assignments: Problems are given at the end of units for students who finish early and wish extra credit.

Unit 10 ■ Learning to Format Personal/Business Papers

(Lessons 71–80)

Learning Goals:
1. To further the development of basic keying techniques.
2. To further the development of basic keying skills.
3. To continue to improve language arts and composition skills.
4. To continue to develop appropriate related understandings and skills.
5. To format and key a variety of personal papers, such as invitations, acceptances, thank you notes, personal/business letters, and schedules.

General Directions

Use a 70-space line for all lessons in this unit (center – 35; center + 35 + 5) unless otherwise directed. SS sentences and drill lines. DS paragraph copy. Set machine for a 5-space paragraph indention.

Your teacher will tell you whether or not to correct errors when formatting problems.

LESSON 71
70-space line

5 minutes   **71a ● Keyboard Review**

Directions: Key each sentence three times SS. DS between 3-line groups.

keep arms and wrists quiet

alphabet Pam was very quick to just relax in the good fall sunshine and breeze.

figures I moved the business from 2389 Smith Street to 190 East Beacon Avenue.

adjacent keys Twelve oil wells were just opened, saving the nation for new shippers.

easy It is very easy to do most all work fast and have more fun in the sun.

| 1 | 2 | 3 | 4 | 5 | 6 | 7 | 8 | 9 | 10 | 11 | 12 | 13 | 14 |

70d ● Formatting Problem: Report with Short Table

Directions: 1. Key the unbound report below on a 60-space line DS. Use a 2″ top margin. Center the heading over the copy. QS below main heading. (Refer to page 100 if necessary.)

2. Leave 12 spaces between the columns of the table SS. DS above and below the table heading. Center the table and heading horizontally between the report margins.

PRESIDENTIAL TRIVIA
_{QS}

Here are some little known facts about the people who have held the highest office in our land. You may find them helpful when election time rolls around.

The majority of the 40 different persons who have been President of the United States are natives of the eastern part of our nation. Eight were born in Virginia. Native states of the most recent Presidents are shown below:

NATIVE STATES OF RECENT PRESIDENTS
_{DS}

George Bush	Massachusetts
Ronald Reagan	Illinois
Jimmy Carter	Georgia

_{DS}

A number of chief executives were related. James Madison and Zachary Taylor were second cousins; Franklin and Theodore Roosevelt were fifth cousins. John Quincy Adams was the son of John Adams, and Benjamin Harrison was the grandson of William Henry Harrison.

These final bits of trivia are sure to help you win the next game of Presidential Pursuit with your friends. James Madison weighed the least, 100 pounds; William Howard Taft was the heaviest, tipping the scales at more than 300 pounds. Theodore Roosevelt was the first U.S. President to ride in an automobile or an airplane, or to submerge in a submarine. George Washington, the father of our country, had no children of his own.

70e ● Extra Credit

Directions: Problem 1

1. Key the names of students in your keyboarding class by rows.
2. Use your course title as the main heading; use Row 1, Row 2, etc. as column headings. Arrange the columns and center the table on a full sheet of paper.

Directions: Problem 2

1. Key the report in 70d above, omitting the table but incorporating the ideas from it.
2. Use the directions in 70d for keying your summary.

Directions: Problem 3

1. Key the first ¶ in 70c, page 126, as many times as possible in the time that remains.
2. Submit the paragraph on which you made the fewest errors.

Vertical Centering

Centering material so that it will have uniform top and bottom margins is called *vertical centering*.

1. Count the lines in the copy to be centered. If your copy is to be double spaced, remember to count the spaces between the lines. There is one line space following each line of copy when material is double spaced.

2. Subtract the total lines to be used from the lines available on the paper you are using. (There are 33 lines on a half sheet, 66 on a full sheet.)

3. Divide the number of lines that remain by 2. The answer gives you the number of lines in the top and bottom margins. If the result contains a fraction, disregard the fraction.

4. Space down from the top of your paper or screen the number of line spaces obtained in step 3. Start keying one line space below the number you calculated for your top margin.

Vertical Centering (Backspace from Center Method)

1. Insert paper to line 33 (vertical center of a piece of paper 11″ long). Roll cylinder (5) back (toward you) one line space for each two lines in the copy to be keyed. This will place the copy in exact vertical center.

2. To key a problem off-center or in *reading position,* roll cylinder back two extra line spaces.

3. Another centering method is to fold the paper from top to bottom and make a slight crease at the right edge. The crease will be at the vertical center (line 33). Insert the paper to the crease, roll the cylinder back one line space for each two lines in the copy.

Horizontal Centering

Centering material so there will be equal left and right margins is called *horizontal centering*.

1. Check the placement of the paper guide (2). Turn to page xi and read the directions for adjusting the paper guide.

2. Clear tab stops (27). Set tab (28) at center point of paper (elite 51; pica 42) for paper 8½ inches wide.

3. Backspace (12) from center point once for every 2 characters or spaces in the line to be centered. If there is one character left, do not backspace for it. Begin to key at the point where you complete the backspacing.

 Note: Microcomputers and some typewriters are equipped with automatic centering. To center horizontally on your particular machine, consult the user's manual.

Horizontal Placement of Tables

1. Insert paper into the machine with left edge at "0."

2. Move the left and right margin stops to the ends of the scale. Clear all tab stops.

3. Move the printing point to the center of the paper.

4. Determine number of spaces to be left between the columns (if a specific number of spaces is not given).

5. Spot the longest word or entry in each column.

6. From the center of your paper, backspace once for each 2 letters, figures, spaces, or punctuation marks in the longest word or entry in each column. If you have an extra character in any column, add that character to the first character of the next column. If one space is left over

after backspacing for all the columns, disregard it.

7. Backspace once for each 2 spaces to be left between the columns. If one space is left over, disregard it.

8. Set the left margin at the point at which you stop backspacing. This is the point where the first column will start.

9. Space forward once for each letter, figure, space or punctuation mark in the longest entry in the first column and once for each space between Columns 1 and 2. Set a tab stop for the second column. Continue in this way until stops have been set for each column.

Centering Columnar Headings

1. Set the carrier or cursor at the point a column is to begin.
2. Space forward 1 space for each 2 spaces in the longest line in that column.
3. From that point, backspace once for each 2 spaces in the columnar heading.
4. Key the heading. It will be centered over the column.

Finding Horizontal Center Point for Odd-Size Paper or Cards

1. Insert paper or card into the machine.
2. Add the numbers on the line-of-writing scale (10) at the left and right edges of the paper or card.
3. Divide the sum by 2. The resulting figure is the horizontal center point of the paper or card.

 Note: To do this on a microcomputer or an electronic typewriter with automatic centering, you will need to reset your margins for a 5½" line. Check your user's manual for assistance.

Keying Left-Bound Reports

1. Leave a 2" top margin and a 1" bottom margin on the first page, 1" top and 1" bottom margins on all following pages.
2. Set a 1½" left margin (pica, 15 spaces; elite, 18 spaces) and a 1" right margin (pica, 10 spaces; elite, 12 spaces). Move the center point 3 spaces to the right to allow for the wider left margin.
3. Double-space the body, using 5-space paragraph indentions. Retain at least 2 lines of a paragraph at the bottom of a page and carry forward at least 2 lines of a paragraph to a new page if possible.
4. Indent long quotations of 4 lines or more 5 spaces from each margin and single space them.
5. If the first page is numbered, center the number ½" from the bottom. Place the following page numbers 6 line spaces from the top and align them with the right margin.
6. Place the heading on line 13, leaving a quadruple space between it and the body of the report.

---

leave 2" top margin

WRITING A LEFTBOUND REPORT

Famous authors do not become writers overnight. The pro-cess almost always begins with a desire to write about an idea, topic, or feeling that interests the writer. This strong desire is followed by a process that includes writing, starting over, rewriting, and perhaps coming out with a good page. Yes, many of our great writers probably had more paper in their waste-baskets than they had finished copy on their desks.

1½" left margin   1" right margin

Most of us do not have any burning desire to become great literary geniuses. Even if we did, it is not likely that we could do so easily. The great writers whom we know about have worked long and hard at perfecting their writing skill. We can, however, learn how to write a short paper that is clear and in-teresting without having to master the skills of great authors. Let's see how you might go about this task.

Steps for Preparing a Report
Choose the right subject. To begin with, you need to select a subject you know something about. One authority says such a choice may be the most important decision you make in planning and writing your composition.[1] You can't write about

[1]John E. Warriner and Sheila Laws Graham, English Grammar and Composition, Second Course, (New York: Harcourt Brace Jovanovich, Inc., 1987), p. 376.

approximately 1"

Keying Superscripts and Subscripts

1. For placement of a superscript (superior number), press the paper down key (14).

2. Key the figure or symbol, then press the paper up key (13) to return to original position.

3. For a subscript, press the paper up key (13).

4. Key the subscript, then press the paper down key (14) to return to original position.

 Note: Some microcomputers have special function keys that can automatically set codes for superscripts and subscripts to be printed. If your machine cannot key these figures, place figure between two diagonals with no spaces before or after figure: /2/. Check your user's manual.

Keying Footnotes

1. Key a superior number immediately following the material in the report which will be documented by a footnote.

2. Draw a light pencil mark on your paper to mark the 1″ bottom margin. Space up 2 or 3 lines from that mark for each footnote. Leave an extra line space for a DS between two or more footnotes; then space up 2 additional lines and draw a second pencil mark. This is where you will key the divider line.

3. After completing the last line on the page, double space, then key a 1½″ divider line (15 spaces pica; 18 spaces elite) at the point where you have your second pencil mark.

4. After keying the divider line, double space, indent 5 spaces and key the footnote reference. Single space each footnote; double space between footnotes.

Keying Reference Citations

1. After keying the quoted material, place within parentheses the author's last name, date of publication, and page number of the cited material.

2. At the end of a report, quadruple space and center the word ''References.'' Quadruple space and key in alphabetical order (by author's last names) each complete reference.

Keying a Bibliography

1. Use the same top and side margins used for the first page of your report. Center the heading over the line of writing.

2. Start the first line of each reference at the left margin. Indent other lines 5 spaces. Single space the entries; double space between entries.

```
                        BIBLIOGRAPHY
                               QS
      margin
        ↓
indent    Croyderman, Elizabeth C.   Using the Thesaurus.  Knoxville:  Barston
5 spaces →   and Company, 1987.
                       DS
          Laughlin, R. M.  "Fun in the Word Factory:  Experiences with the
             Dictionary."  Language Arts (March, 1988), pp. 319-21.
                                                          DS
          Marston, John M.  Ginn Elements of Good English.  Lexington:  Ginn
             and Company, 1984.
                         DS
          Pollock, Thomas Clark, and Richard L. Loughlin.  The Macmillan English
             Series.  New York:  Macmillan, Inc., 1983.
```

Keying a Postal Card

1. Set margin stops 4 spaces from each edge of the card. Set a tab stop at horizontal center.

2. Begin the dateline on line 3. Use block or modified block style.

```
1                    begin 3 lines from top
2
3                              ↓  June 20, 19--
4                              ↑                QS
5   → 4 spaces                 └ center point
6
7      Dear Grandmother
8                          DS
9      Thank you very much for the check you sent for my
10     birthday.  You are certainly a generous lady.
11                                             DS
12     I am planning to save the money and buy school
13     clothes with it this fall.  I'll let you know
14     what I get.  Have a good summer.
15                          DS
16           center point ——→Cheryl
17
18
19
```

Addressing a Postal Card

1. Key the return address and the address of the recipient on the opposite side of the postal card.

2. Begin the return address on the second line from the top of the postal card and 3 spaces from the left edge.

3. Begin the address of the recipient about 2″ from the top of the card and 2″ from the left edge.

Note: Addresses may be keyed in all caps with no punctuation or in both caps and lower case.

```
Cheryl Scalia
638 Eleanor Court
Little Rock, AR  72212-8899



                    MRS MARIE HANWELL
                    3354 MOHAWK DRIVE
                    JEFFERSON CITY MO  65101-7478
```

Two-Letter ZIP Code Abbreviations

Alabama	AL	Indiana	IN	Nebraska	NE	South Carolina	SC
Alaska	AK	Iowa	IA	Nevada	NV	South Dakota	SD
Arizona	AZ	Kansas	KS	New Hampshire	NH	Tennessee	TN
Arkansas	AR	Kentucky	KY	New Jersey	NJ	Texas	TX
California	CA	Louisiana	LA	New Mexico	NM	Utah	UT
Colorado	CO	Maine	ME	New York	NY	Vermont	VT
Connecticut	CT	Maryland	MD	North Carolina	NC	Virginia	VA
Delaware	DE	Massachusetts	MA	North Dakota	ND	Washington	WA
Florida	FL	Michigan	MI	Ohio	OH	West Virginia	WV
Georgia	GA	Minnesota	MN	Oklahoma	OK	Wisconsin	WI
Hawaii	HI	Mississippi	MS	Oregon	OR	Wyoming	WY
Idaho	ID	Missouri	MO	Pennsylvania	PA		
Illinois	IL	Montana	MT	Rhode Island	RI		

Keying Personal/Business Letters

1. Set your machine for single spacing.

2. Set the margins. The margins vary according to the length of the letter.

3. Space down to begin the return address. (The number of lines to space down varies with the length of the letter. The longer the letter, the fewer the number of lines.) For a modified block style letter, start the return address at the center point of the paper. For a block style letter, start the return address at the left margin.

4. Space down 4 times below the return address to the letter address.

5. Begin the salutation a double space below the letter address.

6. Begin the body of the letter a double space below the salutation. Single space the paragraphs; double space between paragraphs.

7. Begin the complimentary close a double space below the body of the letter. For a modified block style letter, start at the center point. For a block style letter, start at the left margin.

8. Key the name of the writer on the 4th line space below the complimentary close. (The keyed name of the writer is optional.)

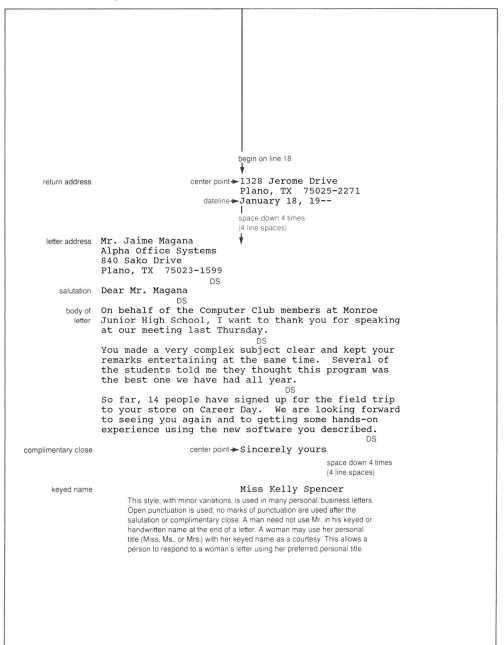

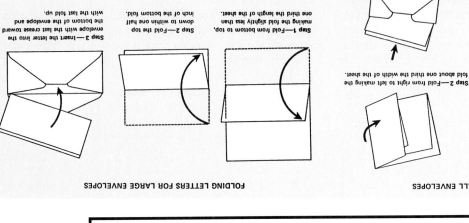

FOLDING LETTERS FOR SMALL ENVELOPES

Step 1—Fold the lower edge of the letter to within half an inch of the top.

Step 2—Fold from right to left making the fold about one third the width of the sheet.

Step 3—Fold from left to right, leaving about a half-inch margin at the right in order that the letter may be opened easily.

Step 4—Insert the letter into the envelope so that the left-hand creased edge is inserted first and the last side folded is toward the backside of the envelope.

FOLDING LETTERS FOR LARGE ENVELOPES

Step 1—Fold from bottom to top, making the fold slightly less than one third the length of the sheet.

Step 2—Fold the top down to within one half inch of the bottom fold.

Step 3—Insert the letter into the envelope with the last crease toward the bottom of the envelope and with the last fold up.

Addressing a Small Envelope

1. Key the writer's name and return address in the upper left corner as shown in the illustration. Begin on the second line space from the top edge and 3 spaces from the left edge.

2. Key the receiver's name about 2 inches (line 12) from the top of the envelope. Start about 2½ inches from the left edge.

3. Use block style single spacing for all addresses. Addresses may be keyed in all caps with no punctuation or in both caps and lower case. City and state names and ZIP Codes (see p. RG4) must be placed on one line in that order.

4. The state name may be keyed in full, or it may be abbreviated using the standard abbreviation or, preferably, the 2-letter state abbreviation.

Addressing a Large Envelope

1. A large envelope (9½" × 4⅛") is usually prepared for business letters or for letters of more than one page.

2. Key the writer's name and return address as directed on the illustration of the small envelope.

3. Begin the name and address of the receiver 2½" from the top and 4" from the left edge of the envelope. Use block style and single spacing.

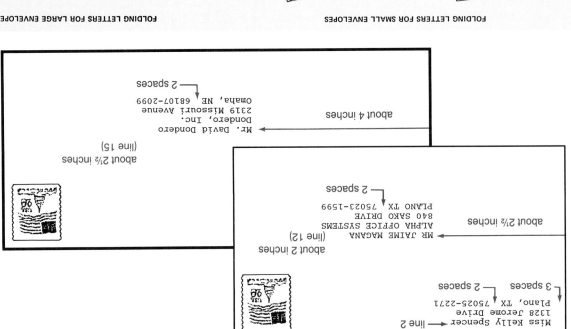

Large envelope:

Mr. David Dondero
Dondero, Inc.
2319 Missouri Avenue
Omaha, NE 68107-2099
— 2 spaces
(line 15)
about 2½ inches
about 4 inches

Small envelope:

Miss Kelly Spencer — line 2
1328 Jerome Drive
Plano, TX 75025-2271
3 spaces   2 spaces

MR JAIME MAGANA (line 12)
ALPHA OFFICE SYSTEMS
840 SAKO DRIVE
PLANO TX 75023-1599
— 2 spaces
about 2 inches
about 2½ inches

Formatting/Keying Business Letters

General Information

Letter Styles: With slight variations, the modified block style shown on page RG8 is the most commonly used style for business letters. Other styles that continue to grow in usage are the block style and the simplified style illustrated on pages RG9 and RG10.

Punctuation Styles: Two commonly used punctuation styles are *open* and *mixed.* In *open* punctuation, no punctuation marks are used after the salutation or the complimentary close. In *mixed* punctuation, a colon is placed after the salutation and a comma after the complimentary close.

Vertical Placement of Dateline: Vertical placement of the date varies with the length of the letter. For short to average business letters, the date is placed on line 18. The address begins on the 4th line space below the date.

Margins: The line length used for business letters varies according to the number of words in the letter. A 50-space line works well for most short letters; a 60-space line works well for most average-length letters. If you prefer, set 2″ side margins for short letters, 1½″ side margins for average-length letters, or 1″ side margins for long letters.

Titles in Addresses: As a mark of courtesy to the person to whom a letter is addressed, you may use a personal or professional title on a letter, envelope, or card: *Mr. Robert Wertz, Dr. Ann Hendricks.* When a woman's preferred title is unknown, use *Ms.* as the personal title.

Abbreviations: Excessive abbreviations should be avoided. It is preferred, however, to use the two-letter state abbreviation in an address when using a ZIP Code. Leave two spaces between the state abbreviation and the ZIP Code.

Reference Initials: Reference initials of the typist should always be placed at the left margin, two line spaces below the keyed name of the writer of the letter.

Stationery: Most business letters are prepared on 8½″ × 11″ stationery that has a letterhead which includes a name and address of the company.

Envelopes: Either large or small envelopes may be used for one-page letters. Large envelopes should be used for two-page letters and in instances where materials are enclosed with the letters.

Attention Line

An attention line is used to direct a letter to a particular person. The attention line appears as the first line of the letter address. Key the attention line immediately above the company name on the envelope.

```
Attention Miss Carol Key
Largo & Key, Inc.
2573 Winsome Drive
Charleston, WV  25312-1078
```

Subject Line

When a subject line is used in a letter, it appears on the second line below the salutation. It may be centered on the line, or it may be keyed at the left margin.

```
Mr. Rodger Avion
361 Oakman Avenue
Lynn, MA  01905-1206
        ←—DS
Dear Mr. Avion
        ←—DS
SUBJECT:  Accounting Software
```

Enclosure Notations

An enclosure notation is used when some item (or items) is sent with a letter. The notation appears at the left margin a double space below the reference initials. If two or more items are enclosed, use the plural *Enclosures.*

```
Lonnie Evans
Director of Sales
    ←—DS
xx
    ←—DS
Enclosure
```

Postscript

A postscript is the last item in a letter. The postscript appears a double space below the enclosure notation (if used) or the reference initials if an enclosure notation is not used. The postscript need not be preceded by the letters *P.S.*

```
xx
  ←—DS
A video tape of your
```

2119 DEL RIO DR., SAN JOSE, CA 95119-3348 (408) 272-8327

50-space line; mixed punctuation

|center point
↓
begin on line 18 ──→ April 17, 19--

                                                                            words
                                                                              3

                            return 4 times

letter address Mr. Jay Kaczmarski   7
                Modern Shipping, Inc.   11
                4756 W. State Street   15
                San Diego, CA 92110-1374   20
                            DS
salutation Dear Mr. Kaczmarski: 24
                      DS
body Thank you for inquiring about the services that we   35
      provide at Creative Consulting.   41
                            DS
      Creative Consulting is a firm totally dedicated to   51
      analyzing the staffing and the training needs of all   62
      sizes of business firms. In addition, we provide   72
      suggested solutions to help firms meet those needs.   83
                            DS
      Our staff is highly trained to provide confidential   93
      consulting services. We often can do in days what   103
      otherwise might take an in-house staff months.   113
                            DS
      If you need more information, please give me a call.   123
                            DS
complimentary   center point ──→ Sincerely yours,   127
close
                            return 4 times

keyed name and
official title   Ms. Roxanne Ray, Manager   131
                                    DS
reference initials db   132

Business letter in modified block style

2119 DEL RIO DR., SAN JOSE, CA 95119-3348 (408) 272-8327

50-space line; open punctuation

words

March 5, 19-- ◄——— begin on line 18   3
              return 4 times

letter address   Mrs. Pamela Davidson   7
                  Advanced Video Services   12
                  754 Timberline Street   16
                  Chula Vista, CA 92011-5097   22
                                      DS
salutation   Dear Mrs. Davidson   26
                              DS
body   I am pleased to have this opportunity to respond to   36
                  your questions regarding the charges for consulting   46
                  services at Creative Consulting.   53

                  Our fees for researching and analyzing the staffing   64
                  and training needs of your firm are billed at $90 per   74
                  hour plus expenses. Our training seminars are billed   85
                  on a daily basis of $500 per day plus the costs of   95
                  materials.   98

                  We will be happy to provide you a free appraisal of   108
                  your needs and to identify all our charges.   117

                  Please contact me if I may be of further assistance.   128
                                              DS
complimentary   Sincerely yours   131
close   DS
company name in   CREATIVE CONSULTING   135
closing lines
(all CAPS)   return 4 times

keyed name   Preston Price   138
official title   Assistant Manager   141
                              DS
reference initials   rs   142

Business letter in block style

///lllhendrix consultants, inc.

115 Gateway Drive
Seattle, WA 98168-4301
(206) 559-0182

Business letter in simplified style · 50-space line; open punctuation

		words
All Major lines begin at left margin	April 17, 19-- ——→ begin on line 18 return 4 times	3
Address in all caps with no punctuation begins on the fourth line below date	MISS MARIA GARCIA DIRECTOR OF WORD PROCESSING CLAY & SMITH LEGAL SERVICES 146 ACCESS DRIVE SPOKANE WA 99216-6792	7 12 18 21 26
Omit salutation	DS FORMATTING THE SIMPLIFIED LETTER	32
Subject line in all caps; double-space above and below it	DS Our consulting firm has found the simplified letter to be the most efficient in terms of production time. It is formatted as follows:	43 54 59
Begin enumerated items at left margin	1. Use a block format.	64
	2. Begin the address (in ALL CAPS with no punctuation) on the fourth line below the date.	74 83
	3. Do not use a salutation or complimentary close.	93
	4. Always use a subject heading keyed in all caps, a double space below the address. The body of the letter begins a double space below the subject line.	104 114 124
	5. Begin enumerated items at the left margin.	134
	6. Indicate the writer's name and title in all caps on the fourth line below the body of the letter.	144 154
	7. Key only the operator's reference initials in lower case a double space below the writer's name.	164 174
Omit complimentary close	Firms using this letter format like its efficiency. return 4 times	185
Writer's name and title in all caps on the fourth line below letter body	DS PHILIP WANG, SUPPORT SERVICES MANAGER DS ez	192 193

Capitalization Guides (pp. 86, 105, 120, 234)

Capitalize:

1. The first word of a complete sentence.
2. The first word of a quoted sentence. (Do not capitalize fragments of a quotation resumed within a sentence.)
3. Languages and numbered school courses, but not the names of other school subjects.
4. The pronoun *I*, both alone and in contractions.
5. Titles of organizations, institutions, and buildings.
6. Days of the week, months of the year, and holidays, but not seasons.
7. Names of rivers, oceans, and mountains.
8. *North, South, etc.,* when they name particular parts of the country, but not when they refer to directions.
9. Names of religious groups, political parties, nations, nationalities, and races.
10. All proper names and the adjectives made from them.
11. The names of stars, planets, and constellations, except the sun, moon, and earth, unless these are used with other astronomical names.
12. A title when used with a person's name.
13. First words and all other words in titles of books, articles, periodicals, headings, and plays, except words which are articles, conjunctions, and prepositions.
14. The first and last words, all titles, and all proper names used in the salutation of a business letter.
15. Only the first word of a complimentary close.
16. All titles appearing in the address of a letter.
17. The title following the names of the dictator in the closing lines of a business letter.

Spacing Guides (pp. 5, 14, 15, 20, 26, 28, 55, 56, 60, 63, 131, 139)

1. Space twice after a period that ends a sentence, except when the period comes at the end of the line. When it does, return the carrier without spacing.
2. Space once after a question mark within a sentence; twice after a question mark at the end of a sentence.
3. Space twice after an exclamation point at the end of a sentence.
4. Space twice after a colon except when stating time.
5. Space once after a semicolon or comma.
6. Space once after a period that ends an abbreviation; twice if that period ends a sentence. (Do not space after a period within an abbreviation.)
7. Space once between a whole number and a "made" fraction.
8. Do not space between the $ and the number which follows it.

9. Do not space before or after a diagonal.
10. Do not space between a number and a following % sign.
11. Do not space between parentheses and the material they enclose.
12. Do not space before or after the apostrophe unless the apostrophe is at the end of a word.
13. Do not space between quotation marks and the material they enclose.
14. Do not space before or after a dash.
15. Do not space before or after the hyphen in a hyphenated word.

Number Expression Guides (pp. 134, 157, 163, 205, 216)

1. Key even sums of money without decimals or zeros.
2. Key distances in figures.
3. Use figures to key dates. When the day comes before the month, use a figure and follow it with *th, st,* or *d.*
4. Spell a number beginning a sentence even though figures may be used later in the sentence.
5. Use figures with *a.m.* and *p.m.* Use words with *o'clock.*
6. Key amounts of money, either dollars or cents, in figures.
7. Key policy numbers without commas.

Word-Division Guides

Divide:

1. Words only between syllables.
2. Hyphenated compounds at the point of the hyphen; for example, *self-control.*
3. Words so that *cial, tial, cion, sion,* or *tion* are retained as a unit.
4. A word that ends in double letters after the double letters when a suffix is added, such as *fill-ing.*
5. A word in which the final consonant is doubled when a suffix is added between the double letters, such as *control-ling.*

Do not:

1. Divide words of one syllable, such as *thought.*
2. Separate a syllable of one letter at the beginning of a word, such as *across.*
3. Separate a syllable of one or two letters at the end of a word, such as *ready* or *greatly.*
4. Divide words of five or fewer letters.
5. Divide the last word on a page.

Punctuation Guides

Dash and Parentheses (p. 184)

1. Use a dash to show a sudden break in thought.
2. Use a dash before the name of an author when it follows a direct quotation.
3. Use parentheses to enclose an explanation.

Period, Question Mark, Exclamation Point (p. 139)

1. Use a period after a sentence making a statement or giving a command.
2. Use a period after each initial.
3. Use a period after most abbreviations. (Nicknames are not followed by periods.)
4. Use a question mark after a question.
5. After requests and indirect questions, use a period.
6. Use an exclamation point to express strong or sudden feelings.

Quotation Marks (p. 188)

1. Place quotation marks around the exact words of a speaker.
2. When the quotation is broken to identify the speaker, put quotation marks around each part. If the second part of the quotation is a new sentence, use a capital letter.
3. Use no quotation marks with an indirect quotation.
4. Use quotation marks around the titles of articles, songs, poems, themes, short stories, and the like.
5. Always place the period or comma inside the quotation mark.

Semicolon (p. 170)

1. Use a semicolon between the clauses of a compound sentence when no conjunction is used. (If a conjunction is used to join the clauses, use a comma between them.)
2. Use a semicolon between the clauses of a compound sentence that are joined by such words as *also, however, therefore,* and *consequently.*
3. Use a semicolon between a series of phrases or clauses that are dependent upon a main clause.

Apostrophe (p. 204)

1. Use an apostrophe in writing contractions.
2. *It's* means *it is. Its,* the possessive pronoun, does not take an apostrophe.
3. Use the contraction of o'clock (of the clock) in writing time.
4. Add *'s* to plural nouns that do not end in *s.*
5. If a plural noun does end in *s,* add only an apostrophe after the *s.*
6. The apostrophe denotes possession. Do not use it merely to form the plural of a noun.
7. Use *'s* to form the plural of figures, letters, signs, and words referred to as words.

Colon (p. 178)

1. Use a colon to introduce a list of items or expressions.
2. Use a colon to separate the hours and minutes when they are expressed in figures.
3. Use a colon to introduce a question or long quotation.

Comma (pp. 143 and 168)

1. Use a comma after each item in a series, except the last.
2. Use a comma to separate consecutive adjectives when the *and* has seemingly been omitted. Do not use the comma when the adjectives do not apply equally to the noun they modify.
3. Use a comma to separate a dependent clause that precedes the main clause.
4. Use a comma to separate the independent parts of a compound sentence joined by *and, but, or, neither, nor.*
5. Use a comma to prevent misreading or confusion.
6. Use a comma to set off a direct quotation from the rest of the sentence.
7. Do not set off an indirect quotation from the rest of the sentence.
8. Use commas to set off parenthetic expressions that break the flow of a sentence. If the parenthetic expression begins or ends a sentence, use one comma.
9. Use a comma to set off *yes, no, well, now.*
10. Use commas to set off appositives that give additional information about the same person or object and that can be omitted without changing the meaning of the sentence.
11. Use commas to set off the name of the person addressed.
12. Do not use a comma to separate two nouns, one of which identifies the other.

ALPHA referring to letters of the alphabet.

ALPHANUMERIC pertains to a character set that contains digits, punctuation, and symbols.

APPLICATION a task or problem for which the computer can be used.

BACKUP FILE a duplicate of an existing production file.

BLOCK a segment of text that can be marked for deletion or moving to a different location.

BOOTING UP starting the computer.

BYTE a group of adjacent bits set up to represent a character.

CHARACTER a unit of alphanumeric data.

CPU (CENTRAL PROCESSING UNIT) the internal operating unit or ''brains'' of an electronic computer system; also ''the little black box.''

COMMANDS combinations of keystrokes that tell the computer to perform certain functions.

CONTROL KEY (CTRL) a special key that is pressed at the same time another key is struck, causing that key to perform a special function.

CRT (CATHODE RAY TUBE) see **VDT**

CURSOR a dot, line, or square of light that shows the point on a display.

DAISY WHEEL a printing wheel shaped like a daisy used on some typewriters and printers.

DEFAULT preset instructions on the system disk.

DELETE to remove from text a segment of copy (a character, a phrase, a line, a sentence, a page).

DISK (DISKETTE) DRIVE the unit into which a diskette is inserted to be read or written by the CPU (central processing unit).

DISKETTE (DISK) a magnetic, Mylar-coated record-like disk (encased in a square protective envelope) used for recording, reading, and writing by the CPU (central processing unit).

DISPLAY SCREEN see **VDT**

DOWNTIME the time when a computer system is not operational.

EDIT to rearrange, change, and correct existing text; editing includes proofreading but is not limited to it.

ELEMENT a ball-shaped printing device.

ENTER to input keystrokes; see **KEY**.

ENTER KEY see **RETURN KEY**.

ESCAPE KEY (ESC) a key on some computers which lets the user leave one segment of a program and go to another.

FILE NAME code used to identify stored data.

FOOTERS notations that print below the text, such as page numbers or titles.

FORMAT the style (arrangement, placement, and spacing) of a document.

FORMATTING the process of arranging a document in proper form.

FUNCTION KEYS special keys on typewriters, computers, and word processors that when used alone or in combination with other keys perform special functions such as setting margins, centering copy, and so on.

GLOBAL SEARCH AND REPLACE to direct a computer or word processor to find a repeated series of characters and replace it with a different series of characters automatically throughout a document (for example, find and replace Co. with company).

HARD COPY a readable printed copy of computer output.

HARDWARE the physical equipment that makes up a computer or word processing system.

HEADERS notations that print above the text, such as page numbers or titles.

ICONS pictographs that are used in place of words or phrases on screen displays or in printed copy.

INFORMATION PROCESSING the job of putting text and data into usable form (documents).

INPUT text and data that enter an information system; the process of entering text and data.

INSERT, INSERTION new text that is added to existing text; also the process of adding new text to existing text.

KEY to strike keys to record or display text and data; also enter, key in, keyboard, input, and type.

KEYBOARD an arrangement of keys on a ''board'' that is attached to or apart from a machine such as typewriter, computer, or word processor; also the act of keyboarding or typing.

MEMORY storage location in a computer, word processor, or electronic typewriter.

MENU a list of options from which a keyboard operator may (or must) choose when using a word or data processing machine.

MERGE to assemble new documents from stored text such as form paragraphs; to combine stored text such as a form letter with newly keyed text (names, addresses, inserts).

MICROCOMPUTER a small-sized computer with a keyboard, screen, and auxiliary storage; its central processor is usually a single CPU chip; also "computer on a chip."

MONITOR see VDT

MOVE to reposition a heading or text up or down the video screen; when a block (paragraph) of copy is moved, it is a "block move."

OUTPUT useful information that leaves an information system, usually presented to the user as a screen display or a printout.

PRINT to produce, using a printer, a paper copy of information displayed on a screen or stored in computer or word processor memory.

PRINTER a unit attached to a computer or word processor that produces copy on paper.

PRINTOUT the printed paper output of a computer, word processor, or electronic typewriter.

PROMPT a message displayed in the window of an electronic typewriter or on the screen of a computer or word processor telling the user that the machine is awaiting a specific response.

RETRIEVE to make stored information available when needed.

SEARCH to locate an editing or correcting point within a document by matching a series of characters or words.

SOFTWARE instructions or programs that tell a computer or word processor what to do.

SOURCE DOCUMENT the original hard copy from which data are entered.

STORE to save information on magnetic media so that it may be used later.

TASK the basic unit of work for a processor.

TERMINAL any device capable of sending or receiving data over a communication network.

TEXT (DATA) ENTRY the process of getting text and data from the writer's mind or from a written or voice-recorded document into the computer or word processing system.

VDT (VIDEO DISPLAY TERMINAL) a TV-like picture tube used to display text, data, and graphic images; also called CRT, display screen, and monitor.

WINDOW a rectangular section of a display screen that is dedicated to a specific activity or application.

WORD PROCESSING the writing and storing of letters, reports, and other documents on a computer, electronic typewriter, or word processor; may also include printing of the final document.

WORDWRAP a feature that allows the computer, electronic typewriter, or word processor to carry words to the next line without the necessity of striking the return key (enter key).

Keyboarding Mastery Techniques

positioning body and hands
xiii, xiv, xv, 2, 3, 4, 6, 7, 9, 11, 12, 13, 14, 15, 17, 18, 19, 20, 21, 23, 25, 26, 27, 35, 38, 39, 41, 43, 54, 56, 58, 60, 62

learn the spatial arrangement of the keyboard
vii, viii, ix, 3, 5, 7, 10, 12, 14, 17, 19, 21, 24, 26, 27, 38, 39, 41, 42, 44, 54, 56, 58, 60, 62

strike keys with correct fingers
xiv, xv, 3, 5, 7, 10, 12, 13, 14, 15, 17, 19, 20, 21, 24, 26, 27, 38, 39, 41, 43, 45, 54, 55, 56, 58, 60, 62

operate various machine parts
vii, viii, ix, x, xi, xiv, xv, 2, 3, 4, 14, 15, 20, 21, 24, 25, 27, 47, 49, 51, 53, 146, 172, 186

proper care of equipment
xi, xii, xv, xvi

Speed and Accuracy in Keyboarding

read and key response patterns
4, 6, 8, 11, 12, 13, 14, 17, 19, 20, 21, 24, 26, 27, 28, 29, 30, 31, 32, 36, 38, 41, 44, 48, 51

key skill-comparison writings
52, 106, 112, 116, 123, 186, 204, 227

control the pace of keying for accuracy
30, 31, 33, 35, 36, 38, 39, 43, 58, 60, 71, 87, 171, 180

push for higher speed goals
55, 61, 70, 130, 132, 137, 147, 157, 159, 161, 164, 167, 168, 171, 174, 179, 182, 187, 190, 200, 202, 205, 209, 210, 214, 220, 222, 227, 230, 235, 237

sustain speed on longer writings
32, 33, 35, 36, 40, 45, 132, 135, 145, 155, 163, 167, 169, 177, 182, 185, 190, 193, 194, 196, 198, 211, 222, 225, 233, 240

Copy Arrangement Skills

center horizontally and vertically
RG1, RG2, 67, 69, 73, 98, 123

tabulate in columns
RG1, 53, 114, 117, 119, 122, 123, 125, 223, 231, 232, 233, 238, 240, 242, 245

balance letters on page
RG5, RG8, RG9, RG10, 87, 88, 89, 91, 92, 94, 95, 136, 137, 140, 142, 145, 211, 212, 214, 215, 217, 218, 219, 221, 223, 224, 225

follow correct form in keying themes/reports
RG3, 65, 100, 101, 102, 106, 108, 109, 110, 111, 127, 149, 150, 151, 153, 154, 155, 165, 166, 167, 169, 194

apply correction techniques
71, 72, 146, 156, 164

Communication Skills

practice proofreading
30, 66, 76, 77, 85, 87, 96, 98, 101, 106, 109, 116, 117, 122, 123

divide words at end of line
RG11, 130

punctuation sentences
RG12, 63, 139, 143, 168, 170, 178, 184, 188, 204

compose at the keyboard
67, 105, 124, 165, 210, 220, 222, 240

Formatting Problems Skills

follow directions (problem keying)
71, 77, 79, 81, 87, 91, 94, 101, 102, 110, 114, 117, 119, 123, 127, 131, 135, 136, 137, 140, 142, 143, 144, 145, 148, 150, 155, 158, 159, 160, 161, 162, 165, 167, 169, 172, 175, 176, 177, 182, 184, 186, 189, 190, 191, 192, 193, 194, 196, 197, 198, 211, 214, 218, 223, 224, 228

fill in simple forms
143, 144, 231, 232, 240

outline and prepare manuscripts
RG3, 65, 100, 102, 106, 107, 108, 109, 110, 111, 127, 148, 149, 150, 151, 153, 155, 165, 167, 169, 194

key from rough draft
72, 74, 83, 84, 87, 98, 106, 109, 116, 184, 186, 192, 216, 224

Electronic Information Processes
efficient information flow
147, 182, 202, 220